HOPE

FOR

CARSONVILLE:

A DAUGHTER'S MEMOIR

BY

ERIN Q. HARTMAN

A

ARBUTUS PRESS
TRAVERSE CITY

978-1-933926-00-1 Hardcover
978-1-933926-01-8 Paperback

Library of Congress Cataloging-in-Publication Data

Hartman, Erin Q. (Erin Quinlan), 1956-
  Hope for Carsonville : a daughter's memoir / by Erin Q. Hartman
    p. cm.
  ISBN 978-1-933926-00-1
1. Hartman, Erin Q. (Erin Quinlan), 1956 —Childhood and youth.
2. Quinlan family. 3. Carsonville (Mich.) Biography. I. Title.

CT275.H38679A3 2007
977.4"43043092—dc22
[B]

                    2007009710

            Printed in the United States

      Cover art: Jim DeWildt

          Quinlan Island Press
          3149 S. Lee Point Road
          Suttons Bay, MI 49682
          eqhartman04@gmail.com
          ISBN 0-9841981-0-5

Dedication

To my loving husband Randy
and our beautiful daughters
McKenzie, Bryanne, and Morgan.

CONTENTS

Author's Note

As a mother, you seldom get to share your childhood with your own children, and in a lifetime you can't tell your family all the love you have for them. There are no words for it. This book is, first and foremost, a gift of love. I feel honored to be able to share who I am with my family. I have been blessed with memories that for a time were lost. Now, remembering my childhood, my heart is full of wonder.

My parents were love itself to me, and their expressions of love were part of life's lessons. These stories are my experience of how it felt to grow up in such a large, loving, hard-working family.

Many nights, for two years, I was wakened by a small girl standing in my room, wordlessly insisting that I write the story of my life. I did as I was told: memories started flowing out of me. This has been a journey of my soul. These are my memories and my emotions, the way I saw my childhood as I lived it.

I am grateful for the encouragement and support of my brother Tony and his gift to me of a computer when I decided to write this book. He has been my constant cheerleader. My sister Pat and brother Paul have been sounding boards as I wrote about things that were at times painful. Additionally, there were friends who read my stories in their rough original format and encouraged me to keep writing.

How do you thank those who have contributed to the fulfillment of a dream? My sister Marianne, my friend JoAnn Overzet, and Shirlee Hartman generously offered much practical advice and help. JoAnn and Marianne contributed many hours of hard work and love to this book, editing my stories, making my voice clearer. Without them, this book would be less.

Erin Q Hartman
2006

Prologue

Welcome Home.

The harbormaster calls out to the big boats, "Welcome, Captain! Welcome to Port Sanilac!" I stand on the dock, remembering.

Port Sanilac is a "safe harbor." The boats are big, with welcome mats in front of their entrances. American flags are blowing from the north, standing straight out, and flowerpots are tipped over, toppled by the wind. The sailboats are like small floating houses. Their occupants are tucked in below, in the dark places they call home, waiting for the storm to blow over. I feel the wind in my hair and cheeks, and my lips are tingling with delight. Lake Huron's waves, one at a time, flow over my heart.

I'm home again, not with Hope and Bill but with my godmother, Hazel, who is whispering that she has a story to tell me.

Sitting at Hazel's kitchen table, drinking her hot coffee (she uses the cup used by her deceased husband Richard with his name on it), she says to me, "Yes, I'm your godmother, Erin. I'm kind of surprised, at this late time in your life, that you don't already know about this."

"I knew you were my godmother, but you said there was more to the story," I reply, sliding my chair closer. Even with just the two of us here, there is tension in the room. Hazel folds her arms on her lap as she starts to speak, but I can't hear everything she is saying. My mind has flashed back to a recurring dream.

Many nights I awakened with the feeling of ants climbing on my body, to find nothing there. In the dream the floor is hard, sandy; I crawl fearfully, with no place to hide. Hundreds of ants are crawling in circles. I can't keep my eyes off the ants. I want someone to pick me up, to save me from them. They are climbing up my white high-tops and into my diaper. When I put my hands down on the floor to crawl, they're on my fingers. I'm crying, waiting for someone to pick me up. Finally Hazel rescues me. Smelling like sweet cream, she wipes the ants off me, saying, "Now, there now, there, these little ants won't hurt you."

Hazel is speaking now as I come back from my daydream.

"I drove over to see Hope and Bill one windy evening," she is saying. "The storm door on their house was swinging in the wind. Opening the door, I saw the plastic curtains blowing in the windows. Your mother was in a back bedroom resting from having a heart attack after giving birth to Charlie. The sink was full of dirty dishes. Your brothers Mike, Butch, and Tony, were playing kick-the-can, while your brother Brian was chasing your sister Marianne with a kettle of hot water for a trick she'd played on him in school that day. 'Where is baby Erin?' I thought to myself.

"I crept up the gray painted steps, smiling as I looked out the bare window, seeing your brother Joe and sisters Pat and Shannon playing in front of the chicken coop, trying to put doll clothes on the chickens. But then I thought for the second time, 'Where is the crying coming from?'

"I started to panic, moving swiftly through the upstairs, looking for you. When I walked into your room, Erin, my heart sank. Denise was feeding you her bottle. She was only two years old, but she was trying to stop your crying. I felt sick. You had a red face, full diapers, and a horrible cough. Picking you up and changing you would not fix the situation. I stood there looking at you, Erin, and I said to myself, 'I'm taking this baby out of here now!' I stepped over the clothes on the floor and found a bath towel, changed you, and then wrapped you up. I gave you a water bottle with sugar in it. I walked right out that front door, too upset to have a conversation with your mother at all right then. I knew Hope was in over her head. But to be honest, I was madder than a wet hen. I had so much time and love for kids, while Hope just seemed to be having babies and not taking care of them.

"It wasn't that they didn't love you kids, Erin. They wanted all of you. It was just that it was hard times for them, and Hope's heart wouldn't allow her to keep up the pace.

"Well, when I got home, I called your mother. I told her, 'I've taken Erin. She has the whooping cough, and she needs medical attention. I realize that with all of those kids you are unable to get proper care for her, so I'm taking her until you feel stronger. Hope, I'm her godmother, and you're my friend, and I'm happy to do this for you.'

"Hope paused and said, 'Yes, you are a godsend, Hazel.'

"Erin, I kept you for over a year. You had your own room. Come with me."
I follow her to the back bedroom, where she shows me a picture of myself in my crib. "Erin, I taught you how to walk. You even slept in your shoes. I loved you, Erin. You were a gift from God. Such a happy little baby!" She reaches over to me, touching my face as if she is blind, feeling her way. "On Sundays, after church, Hope came over for a cup of tea and watched you crawl around."

"Well, Erin, I started to believe you were my baby. Fourteen months passed, and in December of 1958, for your second birthday, I decorated the house and made your favorite chocolate layer cake. Then came a knock on the door. Another guest, but not a party guest. It was Hope. I reached out to hug her, but she didn't hug back. Instead she started to cry.

"'Hazel, you have done so much for me. In a lifetime, I could not thank you enough for the life you've given Erin. But she's grown up here for almost fourteen months, and she thinks this is her home. I can't live with that! I can't live without my baby. I'm afraid you're too attached. Erin thinks you're her mother, and that won't do.'

"I started to cry, Erin. Hope was right.

"'Please forgive me,' she went on, 'but I have to reclaim my daughter. No matter how many kids you have, you can never spare a single one.'"

Tears stream down my own face now, and I wipe them away with my sleeve as I look into Hazel's eyes. "Hazel, please explain how my mother could have let me stay with you that long!"

"Well, Erin, it was like this. Hope and Bill had hard times in their lives. They struggled more than most. It wasn't just that they didn't have money: they were also dealt some very sharp turns. They had a lot of pain in their lives.

"Don't judge them, honey. They were God-fearing people, and your father was the proudest man I have ever met. You children were really all they had to keep them going. After Shawn died, your father was ready to dig his own child's grave until his family paid for the grave and headstone. Erin, that is a family on hard times."

Hazel reaches for my hand saying, "Yes, Erin, I was devastated when I lost you. But your parents wanted you even more than I did."

I hug Hazel. She is soft, smelling of a special cream I haven't smelled in over twenty years. I don't know, really, what to say. I just thank her, both for being a mother to me and for allowing me to go back to Hope, my real mother. I know that no matter what struggles my family ever has, home is always better for me. I'm a Quinlan.

Holding both Hazel's hands in mine, I kiss her on the cheek, saying, "I feel overwhelmed, Hazel, and I need to go now. I'm very moved, but I'm confused, too." I realize that both Hazel and Hope made sacrifices for me, but there's so much to sort out.

Hazel walks me to the front door, and in my confusion I look down at the floor. There are hundreds of red ants crawling around in a circle! I know that I crawled on my hands and knees on this floor as a baby, right here in this house. I know that Hazel loved me.

I stay in contact with Hazel until she dies on June 30, 2002.

Annie Gets Her Gun

HOPE MOVES THE OXTAIL to the side with her big wooden spoon as she dishes out the bean soup. The soup is hot, and steam rises from the bowls. I whisper to Charlie, "I hate to have the oxtail touch my soup."

Swinging my legs under the table, looking outside (it is almost dark), I can see the neighbor kids running from door to door under the streetlights. I hear them yelling next door, "Trick or treat!" They have big bags with witches drawn on the outside. Probably made them in school, I think.

At our house, the big white mixing bowl sits on a chair in the front doorway. When Hope answers the door she tells the trick-or-treaters they can reach into the bowl and each take one piece of candy. Charlie and I watch out the window. Some kids are witches, some are ghosts. One kid has a pretend hook for an arm. He has a patch over his eye, and when he talks you can see a black tooth. The kids have their mothers with them. Rain is coming down the window, and inside, on the windowsill, is a small puddle of water. I slide my finger through the water, lick it off my fingers, and watch the kids run to the front door of our house. "Trick or treat, trick or treat!" they yell. Some kids say, "Trick or treat! Smell my feet! Or give me something good to eat!"

My older brothers and sisters are upstairs. Only Charlie, Denise and I are downstairs with Hope. Hope holds out the bowl of candy to each group of trick-or-treaters, smiling at the kids before shutting the door behind her and turning to us. "Who in the hell would let their kids learn to be beggars?" she says to us. "I don't believe Halloween is a holiday at all! Here comes another kid, Charlie. He is all blackened in his face and has holes in his clothes. His mother burnt a cork to black his face," Hope says, pulling back the curtains. "It is ridiculous that a parent would carry on like this!"

We stand watching out the window. "Look, Hope! Look at that kid!" Charlie and I laugh. "He's a big round orange pumpkin, with small legs hanging out. He can barely run!" The trick-or-treaters are pushing each other, laughing, having fun. The parents are talking to each other in groups separate from the kids.

"I see him," Hope says. She shakes her head as she rests her folded arms against her breasts. "That costume is store-bought, kids. Some fool actually went to a store to buy that one. At least they could have taken the time to make the costumes at home. Those will only last one night, and that is a huge waste of money!"

"Hope, how old do you have to be to go trick-or-treating?"

"It's for all ages, Erin, but you are not going on my watch. You and Charlie are too young to go out alone, and I sure as hell am not going to take you around town dressed like fools to teach you to beg. I don't believe in Halloween." We stand and watch for a long time.

The front door opens wide again. This time it is Brian, my older brother, standing there with a big bag from the store in his hand. He's laughing out loud.

"Erin and Charlie, come over here! I have a surprise for you guys." Charlie runs to the door. He knocks over the dish of candy, and candy flies all over the floor. The bowl breaks into three big pieces. Brian gets on his knees to pick up the pieces. "Don't worry, Hope," he says, "I'm rich now. I can buy you a new bowl. I got paid today at my new job. It's my first paycheck and I'm spending it on the kids. My checks will help out a lot, Hope, but this first check is for my little brothers and sisters."

I run and jump into Brian's arms. "Yippee, yippee, we are going to play hide-and-seek! And get scared! It's Halloween!" For hide-and-seek, the big kids chase Denise, Charlie and me all through the house while we try to not be found. It's lots of fun!

"Nope, not this Halloween, Erin. We are not going to play hide-and-seek. We are going out trick-or-treating! There's not much time left, but I got you costumes like the other kids. Run and put this on," he says, throwing a shiny bag at me. "I know you will love it, kids. It's fun to go out on Halloween, and I will take you all!"

My brother Brian is seventeen years old. He's tall and has black curls that fall in his face. He has beautiful green eyes, and he laughs at us little kids all of the time.

The older kids, hearing Brian's voice, have come downstairs to see what's going on. I rip open the bag to find a skirt with small bits of white stuff on its edge. Pat grabs the bag, laughing, and says, "Erin, it's a cowgirl skirt! You're a cowgirl!" I'm not sure what a cowgirl is supposed to look like, but I love my new skirt.

"Here, put her hair in braids, Marianne," Pat says, "one on each side. Yeah, that's how Annie Oakley looks." Marianne looks at me critically as she evens out my braids.

"Hurry up, Cowgirl, hurry up!" Denise yells, pulling on her long black dress with wild colors on the sleeves. Pat wraps a purple headband around her forehead. It hangs down on the sides.

Shannon is dancing around. She's a ballerina. Her skirt is stiff and sticks straight out.

Marianne is a princess, Pat is a nurse, Joe is a bad guy, Denise is a gypsy, and Charlie is Davy Crockett. He has a hat with a long fur tail on it and a knife on his leg, strapped onto his pants.

I'm Annie Oakley. My vest matches my skirt. My boots are white.

"Hey," my sister Pat says to Brian, "that's real fringe on Erin's vest!"

Two guns hang at my waist in a brown plastic holster. Brian takes out my guns and waves them in the air. "Do like this, Erin." He shoots the guns. They have caps that make noise when you shoot.

Hope is in the kitchen doing dishes, yelling at us. "Kids, this is not my idea! Brian wants to treat you all to a fun Halloween." Shaking her big spoon from the bean soup, she says, "Brian, they're your charges, and it's pretty dark out there already, so go now. And be careful not to get hit by a car or anything! Hold Erin and Charlie's hands. This is a lot of kids for you to watch in the dark."

Brian throws me over his head, putting me up on his shoulders. He is not in a costume, and I can smell the greasy stuff he always puts in his hair to hold it back on the side. He smells good to me. His jeans are rolled up at the ankle, and I can see his white socks. His white t-shirt hangs over his black belt. His big fur-collared coat makes him look like a father. I'm high enough to see into all of the windows. I'm Annie Oakley, and my guns really make a loud noise as we walk into the dark with Brian.

We pass lots of tired kids, wanting to go home, but we are just coming out. Davy Crockett is by my side, looking up at me. Denise, the gypsy, is holding Brian's other hand. It is cold, my nose is cold, and I can feel the rain hit my vest, but I don't care because I'm Annie Oakley.

The first house we go to is dark, all the lights turned off. One of Brian's friends lives here. Brian pounds hard on the window, yelling, "Come on, Chris, open up! I have my little brothers and sisters all dressed up! Open the door! I know you're in there! I need some help with all these kids!"

The porch light comes on, and Chris is standing in the doorway in just his jeans and socks. "Come on, Brian, they're your little sisters and brothers! It's cold out! I don't want to go. Here, give them some candy and take them back home."

"No, I'm not going to do that, Chris. They're going out tonight and filling their bags! This is a big night."

Chris gets his shoes on to come with us. We walk up and down the streets, and I get to ride on Brian's shoulders. Brian takes us to all his friends' houses to show off our costumes. Some pretty girls come with us and follow us up and down the streets. It's fun!

Some houses have doorbells, and I get to ring them. When our hands get cold, Brian pushes them into the bags of candy to warm them up. Some people are really nice and let us come into their houses to get warm.

After Brian's neck gets sore from carrying me, one of his friends goes home and gets a wagon for Denise, Charlie and me to ride in. The rain pours, the lights are all getting turned off, but we're still out getting candy. Brian's friends are dancing under the streetlights and kicking broken-up pumpkins.

At last Brian says, "Well, you guys had a good time, didn't you?" We cuddle together in the wagon as Brian pulls us home.

Hope, standing in the kitchen, says, "Look at how cold these kids are, Brian!"

"I know, Hope, but they were having so much fun! Besides, we didn't make them walk. We pulled them in Chris's wagon so their feet wouldn't get wet."

Turning back to us kids Brian says, "Now comes the best part of the night! Empty your bags in a huge pile and sort the candy out. Match all of the candy bars up, like they're little cars. Count them, and let's see who got the most candy. Whoever has the most gives some to me."

Sitting on the floor, we pour out the candy and pile it up high. "Yea! This is so fun, Brian! You are the best brother ever!"

Our noses are frozen, my fringe is wet, and my socks are stuck on my feet. Then my face is down in the pile of candy somehow, and I'm falling asleep. Brian throws me over his shoulder and carries me upstairs. I pretend to be all the way asleep so I don't have to walk. Brian tucks me in and says, "Good night, Annie, I hope your belly is full." I smile as he winks at me in the doorway.

I cuddle with my sisters to keep warm, and we all sleep in our Halloween costumes. My Annie Oakley costume is my new pajamas. I can hear the big kids all laughing downstairs in the kitchen with Brian's friends. I'm warm now, full of candy, happy to have Brian as my big brother.

Fire

LYING UPSTAIRS, LOOKING OUT the windows that face the street, I can see the tree branch moving against the roof like a monster's hand. It moves and scratches most nights. I cuddle closer to my four sisters, touching my sister Denise's back with my bare chest, smelling her hair. I try to go to sleep.

It is a cold night; I can see my breath when I breathe. Hope and Bill, our parents, don't heat the upstairs of our house. My sister Pat is lying in bed pretending to smoke cigarettes. Snuggled in the deep round nest our mattress makes, I can feel the mattress buttons against my skin. I'm Erin, four years old. Down the hall, in my brother's room, they're probably sleeping the same way, with just skivvies on, cuddling for warmth.

Facing the window, under lots of thin blankets piled high, I listen to the scratching of the tree branch. Then I hear noises in the hall and the sound of feet hitting the gray painted floorboards. Hope is screaming "Fire! Fire! Fire! Oh, dear God, we're going to die! I can't let this happen! Get out! Get out now!"

My older brothers and sisters are running around frantically, trying to find clothes to put on. They don't want to be seen half-naked by the neighbors. The big kids are pushing each other, trying not to have to move out onto the cold roof. We are all crying, and I beg, "No, Hope, please don't make me go out there. I'm a scared!"

I grab at her hand. She shakes me loose, saying, "Do as your goddamn told!"

Holding onto each other, we cry, "We can't see! Hope, we can't—! It's too dark!" I'm crying. Hope is yelling at us kids. She seems really mad.

I stand next to the window. Fear holds me still. Hope is still screaming. Joe is trying to find another window we can use to get out, but they're all painted shut. We have only two windows upstairs that open. We can smell the smoke but can't really see it. "Faster, faster! The fire is coming up the stairs!" Hope yells as her strong arms urge us forward. She forces a baseball bat into the window opening to hold the window up.

I'm first to go out. Hope picks me up, and my heel clips the sill as I am dropped on the other side. The wind is blowing my hair; it feels like snakes on my face, burning as it hits my cheeks. I have never been on a roof before. I hold Charlie's hand, dragging him behind me. I hear Hope yelling, "Move down, move down! Make room for the others!" I am a scared to look back. Someone might fall off! It is so slippery out here! Dark dark, cold cold crying crying....

We are sitting on the slanted roof, with the porch under us, and I look up at the monster tree. It doesn't seem so scary now that we're outside with it. It watches us press ourselves hard against the side of our house, taking up space that only the night should have.

"Don't look down. We'll be okay. We'll be saved soon," Hope says calmly, as she wipes her forehead with her nightgown. "The hardest part is done. Now they will see us up here, and the firemen will save us. Don't hold hands, kids, even if you are afraid. It will make you stick out too far from the dormer. The firemen will come and save us." Hope's voice is clear now. I press my ponytail so hard against the house that my rubber band breaks.

Denise whispers to me, "Erin, don't be scared. Hold on tight. The roof is wet." I want so bad to be back in my warm bed!

"Move down, move down," the big kids are saying. I look for Denise. Her wavy hair makes her look like an angel.

Charlie is looking forward, staring at the tree. He stutters as he says to me, "Erin, are you a-sc-sc-scared?" I don't answer.

Hope says calmly, "The neighbors will see us up here even if it's two o'clock in the morning. Someone coming home from work or the bar will see us. They will call the fire department for us. We are going to make it! Just don't move."

The tree seems to stare at us. I think that tree likes us. We are all watching to see what happens next, and the tree seems to be listening to our fears, wanting to help us. Our backs are getting hot. I smell my baby dolls burning behind us in the house. Then loud horn sounds come from the next street-lots of loud, special horns. Hope yells, "That is the fire truck! No, don't look down! I can see them on the next street. We are going to be saved." I wonder if God is driving the truck. We try to look in its direction, but Joe says to keep looking straight ahead. We can hear the siren, and then we can see the trucks, but they don't get closer.

We hear the men yelling and swearing at each other. They're trying to push the truck out of the sand. It won't move.

There are hot tears now, dirty on our faces. Hope slowly moves her head forward to see my brother Joe. "Joe, Joe," Hope repeats. "They're not going to make it! We'll burn to death up here! We need to save ourselves. You've got to get hold of that branch and pull yourself across the roof. That branch is strong enough to hold you." Joe is only eleven years old. "Go to Hardgrave's house! They'll have a ladder leaning against the garage. I saw the roofers there today. You'll need to run as fast as you can and get the ladder for us. If you don't, we'll die up here! The fire is getting higher and higher!"

Her nightgown is flying up, but Hope is calm. She looks at all us kids lined up like wet pop bottles. She says, "We need to save ourselves. Joe, don't be afraid. You can do this. I need you to listen carefully. Run, and don't stop until you get back here with the ladder! Put it against the house. We will all climb down. I'm afraid the hoses won't reach from where the fire truck is stuck."

Joe listens to Hope, and he doesn't look scared. "Okay, I think I can do it," he yells back. He crawls across the roof to the monster tree's branch. The monster tree is now our friend and is watching over us kids. If we slip on the wet roof, its branch will stop our fall. Joe pulls on the branch as hard as he can, throwing his body against the trunk, sliding as fast as he can down to the cold dark wet grass. We watch his white skivvies run into the dark. We cry silent tears. My lips are shaking, watching him go.

Yippee! He's back! Joe leans the ladder against the edge of our roof. Hope moves to the edge, holding onto the tree to steady herself as Joe scurries up the ladder. We stop crying to do what Hope tells us to do. I want to tell someone I'm cold, but I keep quiet. Hope slides to the edge, Joe reaching for her hand, but she shakes her head and pulls back. "No, I can't go yet. We need to get the kids down first. Don't look down," I hear her say to all of us on the roof. "We can do this."

I can't see. My eyes are crying. They sting. I hope I'm next to go. Hope reaches for Denise, then me. Someone grabs Charlie. We are all on the edge, waiting to slide down the roof to be saved from the flames. Marianne is holding one side of the brown painted ladder as we all take our turns getting down.

I'm halfway down the ladder when a big man grabs me. He throws me over the shoulder of his wet plastic coat. His coat has yellow stripes around his armpits. His hard hat moves up and down like one of those dolls I've seen in the back windows of some people's cars. He grabs Denise, putting her over the other shoulder, backing down the ladder with us. Bouncing, we look at each other and smile—dirty tears, dirty faces, and bare chests we don't want anyone to see.

Joe is leaning against the ladder with his hand reaching out. He keeps moving kids off the roof. A huge man steps forward to help and asks, "How old are you, son?"

"Eleven," Joe says.

"Our truck got stuck on the turn near the beach. The sand is soft, and our wheels got buried. Our hoses and ladders wouldn't reach you. It would have been too late — without you thinking so fast. Your mother must be proud of you."

At last Joe, in tears, sits at the bottom of the ladder, staring at the neighbor's house. We kids are happy to be safe. I can see Joe through the window of the fire truck where they put Denise, Charlie and me. The lights inside the fire truck are all yellow and red and green. Buttons and knobs are everywhere. Men are talking on the radio. The big hands of the fireman and the look in Joe's eyes are like pictures in my head. I see some of the neighbors, wearing nightgowns that blow in the wind. It is almost turkey day, and it is cold outside. Some neighbors have coats over their nightclothes. I climb out of the truck to see the big people.

I lean against Hope in a coat someone gave me to wear and put my hands in the pockets to keep warm. Hope stands looking at the flames, saying nothing. The fireman asks Hope, "Are you a smoker, Mrs. Quinlan?"

"No, sir, I'm not," she says.

"What happened here tonight?" the huge man asks.

Hope rubs her hands up and down her arms, fast, to warm up and says, "My friend Lee and I were having a few drinks. She's a smoker."

"Well, where is your friend now?"

Hope looks as if she doesn't understand the question. Then I hear her say, "I think she left about eleven. Well, we were having a few drinks. She must have fallen asleep in the chair. Hell, I don't know! I went to bed. I figured she would sober up and drive home." She wipes tears off her face, her voice shaking. "I left her sleeping in the chair. Maybe earlier, when we were talking, she let a hot ash fall between the arm and the seat of the chair. I'm not accustomed to babysitting adults."

The fireman looks at Hope, and then walks away. He comes back a few minutes later, covered in black soot. He says, "Well, the fire started in the chair, all right." He looks mad. "That ash must have smoldered there until about two this morning. The chair is in the living room, and there's nothing left but metal springs. Mrs. Morgan is the one who caused this fire, and she was fortunate to get out before it started. The flames followed the draft upstairs, but that closed door at the top of the stairs slowed it down long enough for you to gather the kids and get them out the window. We call that a back draft. You must believe in miracles!"

"I don't believe in miracles, but I do believe in God!" Making the sign of the cross, she pulls all the kids she can reach into her arms. I hear her say, "I believe in my kids, too, and one of them saved us tonight."

Neighbors take us into their homes for the night and give us fresh clean pajamas. We kids are split up, because no one wants more than two kids. The bed I get to sleep in has two sheets and smells like soap. I wish I had my doll, but the lady says, "Don't worry, we'll get you a new dolly tomorrow. Tonight you can sleep with my daughter's dolly, okay?" Denise gets a teddy bear to sleep with. I'm so glad that Denise is with me! She is warm to sleep with.

People come the next day and start getting all the old burned stuff out of the house. We kids watch from the other side of the street where we're playing with our friends. We are ready to get back to our own beds as soon as they let us.

Later on, I watch out the window of the neighbor's house to make sure no one hurts the monster tree. I love that tree now.

The Last White Horse

MY TOOTH IS MOVING around in the front of my mouth. My tongue is trying to escape my mouth through a new hole it is trying to make. I can also kind of whistle. "Hey, Charlie, watch this!" I say as I push my tongue out against the gum under my front tooth. I move it back and forth. I can also make it move from side to side. I am going to have the tooth fairy take it out of my mouth tonight when I'm sleeping. Mrs. Kelly, the first-grade teacher, said that you go to sleep and while you are sleeping the tooth slips under your pillow, and when you wake up it doesn't hurt at all and you get a dime or a quarter. If you don't have a black mark on it, it is worth more.

My birthday is coming, too. "I can get a birthday present and have money from the tooth fairy," I say to Denise.

"I don't think so, Erin. You don't just go to bed and have the tooth fairy pull it out. Hope is the tooth fairy around here, and it's no fun to have a tooth pulled out."

"I don't believe you, Denise. There is a fairy, and I think she comes in through our bedroom window with small wings and has a wand. I know some kids in school said that the tooth fairy came, and when they woke up the tooth was gone."

"Yeah, gone from the pillow, not from your mouth, stupid," she replies, pushing my shoulder.

"One kid had a dollar under her pillow."

"Well, Erin, that was not at our house. I've never seen a fairy around here, and I sure have not had any fairy pull out my teeth when I was sleeping. I think you better ask Hope."

"Charlie, Charlie, look at this! I can move my front tooth back and forth, and my tongue fits under it! I'm going to be getting some money in a day, so we can spend it. I just have to write a note to the tooth fairy and ask her to pull my tooth while I am sleeping so it doesn't hurt."

"Keen, Erin! I hope all my teeth get pulled by a fairy! Does she really have small wings?"

"I've never seen her, Charlie. I just know. But how else could she fly, stupid? At school today, Linda came with her front tooth missing, and the teacher said, 'What did the tooth fairy bring you?' Linda opened her hand, and there were two quarters. I can't believe it! She only lost one tooth but got paid for two! I'm going to go to bed early, and maybe she will pull it tonight."

Looking in the mirror over what we call the "Monstrosity" (the sideboard), I can get really close to my tooth. It has a little blood on it, and there's some on my lip, but it doesn't hurt at all. I get closer to count how many teeth I have.

Hope comes out of the kitchen, saying, "Erin, what are you doing, honey?"

"Well, tonight the tooth fairy is going to come and pull my tooth, so I was just counting how many I have."

"Let me see." Hope takes my hand and pulls me to the middle of the room where there is a bright light. She puts her hand on my forehead and pulls my head back to see my front tooth. She says, "Hold it right there. I need my reading glasses." She walks across the room to where her glasses are lying on a book. "Well, does it hurt honey?" she asks.

I say, "Nope, but it is fun to move around in my mouth. The kids in school say that a fairy comes in the night and takes it out and gives you money under your pillow."

Hope says, "Well, that is partially true, but about the money, it depends what day of the week it happens on. If it's a Friday, for sure it comes, but the other days not always."

Standing in front of her, with a little blood on my green flowered shirt, I ask, "How does it work, Hope?"

"Well, it's like this, Erin. You have to have it pulled out first. Then a fairy comes and gives you the money. The fairy doesn't actually pull the tooth out in your sleep. It's dark in a bedroom, and the fairy couldn't see well enough and might get the wrong tooth. No, I'm the one to pull it. Get me a chair from the dining room and drag it to the front door. I wasn't going to do this today, but I guess we need to get it out."

"Charlie, Charlie, I'm getting my tooth out! I can have the fairy come tonight!" I yell.

Charlie comes running. Hope puts her glasses back on and tells Charlie to get a nice long string from the back room. A kite string would be best, she says. I can't believe it! I'm so excited! Charlie is happy, too. He hasn't ever had a loose tooth, so he wants to know how this tooth fairy business works.

Charlie disappears and comes back with the string. Denise runs upstairs. She doesn't want to watch.

Hope moves the string around the tooth and ties a small knot. I can't talk, and I have to sit really still because she has her hand on my shoulder, kind of pushing down. She takes the other end of the string and ties it to the doorknob of the front door. It's an old knob with a pretty design on it. I'm not sure what is going to happen next, so I just wait. "Get up, Erin," Hope says. "We need to move the chair back some, I think. Yes, we have to, honey. Now sit back down." Hope measures out the string to make sure it isn't tight. "We want it loose, Charlie," she says over her glasses. "I am going to help the tooth fairy out and get this job done today. I want to get the tooth now, because she could swallow it if I don't."

Charlie is excited. Hope goes back and forth, making sure the string and the doorknob are the right distance apart. I'm ready!

"Okay," Hope says. "Erin, this is how it works. You lean your head back, and I tell you what to think about. You think as hard as you can about it, then the tooth is out. It's easy, really. Okay, are you ready?" I can't speak but nod my head up and down. Hope says to me, "Okay, we're ready. Now, I want you to think of the last white horse you've seen." I close my eyes, lean my head back. I try to think of the last white horse I've seen. I can't remember seeing any white horse!

I open my eyes to say, "I have not ever seen a white horse, Hope," but just then our front door slams pretty hard, the glass makes a funny sound, and the curtain flies. I hear a loud snap, feel a pull in my mouth, and I see my tooth flying across the room, then hanging on the doorknob! It is not bloody or anything! I stick my tongue in the hole. I can't believe it: the tooth is gone!

Hope unties my tooth from the doorknob. "See here, honey? We got it," she smiles.

"Hope, there's no blood or anything!"

"That's because it was ready to come out." She leans over the oak chair to hand me my small front tooth. I try to put it back in. "No, don't do that. It is meant to stay out now." She rolls a little wad of toilet paper and puts it in the spot where the tooth used to be.

"Hope, why a white horse?" I ask.

"Well, I knew you had never seen a white horse. Most kids at five years old haven't. I wanted to keep your mind busy."

I wrap the tooth in more toilet paper and put it in my pocket.

Denise comes downstairs. "Did she do her white horse trick?"

"Yep, wasn't that neat?" I say happily.

"Not really," Denise says, walking out of the room.

Charlie and I show our friends the tooth and can't wait until dark to put it under my pillow. After supper I take a shower, to be ready for the fairy in case she has any questions to ask. Like, "When was the last time you saw a black horse?" I try to keep one eye open to see if the fairy comes through the window, flying, maybe on a white horse. I fall asleep waiting for the door to open.

In the morning, I look under my pillow to see two shiny dimes. One for me, one for Charlie. Charlie thinks this is pretty neat, and he says when it's his turn he will share his dimes with me.

My Favorite Christmas

GREEN AND RED CREPE paper chains hang across the hallway. Snow is blowing under the doors. Teachers have bells pinned on their sweaters. My stomach has butterflies. I can hear my teacher, Mrs. Leo, coming to the front of our class. She opens a book and scratches her head as she says, "Today, children, I'm going to read you a story." Clearing her throat, she says, "This is a story about Santa, who lives at the North Pole." She holds up the picture.

I move my hands to the front edge of my desk to pull myself up closer. The lights are all off, and this is our last day of school before Christmas vacation. Everyone knows Santa is coming to town! I look around. "Yep, they all believe in Santa," I think to myself. I do not. Hope has told us that there is no Santa, but I still want to see the picture and hear the story. Maybe he just doesn't come to our house? I want to know more.

Mrs. Leo is a short woman who reads fast and seems to speed from one exciting adventure to the next. Now she is going to stand up in front of this class and read about Santa, when she knows there is no Santa. Mrs. Leo has a Santa hat on, with a white fuzzy ball on the top of the hat that swings over her right shoulder. I stare at her in that hat as she tells of a man who comes down the chimney to put toys under a lighted Christmas tree. I watch the other kids get all excited. They've already had presents that Santa brought to their houses before, so they're sure he is real.

This Santa has a big round belly that jiggles when he says, "Ho, Ho, Ho!" He watches to see who is naughty or nice, is making a list and checking it twice.

I don't understand it. Can a man do this? Mrs. Leo talks about the reindeer pulling the sleigh and elves making toys for all the good boys and girls. I have heard of this Santa before, and he sure does seem nice. He can fly on a sleigh, carrying gifts down a chimney. I keep my eye on Mrs. Leo to see if her face will tell the whole story, about how some believe and some do not, but Mrs. Leo has read this story so many times that she seems to believe in Santa herself. When she finishes reading the story, she puts down the book and smiles. "Well, kids, let's make a list of what toys you want for Christmas. Okay? Santa will be at your house in a few more days."

I take out some of the loose-leaf paper that Hope divvies out to us kids from pack of five hundred sheets on the first day of school. (Along with the paper, we get our own brown work gloves.) The notebook paper has to last until Christmas, so we don't waste it. I don't want to make a list for Mrs. Leo, but she is so excited that I figure I better not disappoint her. I don't want to let people see my face as I pull my pencil out and start to write. I draw a line down the middle of the paper. On one side of the paper, I write pink slippers. On the other side of my paper, I write small radio and battery. I fold up the paper and pass it up to Mrs. Leo. I sit back, wanting to use the restroom in the back of the classroom, and wait for the other kids to make their long lists. As I wait for recess, I put my head down and close my eyes, trying to imagine what it must be like to believe in Santa.

Mrs. Leo unfolds my sheet of paper, looks concerned, and then she asks me to stay behind when the class is let out for recess.

"Sure I will." Am I in trouble? I wonder. I'm kind of scared. The class lets out, and I walk to her big desk, with huge piles of papers from our class stacked up in a neat metal basket.

Mrs. Leo takes a sip from her coffee cup, swinging her legs in front of her desk, with her ankles folded. "Erin, you don't seem to want very much from Santa. Do you believe in Santa?"

"No, ma'am, I don't. Hope told me not to wreck it for the other kids, so I wrote what I wanted, anyway. Is that okay?"

"Why don't you believe?" she asks, barely moving her thin lips as she talks.

"Hope said some people have to have something to believe in, but we don't have to, so she told us the truth. There is no real Santa."

"That's sad, Erin," she says, with tears in her eyes. She looks away, up at the lights.

I pat her scratchy skirt and say, "Christmas is still magic, anyway. All of my family gets together, and Hope makes a big meal, with a turkey, potatoes and gravy, stuffing, and all different kinds of pies. We go to church, and sometimes we're in the balcony, with the candles for the nighttime Mass. We hold candles, and sometimes Charlie and I drop hot wax on the baldheads that are standing below us." The people below look up, and we pull our heads back, not to be seen, but I don't tell Mrs. Leo this part. "Hope said that if we know there is not a Santa, it's better, because she doesn't want us to think we are not as special as the other kids. We might think that we were naughty when we were not. If we make a list, and don't get the toys, we would think it was our fault, and that would wreck Christmas. So instead we all go to midnight Mass, that has candles in the dark, and go right to bed after, so we can open our gifts in the morning. Usually, we get one medium-sized gift, and one small one. It's not sad at all, Mrs. Leo. Really, that's the truth."

The excitement is still in the air for me. I want to see what all of my friends have written down. Mrs. Leo reads the list to the class: kids want bikes, wagons, baby dolls that can wet their pants, snow pants with matching winter coats, ice skates, and sleighs big enough for the whole family to ride at the same time.

After school, I walk home, wondering what I will be getting on my own list. I have a tingling feeling in my stomach. It is almost Christmas.

At home, the smell of homemade fudge is in the air. It is peanut and maple fudge. There is a long piece of wax paper, which Hope has dropped a few pink and green candies onto. It's a real holiday. While Hope drizzles fudge mix into a cup of cold water, she hums a Christmas song; when the drizzled mix turns into a soft ball in the water, it is done, and we have homemade fudge.

My brothers and sisters and I are all excited about Bill coming home with a large tin of molasses cookies from the day-old bakery near his apartment, the place he stays during the week to work. I hate those molasses cookies. They always stick together so you have to eat three at time. But everyone else likes them. On the reel-to-reel recorder, Jim Reeves is singing about Christmas.

Charlie, Denise and I wait for the big kids to come home. They're better than Santa! Our house is full of excitement! It is Christmas, and no Santa could ever make up for what we have behind the steamy hot windows of our house. With dancing, music, special food, and especially being all together as a family, we have more then we need.

Christmas morning we get up, run down the stairs, and slide across the gray plank floor. Hope and Bill are happy, and the house smells of fresh turkey, potatoes and gravy. The windows are all steamed up from the fresh bread, hot out of the oven, to go with the hot cocoa we have on Christmas morning, and dust flies as we put our heads around the corner where the Christmas tree stands. The tree is really big! It is decorated with homemade decorations. Its lights are blinking, and the bulbs have water in the tubes. The water goes up and down, like bubbles.

I can feel the butterflies in my stomach again. Maybe this year will be different, and we won't get even a small present under the tree! I look away, out the window, at the falling snow. It is pretty, but I really want a present—any size at all! Bill leaves the room quietly, walking toward his bedroom. He pulls something out from under his bed to surprise us. He has three sleds for us little kids! They're red, with curved runners, and just our size! So shiny, they must go fast, we think. I don't know if the big kids helped pay for them or not, but this is just like what the other kids at school talked about — a real Christmas story!

We bundle up, as warm as we can, with socks over our brown work gloves and plastic bags over our tennis shoes so they won't get wet. We head to Cowboy Hill! We slide on feet in the snow on our plastic bag boots as we walk. When we get there, we ride our sleds down Cowboy Hill until it's almost dark. We hold hands, side by side, as we scoot down the scary side of the hill, hit a tree and get covered totally in snow. It is so cold and so fun! Finally Denise says, "We have to go now, because we will be frozen by the time we walk all of the way home."

We hold hands in each other's pockets to keep warm. The plastic bags are making the snow pretty slippery. It's hard to stand up, and we talk about how much fun it is as we walk down the snowy road.

I know that the houses we pass have trees lit with colored lights and lots of toys under the trees. But for me, the surprise of the sleds makes me sure that God and Santa worked together on this one.

Every Sunday

HOPE HAS TWO HEADSCARVES. One, her wedding scarf, is a white lace triangle, and the other is black lace—her funeral scarf. I know that black lace is too old for a girl not yet ten years old; still, I must wear a scarf to church. I get excited thinking about Sunday Mass. I don't like having to wear a scarf—or worse — but piling into our old car is part of the fun of going to church.

We are crowded but don't complain much to Hope and Bill. They've been given a car that we don't all fit into, a dark brown 1960 Thunderbird with beautiful red-checkered seats inside meant to hold four people. Bill, my father, who refers to himself as a practical man, took out the back seat of the car, and we kids have to lie in the trunk and put our heads where the back seat used to be. No one is really happy about having to climb into the trunk and ride on top of each other in layers, but I don't mind it as much as the bigger kids because Charlie and I are the smallest. We get to ride on top of our brothers and sisters, and the two of us can see out the windows. Anyway, missing church when you are a large Irish family is not an option but a mortal sin!

Bill also solves the problem of having five girls in the family and only two scarves. He takes two toilet paper squares and folds them into one. Then he puts two big black bobby pins together to make an X or cross. That holds the square in place on a girl's head and really finishes off the look. I feel stupid most Sundays, wearing toilet paper on my head instead of a scarf, until I start to see the humor in the situation.

Hope wears a blue pillbox hat with a black veil that can pull down in front. She pulls the veil down just before she walks into the church, like she is Jackie Kennedy, for dramatic effect—or maybe she is embarrassed at how ridiculous we all look. It never dawns on Hope and Bill to get a few more scarves at the Salvation Army, where we shop most of the time for the extras in life. Every Sunday Hope says, "Oh, girls, this fuss you're making is ridiculous. Most people would not be able to tell the difference between a scarf and toilet paper. You are making a big deal over nothing." We can tell the difference, but arguing gets us nowhere, so we grin and bear it, as always when things are crazy at our house. Respecting God in His home is important to all of us. But what God doesn't know is that His rules make three of us girls look stupid every Sunday. Most of the other people can't take their eyes off the toilet paper on our heads.

Laughing is a huge part of our family life, though. We kids love to laugh at each other. We don't even know what Mass is about.

This week I've found both the white and black scarves, so Denise gets to have a scarf, too. We think it is funny to pretend to be Hope attending a funeral. She goes to them all the time. Hope says you can actually smell death sometimes. I'm glad we can only smell burned food and good homemade bread at our house! I'm dressed in my plaid shirtdress with the bright white cuffs. I'm feeling pretty dressy for church this Sunday.

Going to church is fun. We climb into the back of the car, piling in with our feet in the trunk and our heads towards the front (where most people would sit). It's hot and dusty, and the car smells kind of like oil spilled a long time ago. We only have seven miles to go to the Saint Mary's Church in Port Sanilac, and we are glad it is not farther away.

When we get out of the car, we are happy to be late so no one sees us arrive. I had said a few quick prayers to myself in the car that no one would see our family getting out of this car. The parking lot is quiet, and Mass has already started. I climb out first, because I'm on the tip-top of the pile, and my other five brothers and sisters come out yelling. We march through the double doors, getting strange looks as we enter the church, but at least it isn't raining and we don't have wet toilet paper on our heads.

I know we will be noticed. We kids walk single file to the front pew. Hope and Bill follow, with great pride in our family. Bill is wearing a Western tie with metal tips. It looks like a rope to me. He carries an envelope in his front pocket for the collection at church — a five-dollar check in it that is more then we can actually afford. Hope looks pretty. She has a line drawn up the backs of her legs to make people think she has nylons on like the rich people do, and her dress flows when she walks. Hope has a style like no one else and beautiful cheekbones and a dimple on her right cheek.

Hope and Bill sit in the pew behind us, watching and waiting for one of us to put our butt on the seat at the wrong time or to start laughing at an usher's hair or how someone's dress gets stuck between their butt cheeks when they are at the communion rail. There is so much to laugh at but laughing also make us get smacked on the head with Bill's ex-boxer knuckles. He has it down to a real science: the hit only takes a second but stings for five minutes. Bill is a man of few words. He stutters pretty badly, so he is quick to solve problems without talking. Charlie usually gets smacked first. To hold back and not laugh then is almost impossible, and I usually follow Charlie in punishment because I'm laughing so hard my shoulders jiggle and give me away.

I love church because we get a lot of attention. People seem to admire us and wonder how Hope and Bill have control all of the time. After church, someone will say, "I sure do admire your big family. How many kids do you have? Are they all yours?"

Hope smiles, saying, "Well, when she was born" (pointing to me) "she was as black as a beer bottle. She was born in Pontiac, so they might have switched her at birth. We just call her our Little Black Heart." Rubbing my sore head, I smile at Hope as if I love the name 'Little Black Heart.' Bill is still humming a hymn and having another cigarette while he stands in front of the church waiting for us.

Soon we are the only ones left in the parking lot, trying to remember the order we all rode in the pile coming to church. The bigger kids squeeze in first, and Charlie and I climb on top of them. They start pinching us before we even leave the parking lot of the church, but if we yell it only prolongs the ride home, so we just wiggle and suffer.

During harvest time, my parents drive home very slowly. Bill offers Hope a running commentary on how the farmers' crops are doing. Bill flicks hot ashes out the window, and the ashes fly back into the back seat, adding adventure to the trip. We kids are already sucking down the smoke from his Salem cigarettes, so what are a few hot ashes flying onto the pile of kids? We never complain to Hope and Bill about these rides. They love us and think we should be grateful for getting to go to church.

Back home, we all pile out of the car, relieved that we will not be riding in it for another week.

Hope starts Sunday dinner. This is chicken, fried in a pool of hot grease, mashed potatoes, creamy corn, cornbread, fresh sliced tomatoes, and cucumbers in vinegar. What I love about Sunday dinner is that my father is home and we are truly a family. Relieved to have Mass behind us, eating the Sunday dinner, I think that it doesn't matter how my funeral scarf looks or how stupid my sisters look with toilet paper squares on their heads. God knows we are doing the best we can.

But while everyone else is clearing the table, Denise and I are hiding the scarves for next Sunday.

The Broken Window

AFTER CHRISTMAS, DENISE AND I decide to turn our bedroom into an apartment. Since my older brothers have moved out, there are two whole bedrooms now for us five girls to share.

Denise and I are singing and drinking hot bouillon from coffee cups while we clean our new space. The upstairs is cold. Through the window we can see the Christmas tree at the corner of Joe's gas station. That tree lights our whole town for the long winter. Joe says it is just too pretty to take down.

On New Year's Day we wait in line at Joe's gas station for our bag of candy. It's fun to stand in line with our friends. The townspeople make New Year's Eve a fun time for kids who don't get much at Christmas. I think trading candy is the funnest part. I take the chocolate pills with white inside, and Denise loves the raspberry jelly-filled dark chocolate candies and the striped ones with lines on them. Hope gets the popcorn balls in fancy green see-through paper. With our bellies full, we cuddle up and breathe in the fresh smell of a winter storm coming soon. We can hear our house numbers, 44, swinging around the one nail that holds them, scraping the painted boards of the house as they spin. We know a storm is coming when we hear that sound.

Finally the room is clean, and the only still dirty things in it are the bottoms of our feet as we swing our legs into bed. The bed feels like home. Tired, Denise and I don't cuddle now. Instead we each stay on our own side of the fresh new line we have drawn on the flowered wallpaper—with a small mark on the sheets—to make sure we don't bump into each other. The winter wind is howling. Snow is coming down fast, and I feel a breeze around the window. There is ice on the inside of the window, and the pattern on the glass looks like an ice skating rink for a mouse. We don't think about the cold, though. Sleeping in our new apartment is all we have on our minds.

The next morning, waking up, I notice broken glass in the bed I share with my sister Denise. Snow is all over the bed, and even my dolls are cold.

"Wake up, Denise! Someone must have thrown a rock through the window! The bed is full of snow!"

Denise opens her eyes and yawns. "Yeah, Erin, you were talking in your sleep last night. I guess you were trying to run, too. I'm sure you just put your foot right through the window," Denise tells me. "Don't worry. Just go downstairs and tell Hope what happened. She's always nice to you. She would be really mad at me if I did it because I'm older," Denise smirks.

"The thing is, Denise, my foot is not cut or anything, and I don't have glass on my side of the bed. I think I would have known if I put my foot through a window."

"Well, let's see whose foot fits in the hole," she says. Denise stretches her foot out as long as she can and says, "Nope, not me." She jumps up and says, "Erin, you're making this worse. Just go downstairs and tell Hope and Bill you had a bad night and broke the window, but you are very sorry. Show them your big brown eyes. They always fall for that." Knowing that the window has to be fixed today, since it is a snowy winter Saturday, I snap my hair into a ponytail, pulling off the pink tape that holds my bangs down. As I move to the stairs, Denise yells out, "Good luck, Erin!"

Step by step I try to get a good story going of running in my sleep, but I really am sorry. Bad news to Hope and Bill is just that — bad news. I work up tears to make them feel sorry for me and sort of limp into the kitchen where they're having coffee. "Here's a piece of glass, Hope. It must have been blown in from the storm last night. But don't worry, we're not hurt."

Bill, my father, slams his coffee cup down so hard that coffee splashes out. "Erin, the wind can't do that! Only horseplay can break a window!" I stand there, knowing he is mad and that I'm not excused. I wait until he puts out his cigarette and drinks more coffee. At last he says, "Well, Erin, you might have just outsmarted yourself." I look down, crying, wanting to be let off the hook. Bill feels around for his lighter, stroking his cigarette and tapping it on the orange and yellow tablecloth with old woodstoves printed on it.

Crying, I say, "Last night Denise and I rearranged our bedroom to look like an apartment. We put the bed next to the window. Now there is snow and glass all over the bed. I have no idea how this happened, but the hole is just the size of my foot."

Bill looks at me coldly, like we have never met before. "Erin, we don't have money for this foolishness. You will have to get a snow shovel and shovel sidewalks in town today to earn money for a new window."

"Yes, sir." I spin to get out of his sight. Bill puts on his work boots to go to McPherson Hardware to get the required glass. He says it will cost about three dollars and twenty-five cents.

I'm lucky not to be picking out a tree branch to be spanked with. Instead I get to earn the money — three dollars and a quarter. Denise agrees that I'm lucky. I pull on both pairs of my pants and Denise's also and put plastic bags over my tennis shoes, with rubber bands around the top to keep the wet snow out. I put socks on my hands for gloves.

Outside in the winter storm, every other step is a slide. My nose is cold, but my cheeks are getting pink, and I feel pretty at first as I wander down Main Street asking for walks to shovel. It is nine o'clock in the morning.

Hope's friend Lena, owner of the Carsonville Hotel, is throwing her leftovers into the garbage bin. I ask Lena if I can shovel her walk. She already has a boy to do it but says I can sweep the snow away from the doorway. When the doorway is swept, Lena's bulldog can come in and out when he wants to. I don't tell her I broke a window, figuring she would not trust me even to sweep a porch if she knew how bad I had been. The dog lies in the doorway all day, and as I step over him, he opens one eye and looks at me. The eye is all red. Maybe he has been drinking, I think.

When I finish sweeping, Lena goes to the register and pulls out three quarters. Seventy-five cents. "Warm up now. You know we're expecting more snow today," she says and pulls my scarf up tight around my neck, making a knot.

Sliding on up the street in my plastic bag boots, I see Joe outside his gas station. He has a wrench in his pocket and a lot of grease on his hands. His striped garage suit is black with oil. I walk into the gas station behind him. Joe has a smile for all kids. He crawls under a car as he says, "Erin this is a pretty bad storm. Aren't you cold?"

"No, sir," I say. "These socks are pretty warm. I just wonder if I could shovel your walkway and earn some money?"

"Well, no, I don't need to have the walk shoveled, but you can answer the phone for a while. Just say, 'Joe's gas station, may I help you?' Then come to the garage and get me, okay? It's hard to answer the phone and get anything done."

I'm excited to do this. "Yes, sir!" When the phone rings, I answer it saying, "Joe's gas station. May I help you?" in a deep sexy voice.

Joe hears me answer the phone a few times and finally starts to laugh, "Erin what are you doing?"

"Well, my brothers say I sound like Mae West. I thought if I answered the phone like that, you might give me a regular job here!"

Shaking his head, wiping grease from between his fingers with an orange cloth, he says, "Erin, you are a good kid, but no, I really don't think it would be appropriate to have Mae West answer my phone, even if it would make my gas station busier." He laughs some more and goes over to the register, ringing a bell to pull out one dollar and a big huge red-hot cinnamon jawbreaker. He ruffles my hair with his hand.

I smile, saying, "Thanks, Joe. If Bill ever needs his car fixed, I'll tell him how good you are."

"Fine," says Joe, "but now you better mosey on home, before you get snowed in here and have to work for free. If you want to earn more money first, check across the way. That storekeeper is lazy and might need some cleaning done."

I walk across the street to ask Mr. O'Connell if he needs to have his walk shoveled. "No thanks, Erin, but you can come inside and put all of the candy bars under this glass counter in the right boxes, wipe down the shelves, and do the bathroom sink for one dollar."

It's nice to be out of the cold for a while. When I finish at Mr. O'Connell's it's almost lunchtime, but I don't want to go home until I make the three dollars and twenty-five cents. I now have two dollars and seventy-five cents.

I walk down the street about a mile from our house to see Mrs. Kerns. She is ninety years old and already pays me one dollar a week to clean her house for three hours every Saturday. Mrs. Kerns is a nice old woman with a huge nose and large pores. The black net on her gray hair looks good, I think. She wears an apron too but never seems to cook. Her television is loud and makes a hissing noise that she doesn't seem to hear, and her house is very organized, with magazines to read and Girl Scout cookies, plus bowls of stale candy, on the table next to her chair. It is a quiet house compared to ours. Her bathroom is not like ours, either. The floor in hers is solid, and you can't see through to the basement like we can when sitting on the toilet at our house. Her kitchen doesn't have mice scampering across the floor at night like ours does, either, I bet. Our mouse holes have covers over them. My father uses the shiny tops of can lids on the floor and baseboards, nailing them in a circle.

My grandparents are gone now, and Mrs. Kerns is like a grandmother to me. Her house is a warm, cozy place. I have promised myself I will buy it when I'm old enough.

Mrs. Kerns has one short sidewalk for me to shovel, so I do that. Fifty cents is all she can afford, she says, as she reaches deep down into the pocket of her clean apron and pulls out two quarters. I thank her, smiling as I take my fifty cents, and turn to wave a sock-covered hand as I leave.

I shovel one more sidewalk and after that quickly slide back down the street to get my feet unfrozen and my numb fingers warm, dragging my shovel behind me. Then at last I'm home again!

I walk into the kitchen to give my father the three dollars and twenty-five cents. Bill smiles. "You done good, kid!" He rubs the big bare belly that hangs over his shiny Western belt and baggy jeans. "I've fixed the window, but you girls will have to move your bed. We can't afford broken windows around here."

Hope peels the plastic bags off my shoes. She puts my wet socks on the potbelly stove to dry.

Of all the places I have been today, this is the best place of all. I run upstairs, two at a time, with my snow-wet hair swinging back and forth. I take two bobby pins, hooked together as pretend keys, out of my pocket and use them to open our new apartment door.

Denise is sitting there waiting for me with a cup of hot bouillon. She smiles at me and says, "'Please close the door, for it is warm in here and I greatly fear you will let in the cold and storm!'" She is quoting Robert Service, Hope's favorite poet, and she pulls Hope's shawl up higher on her shoulders as she says the words from the poem. Denise likes to act like Hope sometimes. She has a Suzy Q for me, too. Our favorite treat is Suzy Q cupcakes, and Denise knew I would be out shoveling for almost the whole day, so she went to the store to buy the Susie Qs. She holds her cup of bouillon up to toast me and smiles.

I drink the bouillon in our pretend apartment and tell her my tales of making the money.

"I wanted to help you, Erin," she says. "I feel so bad. I broke the window myself." Looking down at the floor, she says, "Erin, I thought I would have to get a switch to be spanked, and I knew you wouldn't, so I told you that you did it. I'm sorry."

I look at Denise, my favorite sister, in our pretty nice new pretend apartment, and I start to bounce on the bed. "Hey, we got a new window for our apartment too! I'm not mad. The townspeople are pretty nice, really." We raise our cups and toast again. I lean against the window where we have hung out our underwear to freshen instead of having to wash them again so soon.

Charlie knocks on our door, as he does several times a day, "Come on, Erin, let me come in and drink bouillon with you and Denise, please," he begs.

I figure he has to earn the time he spends in our new apartment, so this time I say, "Okay, Charlie, I know what you can do. Steal two red light bulbs off the Christmas tree, and we will let you come into our new apartment. But we're not giving you bobby pin keys because you would just lose them, and besides you might try to bring in some of your friends, and that is against the rules. Just get the red lights, and we'll let you have a cup of bouillon with us."

"It's a deal. I don't care about the bobby pins, Erin," Charlie says, lying in the hallway, talking through the crack under the door. "I just want to see how you fixed up your apartment and what candy you put in the candy dish. I'll be right back with red Christmas bulbs!"

That night we let Charlie join us and light up our new apartment on Main Street with red lights. Suddenly we hear the glass in the front door downstairs move and the paper curtains swing as Hope slams the door. "Erin and Denise, get your butts down here!" Hope yells up the stairs.

"What in the hell are you girls doing with red lights on and underpants blowing from the windows? This is Main Street, for God's sakes! The truck drivers on M-46 might think this is a whorehouse!"

We don't know what a whorehouse is, but it doesn't sound good. We do as we are told, turning off the red lights and taking our underwear out of the window. We whisper together in the dark before we fall asleep in our new apartment for the second night.

Dry Run

WE LIVE ON MAIN STREET. From our windows we watch the big kids in town go to baseball games, and during plum season we hide on the roof and throw plums at them on their way to the school. (No one knows where the plums are coming from.) The funeral home just down the street is where another friend, Carman the undertaker, lives. Hope likes to visit with Carman, who will have a few beers with her and talk about who is being laid out. One day Hope is sitting on our porch with a drink in her hand, visiting with people who pass by, when along comes the undertaker.

"Gene," Hope yells, "who did you lay out today? I know you were working late last night. I saw the lights."

Pulling up his coat collar, Carman stops and replies, "Hope this is one of those days I'm not sure I'm in the right business. I need a drink after what I've just done this morning. Almost too sad to talk about, really," he adds, folding his arms on top of each other, looking directly into Hope's eyes. "Hope, there was a bad car accident last night. A little girl was killed. Her body needed lots of work."

Hope stands up and says, "You are a fine, compassionate man, Carman, and if this upsets you—well, it should. Death is something to be respected. I know you did the best you could have done with a bad situation."

"But Hope, she flew out of the car and was run over! What in the hell do you do with a little girl's body that's gone through all that?" Carman steps up onto the porch to take the coffee Hope hands him, then shakes his head. "Hell, Hope, coffee isn't covering it today!"

Hope puts her arm around Carman and says, "Come on, I'll have a drink with you! You've got a good reason to stop the world today."

Carman and Hope walk to the hotel bar to visit over the sad details.

When Hope comes home later that afternoon, with a sway to her walk, she says, "Erin and Denise, get some nice clothes on. We are going to pay our respects to this little girl, Maria. It is the least we can do for the family."

Mumbling in a low voice, I protest, "But Hope, we don't even know her! Aren't we supposed to know the person in the casket?"

"Not necessarily, Erin. Sometimes you just console the family. I have lost a child myself, and I might be able to help Maria's mother. Besides, it will be good for you girls to go on a 'dry run.'"

Denise and I walk behind Hope, down the street to the funeral home, watching her sway in front of us. I know there will be no other kids there on a "dry run." I don't know what "dry run" means, just that we are going to see a little girl we don't even know, lying in her casket.

The lights are dim, and tissue boxes are everywhere. I work hard not to cry along with the family.

Denise and I walk up to the casket with Hope and look inside. We see a small girl, lying in a long black box with a big shiny gold handle on the side of it. The grown-ups are talking about how Maria was killed going to midnight Mass. A drunk driver crossed the center line and smashed into the car her father was driving. I stand staring at her as my knees start to lock up, holding onto the long handle of the casket and watching her face, waiting to see if she will move or wink. There is thick makeup on her face, stuck in the corners of her eyes and in the creases of her nose. She looks as if she is sleeping, but her stomach is shaped funny. Through her dress I can see the shaped corners of a cardboard box covering her stomach. The dress is a beautiful light blue with a small lace collar. Her dark braided hair comes down over her chest to where her bra would have been if she had been older.

Her father, Mr. Kyle, stands by the casket with his two brothers, telling the story of the blinding snow and how the car flipped, throwing Maria from it. He stands holding his hat in his trembling hand, and tears well up in his eyes as he talks about how he turned the steering wheel as fast as he could but the snow blinded him and he could not see what side of the road he was on.

Mrs. Kyle, Maria's mom, is sitting in a fancy chair. Women from the town crowd around and touch her arm and cry as she tells the story leading up to Maria's death. Mrs. Kyle sobs, telling how she did not want to go to church that night. She had a bad feeling, but Mr. Kyle had insisted, so Mrs. Kyle suggested that they leave Maria and John home. Mr. Kyle said they were too young to be left home. "I should have stopped him," she moans. She falls to her knees sobbing, holding her head in her hands.

"We were going to church! How could God do this to us?" Mrs. Kyle's sweater starts to fall off her shoulders as she turns and explains to her friends, "My Maria was going to be in seventh grade. She was looking forward to wearing a bra and shaving her legs next summer. Now she will never get a chance to go to a high school dance, date a boy, be a cheerleader, or get married." Sobbing uncontrollably, Mrs. Kyle keeps running her hands through her hair, pulling on it. Bits of hair come out in her fingers. "She will never have babies! God has robbed me!" she cries.

Maria's younger brother, Johnny, only eight years old, is at the drinking fountain making the water splash on his dress shoes. He tries to make a game out of the sadness. He hangs around the water fountain and turns the knob for people who come by for a drink of water.

Hope reaches into the casket and touches Maria's hand. She turns to Denise and me, and says, "Come on, I want you two to touch Maria so you don't have nightmares."

I think, I didn't even know Maria until today! If going to the wake of this little girl is going to scare me, how will touching her keep me from being scared? "Hope, you are the one who is scaring me. I don't want to touch her!" I pull my hand back, pleading with Hope, "We don't want to! She's our age. She's just a little girl, too. She won't come to our dreams and scare us, I promise!" But Hope grabs our hands and makes us touch Maria. Maria is cold and hard, and her makeup comes off on our fingers. It kind of stings. I wipe it off on my dress. Hope stands looking at Maria as tears splash off her cheekbones and onto the casket. "Did you know her, Hope?" I ask.

Her hands are shaking as she wipes tears from her eyes. "No, Erin, I didn't know her, but as my mother told me, you don't always cry for the one in the casket. You cry for the loved ones you have lost. I have lost a lot of people."

Hope walks over to Mrs. Kyle and cradles her in her arms. She pushes Mrs. Kyle's soft hair, damp from many tears, out of her face. Hope strokes her hair as Mrs. Kyle weeps, telling her that God did not rob her, that sometimes He takes children to stop them from the pain of growing up and allows them to be at peace. "Cry for the ones left behind," Hope says. Mrs. Kyle whimpers as she looks up into Hope's soft brown eyes. "I have lost a child, Mrs. Kyle," Hope goes on. "Your heart never totally heals. You just learn to live with the pain. I have eleven kids left, but they're not interchangeable, and I still cry for Shawn. That's why I came here to give my condolences." Hope rubs Mrs. Kyle's back and holds her up as she leans into Hope. Hope whispers, "You were a good mom to Maria, and she loved you. Remember, there are no tears in heaven. Maria is no longer in pain. Had she lived, she would have had tremendous pain her whole life from those crushing injuries. God took Maria to protect her from the pain she would have suffered for the rest of her life. He has wisdom we don't have." She adds, "I believe it was Maria's time to die," and Mrs. Kyle pulls away. She doesn't want to hear that.

Hope genuflects and makes the sign of the cross at the holy water dish at the back door. We do too. We leave the room full of crying, grieving adults.

On the way home, Hope says, "Well, ladies, we have done the right thing by coming to the funeral home. I wanted you girls to see what it is like to be at a wake. It was kind of a dry run for you."

"I still don't understand what a 'dry run' is, Hope. What is that?" I ask.

"Well, you did not know Maria, so you were able to be part of a death without pain in your heart. Dying is part of living. You need to have the experience without the pain to understand that. Now you know what to expect, and you will not be so afraid next time."

But Denise and I are upset for days.

"I don't think I like the 'dry run' idea, do you, Denise?" I ask.

"No, I think Hope is nuts for sure now!"

We pretend that Maria is not really dead. She is just playing a game on the townspeople. We make up what we think her favorite games are, and that she is a swimmer, and that she has a boyfriend named Johnny. I think of her when I walk to school, and we make her our ghost runner.

We try to keep her alive because Hope has told us, "You are only dead when you are forgotten."

"Butch has been killed"

August 22, 1966

WITH A BLOODY MARY (ketchup and vodka) in one hand, Hope sits and looks out the living room window, resting up from almost a whole day of baking homemade bread and starting chicken noodle soup for supper. The smell of baking buns has drawn a small crowd of us kids with sticks of oleo in our hands, waiting to spread the oleo on the hot buns when she takes them out of the oven. Hitting the cooling rack, they steam. I can stick my face right over them and feel the heat. I get to spread the oleo this time. It melts over the buns and falls between the cooling racks to be cleaned up later when it hardens. We have cocoa ready to drink with the hot buns.

The big kids have gotten Hope some new living room furniture, and she smiles every time she gets to use her new coffee table. Life magazine is on the top shelf. Her glasses slip down her nose as she reads her third book of the week, her eyes sliding across every word, understanding the writer's point. The wooden arms of her chair are slightly scratched, but she sits there like a queen on her throne. Hope is taking in the feeling of a hot August day half over, her feet up to rest her swollen ankles. We have huge stalks of rhubarb, tall ones; we will make many pies this summer she says. Time now to rest.

The phone rings. It is a man, and he seems like he is in a hurry. "Get me your mother!" he yells, in a voice I have never heard before. "Is she there?"

"Yes, sir." Handing the phone over, I see that Hope is taking a large swallow of her bloody Mary, almost in anticipation of the stranger's voice. We don't get many important calls.

He clears his throat loud enough for us kids to hear through the phone. "Are you Hope Quinlan? Are you the mother of John David Quinlan? Do you live at 44 South Main Street?"

"Yes, that is I." I have never heard Hope talk like that. The phone sits on a bench between two square oak pillars. Hope stands up, still listening, and grabs one of the pillars. She starts to scream, "You son-of-a-bitch! You bastard! What kind of sick son-of-a-bitch are you?" Long, long silence. Hope faints.

I kneel down and start to pick up her head, screaming for help. "It's her heart, you guys! It's her heart!"

Joe runs into the room. "Hope, can you breathe?" She opens her eyes. "Quick, Erin, get a neighbor. She's in trouble," Joe says. He sticks his fingers in Hope's mouth to see if there is something stuck there. Nope, she is not choking.

"Joe, Joe, it's not that! A man called her and said some bad stuff. I think Bill is hurt." Joe reaches for the phone, still dangling from its cord on the floor next to Hope. "I think someone gave her bad news. She was swearing when she fainted."

Joe hangs up the phone. It rings again, Bill this time. I am so happy to hear his voice. "Get your brother Joe on the phone, Erin," he says in a calm, hollow tone. I hand the phone over to Joe. Joe is silent and stands with one foot on the other – he's wearing basketball shoes — his blue eyes closed. Joe is almost grown-up, ready to take his driver's license test. He listens and says, "Yes, sir," hanging up the phone just as Hope is picking up her head.

"Hope," I whisper, "What did the man say?" I say to Joe, "They asked questions about Butch, like, was his real name John David? Why didn't we know that, Joe?"

"Shut up, Erin, this is not the time for twenty questions!! Can't you see Hope is shook-up?" pointing his finger at me to tell me to close my mouth.

We kids pull Hope back up into her chair. I hand her Bloody Mary drink to her and ask what the man said on the phone. She answers, "He said, 'I am going to let you talk to the coroner.'"

"It doesn't sound that bad, Hope, really," I try to comfort her.

Hope takes a drink, saying. "Erin, you only speak to a coroner when someone is dead!"

The phone rings a third time. It is Bill again. Joe answers and says, "Hope is not doing very well. When can you get here?"

Bill says, "I'm calling from Imlay City, Joe, but the traffic is bad. It's a Friday night. I'm doing the best I can. Do not leave Hope's side, Joe. You are the oldest home now, and I need you to stay right by her side."

Hope throws herself around the room as if she is on fire. It is not a cry but a wail. Her nose is running as she tries to talk, but she can't get the words to come out clear. Her black mascara running down her cheeks, she stops for a minute to just stare, walks over to the window and wails more. The big kids come into the room one by one, like God had called them. They stand on the sides of the room as if they are spectators at a bullfight. The top button of Hope's housedress is sprung and lying on the floor.

The sound of the car that will save us comes to the front of our house. It is Doctor Shimon.

"Bill called me," Doc says. "I know you are not afraid of needles, Hopie, and I am afraid if you don't have a shot, we could have a real stress on your heart. Hope, this is a shot to keep you calm."

Hope stands at attention and turns her arm over as if she has been bad. "Go ahead, Doc. They've killed him! Doc, they have killed him! He is a father of two kids. Doc, how could this have happened? They might just as well have killed me. He is my son! I have no children to spare!" She screams. Doc holds her in his arms, and they kind of rock together, back and forth. Doc keeps saying, as he pushes Hope's head onto his chest, "Quiet now, Hopie, quiet now." His arms are strong, and he is calm.

His nurse is opening the doctor's bag, with needles full of clear medicine inside. She shoots a small amount of medicine into the air and hands the needle to Doc behind Hope's back. Hope is sobbing silent tears, her shoulders heaving as if she is being punished for a horrible sin. Doc moves one hand away to pull up the sleeve of Hope's black and pink paisley housedress. He gives a quick smack to her fat arm, the spot turns red, and he pushes the needle in. Her bra strap drops over the new hole in her arm as if to protect her from another surprise. Doc and his nurse walk Hope to the bedroom and put her to bed.

We all stand in silence, watching her try to talk. She doesn't make sense. She keeps saying, "Where is my mother?" over and over again.

"I promise," the nurse says, "she will be okay, kids. She is medicated. Bill called to get us over here so your mother will be safe until he can get home."

Doc greets Bill at the door. "No words," Doc says and reaches out his hand to shake Bill's. "I am worried about her heart. She can't handle many more of life's tragedies. She is a strong woman, but she has been through enough. She will not recover from the loss of Butch if we don't keep her medicated until she is better dealing with it."

Bill pulls off his Carhartts and his boots to have a beer and talk with Doc at the kitchen table after he checks in on Hope. I can still hear her thrashing around in her sleep, but the screaming has stopped.

Bill and Doc drink in silence. "I've never lost a kid, Bill, and I'm kind of out of my league here. And I know that you love your kids. How did it happen?"

No response at first. Bill looks up at the light fixture as his eyes water up. "It don't matter, really, does it, Doc? No, I guess not. I know it was the last pole of the day, they said. But as far as what happened, I'm not sure. I heard he was taken to the hospital DOA. He was electrocuted. I didn't need to know more, I guess."

Doc pulls at the front of his white coat as Shirlee, his nurse, adds the noodles to the soup Hope had started. "I guess you're right, Bill, it doesn't matter. I just thought maybe it was a mistake."

Bill pulls out a Salem cigarette, stroking it in his worn out hands. "I got him the job. I never would have believed it would end like this. He was a great lineman, Doc. I was pretty damn proud of him. He didn't die because he didn't know what in the hell he was doing. He died because some dumb son-of-a-bitch threw a switch for the last pole of the day and Butch was on the pole. He never knew what hit him." Bill starts to cry. "I will never forgive myself," Bill whispers to himself.

Doc puts his hands on Bill's shoulders, saying, "Bill, would you like me to give you a shot, too? I have a few more in my car. It would give you a good night's rest." Bill doesn't answer.

Instead he says, "Turn her up, honey. Play me some Johnny Cash. Tony, Mike and Brian are on their way home." We stand, we watch, we cry. "Thanks, but no thanks, Doc. I need to have my wits about me. I don't want to be drugged. Tonight I just want to be left the hell alone." Johnny Cash is heard throughout the house as we all wail in our separate corners.

Charlie and I run outside to kick all of the telephone poles we can find, yelling, "You killed our brother Butch!"

We were supposed to be getting ready for my brother Tony's wedding to Carol. We had ordered pretty dresses from the Alden's catalog, and I was going to wear a pink dress with two layers to it. You could see through the first layer, but not the second.

When Tony got to the house, he laid the note on the table that my father had left for him at his apartment (the "bat cave"). The note read, "Butch has been killed," signed, "Bill." I see the note but don't say a word.

Mike, Tony and Brian all stand behind the kitchen door with my father. Tony says he has cancelled his wedding and can stay home as long as Bill needs him. He has a whole week off for the honeymoon that is no longer going to take place, and it is not a problem to miss college or anything. All the big boys are at Bill's side. Bill keeps the music on as his mind floats in and out. He goes through, over and over again, what the foreman had said: "Butch has been killed," just as he wrote on the note for Tony.

The big boys are all standing in the kitchen, and we little kids are huddled in the living room by the floor vent. No one makes sense, really. No one. We all cry until we float off to other rooms to be alone. If I could just see Hope's eyes, it would help me. We drift back together and fall asleep like lumps of clay on the living room floor, waiting for more news, for another call that says it is not true. It doesn't come. It is all true.

Arrangements are made in the next few days. We will be wearing our wedding clothes to Butch's funeral. Brian comes home from the Marines, not knowing he is coming for his brother Butch's funeral. He thinks he is going to be the best man in Tony's wedding. Instead he is a pallbearer.

The cars follow each other for miles. Hope says that when a kid dies, even an older married kid, the whole world stops. Our line of cars is about three miles long, I hear someone say at the funeral home. The room is full of flowers, long ones. Yellow roses, red roses, and huge purple dragon flowers. My brother Butch must have had a lot of friends. Everyone is crying. We stand in our wedding clothes, looking at Tony, wishing he were getting married. Brian is in his dress blues. He stands with his white gloves on, proud to be a Marine.

Gloria, Butch's wife, shakes as she wipes away tears with quivery fingers. She walks wobbly, like she has never worn high heels in her twenty-one years. Her large hazel eyes keep looking up at my father. Bill tries to stay clear of her pain. He stares across the room at Hope. Gloria turns her thick gold wedding band in circles on her left hand. Her nails are long and painted pink, her hair blond and fluffy on top with a twist in the back. My brothers try to comfort her, but no one can. Her heart is shattered. I hear her say how Butch kept driving around the block and parking in front of the house. I think maybe he knew he would not see Theresa and John again. Maybe being a father is like being a mother — you just know stuff that does not make sense. But if he knew, why did he still drive off to work? Why didn't he come back in the house and spend the day with the family he loved so much?

Hope is the saddest person in the room. She is unable to stand next to the casket, and someone is always holding onto her. She has her funeral scarf on and keeps her face covered most of the time. One by one we get on our knees and pray in front of the casket. Butch doesn't move except when Gloria's aunt tries to pull him out of his casket. Then his blue shirt and black tie get all wrinkled.

Butch is handsome. He has curly black hair cut in a "waterfall." He has beautiful green eyes — now closed. He had a "chessy cat" grin. He was a good big brother. He loved to chase us kids through the house, scaring us and making us scream. Our undertaker friend Carman didn't take care of Butch; he was laid out in Keego Harbor and buried in a triangle cemetery.

We all cry ourselves to sleep for three nights. Gloria comes up to see us with Theresa and John, my father tries to be more of a father to Gloria, and they cry together. Hope just misses Butch. He was her drinking buddy. Hope always seems to understand boys.

We all talk about Butch as if he is just out of town on a trip. Anything else, especially that he is dead, is too painful to think about. Hope tells stories of times Butch went to jail for fighting or for swallowing razor blades to show how tough he was. He could open a beer bottle with just his front teeth. He chased Tony around with a BB gun in the barn to get him to do all of the chores. Once he gave me a check for my birthday, written out to me, for $2.00. That was twice as much money as Hope and Bill had given me. He told me to spend it on candy and new underpants.

Everyone is sad for a long time. Charlie and I go on kicking poles whenever we see them. People ask us why we're doing it, and we tell stories about our big brother. So he will not be forgotten.

New Bike

BILL COMES HOME TONIGHT for the weekend, the street lights are on. He is never this late, so I run to the back door to see if something is wrong. Bill is wearing the vest he works in. He is smiling, patting us on our heads as Charlie and I stand close to him in the kitchen to see what he is doing home so late.

He clears his throat. "Well, I have gotten you a surprise," he says as he puts his arm around my neck.

"Is it a pair of roller skates?" I ask.

"No, Erin, guess again."

"How about a scooter?"

"No, but you are close."

"Is it something you can ride on? Is it all mine, or do I have to share it?"

"Well, you have to share it, but only with Charlie. In fact, you will need Charlie to ride it with you."

Charlie holds his hands like he is praying to God. "Oh, please say it's a bike, Bill. Please say it is!" Bill grabs Charlie by the hand and leads him outdoors to the trunk of the car. I follow.

We jump around, screaming our heads off. "Please, can we see it now?"

"Not so fast!" Bill says. "I have to tell you that there is a small problem, but with some ingenuity you kids can still have a lot of fun with it."

"What color is it?" I ask.

Bill says, "Hmm, I would say that it is a dark red." We scream even more.

"How big is it?" Charlie puts up his hands to guess the size of a big present.

Bill keeps smoking while he plays the game. "No, it's bigger than that, Charlie, and you can ride it."

"A Radio Flyer wagon, Bill?" I yell.

"No, no," he answers, swaying back and forth with one hand in his pocket, the other smoking his cigarette. "Well, it is a gift, but it's missing a part. In fact, it's broken but I just knew you kids wouldn't mind."

I skip around Bill, begging him to show us the broken toy. At last he unlocks the trunk with his key, and the trunk pops up. Bill folds his arms, standing next to the trunk. "There it is," Bill says proudly.

"It's a bike!" I yell to Charlie.

Charlie starts to help unload the bike from the trunk. Bill laughs a little, admitting, "Well, the missing part is the seat!"

"The seat! Are you teasing us, Bill? How is that going to work?" I think, well, the seat is off, but Bill is playing a joke on us, and it's really in the back seat. Bill likes to kid us sometimes. But it seems this is not one of those times.

"No joke, kids. It's a nice red bike and yours to keep. I could not refuse the deal, and maybe we could just put a bath towel on the metal pipe where the seat used to be."

"Thanks a lot, Bill," Charlie says breathlessly, thrilled that we have a bike. "We love it, and I can put Erin on the handle bars."

Charlie climbs on, excited as he can be. "Erin, it's no big deal," he says to me. "You ride on the handlebars, and I'll stand up while I pedal."

Bill says a seat should be easy to find at a junkyard, but until then at least we can still ride around. Charlie is strong. He is eight years old. I'm nine years old. We ride around town under the streetlights, trying it out.

This bike is perfect! When we play spud, no one ever tries to steal it. Our friends have cards on the spokes of their tires in the front that make a sound like a motor. They have colored streamers that flow from the handlebars and fly in the wind. We have a whole different look — no seat! We do go to the junkyard to look for one, but banana seats are the new style, so regular seats are not to be found.

Charlie and I love the bike. It is fast and fun, and I like riding on the handlebars. Sometimes Charlie even gives other kids a ride. After riding all the way to Cowboy Hill, though, I can see Charlie making faces from working so hard. "Are you getting tired of standing while you're riding the bike?" I ask him.

"Yeah, I am, Erin, but I can't tell Bill. I don't want him to think I'm not happy to have the present. Bill is too excited for me to say my legs are getting tired. What do we do?"

"Well, Charlie, I think we should make some money and buy a brand-new seat."

"Erin, a seat costs a lot of money, and we don't have any money at all!"

"One thing we could do is make perfume and sell it," I say.

"No, Erin. We've never made perfume. Why not try to save pop bottles?"

"No, you idiot! A bottle is only worth two cents. A new bike seat will cost about five dollars, I bet. Nope, we need to make some money fast." We think some more. "I know, Charlie! Mrs. Dryer, the Avon lady, sells perfume. We could ask her for her empty sample bottles. She just throws them away. That would be a start."

Charlie and I ride over to Mrs. Dryer's house. She is just coming out the door with the pretty pink case that holds all her samples. Mrs. Dryer is the best-smelling woman in town. She wears matching clothes, small heels, and a see-through scarf that hangs down behind to make her look good from the back, too. She even has matching hats and purses.

I jump off the handlebars. "Mrs. Dryer, do you have any samples for us?"

"Well, let me see, Erin. I think I gave you most of my sample lipsticks last week."

"Yes, you did, but I'm thinking perfume now."

"I don't usually have samples of that," she says, loading her trunk with her suitcases.

I say, "Would you please look for one or two bottles? We are making some homemade perfume to sell to earn money to buy a seat for our bike. Charlie is getting tired of standing up when we ride."

"Yeah, Mrs. Dryer," Charlie says. "We just need a little bit to make it smell good. We already have a special way of making perfume."

Mrs. Dryer opens a lot of cases. Finally, in the corner of one old suitcase, she finds six small sample bottles of perfume, almost — but not quite! — empty. They have squirt balls on top to squeeze out the perfume. They're so fancy we know right away that all we need to do is finish the bottles off with the crepe paper streamers we made in school.

"That's enough now, kids. No more samples. I have to have them to run my business."

"I promise I won't ask again, Mrs. Dryer."

She puts the almost empty bottles in a paper bag for us, with pink tissue hanging out that matches her scarf. I give her a big smile, thanking her, and stick the bag up my shirt so my hands are free to hang onto the handlebars. We ride home to get working.

Adding water and crepe paper streamers is Charlie's idea. A lot of people have colored bottles of water in the windows of their houses, so that gives us a good idea. Denise and I had already ripped small pieces of crepe paper and put them in each bottle and added water. Soon the bottles has colored water in them. We hide the bottles under our bed, waiting for the water to turn red, blue, and green.

The next morning I get up. "Wake up, Charlie, wake up! The perfume is cooked! You can see the colors now. We're going to be rich!"

Taking the bottles out from under the bed, we mix together the perfume left in each bottle for a new smell. We think it takes two days to make real perfume, and here we did it in one night!

"I'm so happy, Charlie! I know we can sell the perfume with these fancy bottles."

The next day, we load up the six bottles of perfume and start off on our trip to sell them. We stop at Lena's first and ask her if she would like to buy all six bottles to sit on the dresser in her bedroom upstairs above the bar.

Lena is standing in front of the bar mirror with curlers in her hair. (The bar isn't open yet: it's too early to drink.) She gets excited about the perfume and goes right over to the cash register to hit the key with the dollar sign on it. "How much does each bottle cost?" she asks.

"Well, Lena, you are Hope's friend, so you can have them all for four dollars. I know it seems like a lot, but they smell so pretty!"

I think we've got ourselves a deal. I remove the bottles from the fancy tissue paper they were wrapped in. Lena opens them and smells each one. She dabs her neck behind her ears just before we leave. I stand there watching her, waiting to see how pleased she will be, and I notice that now she has a blue streak running down behind her ears. I look at her, don't say a word, and smile, taking the four dollars. Charlie sees the blue streak, too, but we don't let on.

We take the four dollars to Joe's gas station. Joe has been looking for a bike seat for us for weeks, but it's practically the end of the summer already. He yells out his front door, "Hey, Quinlan kids! Come in here." We stop and hop off our bike. Joe has a nice new black seat! He says, "This is a great deal — only two dollars."

"I think the extra money should go back to Lena, Charlie," I say.

"No, Erin, it's our money, and we're keeping it!"

"No, we tricked Lena, and she has blue streaks behind her ears." Charlie is trying out the new bike seat, and I'm walking along beside him. He is so excited he's screaming.

"You're right, Erin," he says when he stops to let me hop on. "We should give some of the money back to Lena."

Stopping at the hotel on the way home, we tell Lena how we made the perfume, and Charlie tells her that we will give back half of her money. Lena taps her cigarette on the table and says, "No, that won't work, Charlie. You will take out the garbage, and Erin, you will sweep the floors. You were not being totally honest. But I'll leave the bottles in the window just for looks. They are pretty, and they do smell good. But it took special soap to get all of the blue dye off of my neck! Did you sell perfume to anyone else?"

"No, we didn't."

"Good! Then let's just forget about it."

"Lena, would you like to see our new bike seat?"

"Sure." Lena pulls her morning curlers out of her hair, slips on her feathered slippers and a see-through robe, and follows us out of the hotel. Sipping coffee, she gives me a wink and knuckles Charlie's head. Then Charlie and I hop on our new bike and ride off to Cowboy Hill.

Bonnie and Clyde

HOPE AND BILL ARE TALKING about turning our home into an adult foster home, and this Saturday morning a man from the State of Michigan is telling them about an old couple found living in the woods without running water or even an outhouse. They were heating their house with a huge log pushed through a window from the outside to a bare spot in the middle of the room. They'd been living like that for years. Now these people, the Johnsons, are angry because the State has taken them out of their home. They need help, the man tells Hope and Bill.

Hope stretches her neck around behind the man's back to look at Bill. Bill strokes his cigarette and taps it on the table with concern. Bill feels that with only six kids still living at home, we can probably do it, but he tells the man it will have to be temporary, and if it doesn't work out they'll have to go, money or no money.

"How much would this job bring in?" Hope asks.

The man says, "Well, we would pay for everything they need and all the food they eat, plus a wage for you."

Ida, bent over a walker, has long white hair to her shoulders and the deepest blue eyes I have ever seen. Her feet slide over the linoleum, one after the other, never leaving the floor. She has one tooth on the top and two on the bottom, and her fingernails are long and yellow. Ida calls her husband "old bastard." He looks just like her except he has Skoal chewing tobacco all over his face and kind of scampers from room to room, quick on his feet.

Well, these are the new members of our family, and to us kids they look like Halloween characters, but Hope tells us, "Kids, this is what we are doing. It is a way to help out with the expenses of the household. You will get used to them, and they will get used to you."

My sister Pat has to help bathe them, and she really hates the job, but Hope persuades her because she wants to be a nurse when she grows up. Hope cooks their meals, and we serve them on TV trays. Ida lets us know if Johnson has an accident or needs something. (He always tells her when he is having problems.) Mostly it's not too bad except for the way they smell, but we use Lysol Spray ten times a day, and that helps.

Every time Johnson and Ida talk to each other, they swear. Charlie and I look at each other with smirks on our faces. They've been married for sixty-five years and still yell at each other all day. Hope is the only one in our family who swears, and she doesn't do it often.

Denise, Charlie, and I love to hear them swear! Sometimes we sneak into their bedroom and take some of the pink and white mints they eat all day, just to get them mad. The mints don't taste good at all, and Ida yells, "Hey, bring back my mints, you little heifers!" We hate being called heifers, but we like to get them to swear. I think they don't really mind us kids that much; they just miss their life in the woods.

Johnson is crude and calls Ida names. She name-calls right back. At night I hear Ida say, "Oh, go to sleep, you old bastard!" Johnson yells back, "Shut up, you old coot!" They're in love, all right!

One winter night Johnson gets up feeling cold and wants to warm up the house a little. He scuffles across the floor and starts piling the furniture into one big heap. We are all asleep and have no idea what is happening until Hope smells smoke. She jumps out of bed in her old worn out nightgown, running to see where the smell is coming from. Ida is leaning proudly on her walker, watching Johnson kneeling down, blowing on the fire as if he is back in the woods again — which is exactly where Hope wants to send them when she sees the fire! Ida and Johnson are surprised to see Hope so mad. Hope yells, "What in God's green earth do you think you're doing? You'll burn the house down!"

Hope tells us that Johnson, in his long flannel shirt, is having an "episode" and doesn't really know where he is. She calls the big kids, and they put all the furniture back where it belongs, but Hope is concerned that Johnson will do it again when she is not home. He is still a strong man and was independent out in the woods until very recently. Hope has an idea. She tells Johnson and Ida that if they want to go home, she will take them back to the woods. She thinks that seeing their old home again will remind them how hard life was there.

So we plan a road trip with Ida and Johnson. It's a school day, but pulling us out of school never bothers Hope. She loads up all the stuff we need to take for the Johnsons, along with food for a picnic for all of us near their old home. Charlie and I are happy to be part of this. We climb into the front seat, and Ida and Johnson are put in the back.

Johnson yells, "Ma! Where are you taking me, Ma?" (He always called Hope "Ma.")

Hope answers repeatedly, "Johnson, you want to go home, so I'm taking you home to live in the woods."

Ida doesn't say much, except for "Shut up!" She says that to Johnson.

The snow is melting, and the roads are clear. Sun beats down on the hood of the car. Hope hums as she drives along.

After an hour or so, we stop at a roadside park to have our baloney sandwiches. Charlie and I help her get Ida and Johnson out of the back seat. It's a tough job. They're strong old people! They call us "little heifers" and poke their long yellow fingernails into our heads.

To go with the sandwiches, Hope has packed two 16-oz. Nesbit Orange pops in glass bottles for Ida and Johnson. Charlie and I each get our favorite tall grape pop, and Hope has a Diet Frosh and vodka. But we haven't even finished our drinks when Hope decides we need to get Ida and Johnson back in the car before he runs away. She tells Charlie and me that she is responsible for their safety, that it's part of her job. So we load the old folks back into the car and drive on down the road, all of us with pop bottles still in our hands. Johnson is yelling, and Hope keeps humming as she drives.

Suddenly, out of the blue, Johnson belts back the rest of his 16-oz pop, turns the bottle upside-down and, holding it by the neck, cold cocks Hope on the head from behind. She loses control of the car, and we swerve all over the road. Then her head drops, and she drives off the road. She is knocked out!

Charlie and I scream, "Hope, are you okay? Wake up, Hope!"

She doesn't answer at first but finally lifts her head and puts the car in park after we hit a ditch filled with high grass. She is not bleeding but has a huge bump on her head. Charlie and I are mad at Johnson, and Hope is furious.

Ida keeps saying, "You old bastard! What did you hit the nice lady for?" Johnson just mumbles.

Hope tells them that now she will not be able to take them to see their old home. She turns the car around so fast that dirt flies everywhere. The sound of our squealing tires can probably be heard for miles. Hope doesn't speak all of the way home. Charlie and I keep a close watch on Johnson.

When we get home, Hope says, "Kids, that is the last ride for Bonnie and Clyde!" And it was.

A year later Johnson got sick and had to go to a nursing home. Ida cried for the old bastard and joined him in the nursing home a few months later. "Bonnie and Clyde" died shortly afterward, one day apart. I guess they did have a special love.

Denise has a Birthday

IT IS A BEAUTIFUL DAY, June fourth. Denise turned nine years old today. I'm sure we are going to have her favorite meal, potato soup with ham in it with fresh hot bread. Denise always chooses the same thing. I hate potato soup. We had made plans for the "Cabaret" at school, but she is backing out now, saying we are not good enough to sing the Buck Owens song, "I gotta tiger by the tail." I want so bad to sing! We have practiced for a year now, ever since last year when we made up our minds we were going to win first place. Now Denise says, no "Cabaret."

Denise says in the morning, "Erin, this is a special birthday. Let's camp in the daytime. Let's sneak out some peaches and corn and hotdogs and bread and have a picnic."

We are excited with our new plan. It is the last day of school, and after school we are going camping. We are going to pack some stuff in a paper bag and go down to Black River to swim. When we get out of school, our friends will want to see if we can play spud, but we can't — we are going to our secret spot! We have Denise's perfect birthday planned, all by ourselves.

At last we are out of school, and we throw our books in the air! "Yea!" Denise says as the teacher is still trying to make plans for the summer. "I'm done for one year!" Denise screams.

After school Hope is waiting at the hotel for us to make sure we get our chores done. She hugs Denise and kisses her on the forehead, handing her a card with one dollar in it. The dollar falls on the concrete as Denise opens the card. I'm jealous. It has been a long time since I've seen a dollar. "Thanks,

Hope," Denise says. "I'm going to buy you a present, Erin. What would you like? Some snowball cakes? Or a big Moe bar?"

"I guess a snowball. It will go best with camping."

We go home to get our stuff together.

"Did you pack your bathing suit?" Denise asks, waving hers around her head. "We have to make sure we have a towel, too, Erin, 'cuz when we get done swimming against the current we're going to be tired and want to rest on the side of the bank."

"Against the current? Why? That's hard, isn't it?"

"Yep, but it's what you do on your ninth birthday."

"Okay, I'll pack a towel. Is Hope going to know?"

"Nope! No one is to know about my birthday party, no one!"

We are going to swim and make dinner over a campfire, Denise says.

"Are you sure? I don't think you can cook, can you, Denise?" I say.

"Well, anyone can make hot dogs, corn and peaches."

"I guess you're right. Have you invited any friends, Denise?"

"Nope, I don't need any, Erin."

Black River is high, the fish moving fast. Men are standing in the water, fishing with long, long lines. The old boards of the swinging bridge creak when we walk across. Kids come and smoke there, and some kiss in the woods. A lot of people come here after school. Today some older boys run across and make the bridge swing to scare the little kids, but Denise and I just hang onto the ropes on the side and let them pass. "Don't bother," Denise says. "They're just bullies. We can have more fun making supper."

I watch Denise start a fire with one of Bill's old lighters she found at home. She picks up little twigs to add to the fire. Denise is so smart: she just knows stuff!

We swim against the current while our supper is cooking.

The hot dogs are good, and the peaches are great. After supper I surprise Denise with a Suzie Q. I got it from cashing in pop bottles. At last we put sand on the fire to put it out and walk home, tired.

Hope is waiting for us. Denise tells Hope she will eat the potato soup tomorrow as leftovers but that she wanted to camp as a nine-year-old. Hope smiles and says, "Well, it's good it was still daytime when you swam and made supper. I wouldn't have supported such an endeavor if it was dark outside."

Denise is lucky she has a June 4th birthday. Mine is December 4th, and it will be too cold to go camping.

Garden of Hope

MR. RICKETT STOPS BY to see Hope, taking off his hat as he comes through the doorway. He and Hope are friends. Mr. Rickett has four farms and is always looking for people to help him on one or the other of them. Hope shuts off the commercial-sized kettle of chicken noodle soup (with no chicken in it), smiles at him and asks, "What's on your mind this time, Bob?"

"Well, Hope, I think we can strike up a deal."

Hope wipes her hands on the apron she wears most days and says right away, "I'm ready to listen."

"Well, Hope, we ran short on help last year—short on manpower, you know—and we couldn't keep our crops attended daily. So this year I was wondering if maybe we could trade labor for land. I was thinking, well, maybe you and a few of your kids could come out to the garden just south of town – it's only about two miles out – and tend to the watering and bring back some vegetables for your family. Hell, you could just plant what you like at the end of the garden, and that would be your pay. Just keep the critters out, keep it watered, weeds pulled. What do you think?"

Hope likes the idea. "Bob, it sounds like a great experience for the kids! Living in town doesn't give them enough to do, really."

And so, our feet just broken in for going barefoot, we are ready to start our own garden.

I'm excited on our first trip out to the farm. I slip a saltshaker into my back pocket as Charlie and I start walking, the pavement hot on our feet. Hope goes ahead, carrying a rake, a hoe, and her dreams. When Charlie and I cross the last field and arrive at Mr. Ricketts' farm, Hope is already walking up and down each row with a frown on her face.

"They're long rows. A hose will not reach," she says, as she stares down the lines disappointedly. "But let's give it a whirl, kids." She pulls the hose out as far as she can. "You just have to use some ingenuity sometimes, that's all," she says as she fills the gray metal watering can. She fills it up as far as the small hole in its side where water starts leaking out, moves to the end of the garden, and starts working. "I'll tell you kids one thing: if this is the only problem we have, we've got it made!" She rubs her eyes. Her face is sweaty and already streaked with dirt.

"Come on, Charlie, we need to get helping so we can go swimming at O'Keif's Pond today," I say, pushing on his shoulder. The watering can is too heavy for either of us to carry, so we each hold a side of it, slopping water as we struggle along. Hope stands at one end of the garden, and Charlie and I run up and down the rows, spilling water in a line.

Hope wipes the sweat off her upper lip and says, "Okay, it's hot. We've done enough for the first trip. Let's head home." Picking up our rakes, hoes, and dreams, we start home. Then, leaving Hope at our house, Charlie and I run off for a swim at O'Keif's Pond.

Without towels, we lie side by side on the hot pavement to dry off. "It's faster this way. Right, Erin?" Charlie says.

"Yep, it is," I say, moving to the next dry spot on the pavement. "It's pretty smart, Charlie. We don't have to carry towels like the other kids or worry about losing 'em."

On the way home, as we come over the top of the road in the hilly stretch, we see all our friends on bikes, roller skates, and scooters. There are twenty kids, totally out of breath, scared and excited at the same time, moving as fast as they can.

Our friend Joel is screaming, "Your mom shot a man!"

Dickey pulls his bike closer to me, eyes squinting, face scrunched up, like we are all in Big Trouble! "There are four men in blue jackets and hats with guns." Dickey puts his kickstand down, parks his bike and spells the word "P-O-L-I-C-E! They're really mad, Erin!"

Charlie is looking at me as if I will know what to say. "Come on, you guys," I motion to the neighborhood kids so we can ride over the hill in a straight line. "I think Dickey means the 'boys in blue,' as Hope always calls them," I say calmly.

Charlie, running next to me, says, "Erin, do you think she knows how to shoot a gun? I think Hope can do anything. She's nuts, isn't she, Erin?"

"I bet it's just one of the big kids who stole another sunflower, Charlie. I don't think she would shoot someone, even if she is a little nuts!" I start to run down the hill.

We reach the house in time to see Hope in front of the police car, the "boys in blue" standing over her as if she is a criminal. They stand there with large guns sticking out of their holsters, just like the Lone Ranger. Officer Mick is talking, trying to reason with Hope as she clings to "Big Bertha," my father's gun, not wanting to turn it over. At last, after a struggle, Hope hands the gun over to Officer Mick, but she presses her face against the window of the back seat to make sure "Big Bertha" is safe in the police car.

Officer Mick asks, "Hope, what happened?"

"Well, Officer, it's like this," Hope says with disgust. "I saw that bastard sitting on my picnic table yesterday, stroking his privates, and I told the son-of-a-bitch if he ever showed up again at my house, I would not hesitate to shoot him! Maybe he did not know who he was dealing with! I have a family to protect. I'm not afraid, I'm mad!"

Officer Mick kind of smiles but says, "Well, Hope, you can't take the law into your own hands. That is our job. If you had called us, we would've arrested him yesterday!"

"I don't trust the police, and I didn't want to leave this one to an amateur! You can't track an elephant in a foot of snow!" Hope says, folding her arms across her chest.

"Well, Hope, we have your gun now, and your old man will have to come down to the station and get it."

Hope is not arrested. I'm happy she is not on her way to jail. My friends are kind of disappointed; they wanted to see the police use handcuffs.

Hope goes inside and sits at the kitchen table, trying to figure out how she is going to tell my father that his favorite gun, "Big Bertha," is at the police station.

"Hope, what really did happen?" I ask.

Pouring wine into her coffee cup, Hope answers, "Erin, while I was changing my clothes from watering the garden, I looked out the window to the side yard, and there was that bastard with his pants down, doing dirty things! I don't have to be told how to handle a pervert. You shoot him! He ran off with his pants down after I shot at him twice. He's damn lucky I didn't want to kill him. I just wanted to let him know I was in charge!"

Charlie and I go out to the picnic table to see if we can find where he had been sitting, and there we find some blood and a piece of skin from his butt.

Bill comes home and listens to Hope's version of the story. He sees where Hope fired the shotgun through the open window, leaving two large holes in the window screen, and he goes out and examines the picnic table. Bill pats

Hope on the back, saying, "You did all right, old girl! Hopie, they don't stand a chance with you and old Bertha here! That son-of-a-bitch is lucky I wasn't home, because I would have aimed for his head. He is one lucky son-of-a-bitch!"

My father seems angry when we drive to the police station to claim his gun. Bill walks straight up to the counter. "Yeah, I'm Bill Quinlan, the owner of that gun." He reaches over the counter to get "Big Bertha" and says, "I can tell you one thing. My wife is a damn good shot, and if she'd wanted to kill the bastard she would have."

"I know, Mr. Quinlan," says Officer Mick. "I was thinking about giving her a job here." He laughs loudly, and then turns serious. "I don't think he'll be dropping his drawers around your house anytime soon. Hell, Bill, I got my own kids. I understand what Hope did. We just have to follow the law."

"I told Hope," Bill says, "don't hesitate the next time — aim for his head, and shoot that son of a bitch!"

Officer Mick raises his eyebrows. "Well, if you do that, you'd better drag him in the house afterward. Sorry, Bill, for taking your shotgun," Officer Mick says as he leads us out the door.

We kids look for the bad guy every day. We have the clues — the blood and a small piece of his butt. Some townspeople tell us to look in the woods. Charlie and I make a trap, a hole disguised with sticks over the top, in front of the picnic table. We talk about how keen it is to have a mother who would shoot a gun to keep bad guys from hurting us.

Hope Gets Burned

I'T'S A COLD WINTER MORNING, and I want to stay asleep to make the time go faster. We are waiting for Ladybird, our dog, to have her first litter of puppies. Then Hope yells up the stairs, "Kids, kids! Ladybird gave birth in the night. Hit the deck! We have work to do!

"We need straw. I heard them crying in the night," Hope says. "Ladybird was howling in pain. I got up and put an old blanket down, but we need it to be warmer. There are eight of them. She's a mother and has to take care of her own kids."

We run out to the unheated back room attached to the house. I'm running with pure joy in my heart. The stairs have three big cement steps, and I skip down the steps to see the puppies.

Hope had gotten up in the middle of the night after she heard three puppies crying for milk and warmth. By now, five more had joined the family. "They will not all live, kids," Hope warns us. "That is just nature's way."

We wonder which ones are not going to make it. Hope says that usually the runts are not as strong as the other puppies, so I try to make the runts work harder to live. I pick them up to make them eat. I'm sad, knowing that some of the cutest ones won't live. They don't fight as hard to get enough milk. Ladybird just lies on her back, looking at the cobwebs.

The room where the puppies are, between the basement and the house, has concrete floors and high windows. We keep stuff in it — a push lawn mower, wringer washer machine, canned vegetables and fruit, boxes of clothes people have given us. The walls are cinderblock and have never been painted. Sometimes we go down there to play the blanket game. That's the game where we wrap up a kid in a blanket, really tight, and drag the kid around the room to try to confuse him. Then we hide him somewhere and make him guess where he is. After he guesses, he can wiggle out of the tight blanket. Charlie is the easiest to trick: he will wiggle around until he falls off the cement step and gets hurt or jump up when he was hidden under a bed and bang his head. Charlie is the most fun to play with but we play this game when Hope is not home.

The backroom is cold and messy. It is not a pretty place to have babies, but it keeps Ladybird out of the cold and wind. We put down straw for her and the puppies and get them all settled down.

"Sometimes, it is worth it just to be left the hell alone!" Hope says of Ladybird. "Well, kids, two bales are a good start and we can just put in fresh straw as we need it," she tells us.

We love the puppies! They're dark brown and light brown with black lines around their eyes like masks and shaggy underbellies. I don't know what kind of dog Ladybird is, but she does look like a lady and is the smartest dog in town. She looks both ways when she crosses the street. She chews gum at baseball games. Our friends give gum to the dogs that come under the bleachers, but Ladybird is the only dog that will chew it for a few hours like a human being. Ladybird is a loyal, loving dog. She doesn't have a collar or a name tag. She is just Ladybird. Hope named her after Lady Bird Johnson whom she admired for her down-to-earth appeal.

Soon the puppies open their eyes and start stumbling around trying to walk. Baby barks are in the air. This is a fun time for us kids.

Then one night the furnace goes out. A few weeks earlier, on another cold night, we had a horrible snowstorm, but this night is different. The wind is howling like Ladybird giving birth, blowing so hard that it blows out the pilot light in our furnace. We cuddle on top of each other like the puppies to get warm on the floor register.

Hope, pacing back and forth, says, "Damn it! I hate that old furnace! It is dangerous as hell! Find the kitchen matches so I can relight it." Hope tears apart the kitchen drawer but can't find a match, so she twists a large piece of cardboard into a tight spiral and lights it from the stove. Dressed in Bill's old work clothes, she steps quickly across the kitchen to the backroom, where Ladybird is sleeping with her new babies, through the backroom and down into the basement, taking the steps one by one and trying not to let the flame go out on the twisted piece of cardboard.

She pushes the furnace restart button down and holds it, waiting for a flame. But, fuel flies out of the hole and hits the twisted cardboard torch she is carrying and blows up in her face. Hope screams like a banshee, running as fast as she can to get out of the basement. But the puppies are lying on straw in the backroom, and Hope, with flames out of control taking over her burning body, slows down as she moves out the back door, not allowing fire to drop on the straw. She doesn't want to hurt the puppies or start a fire in the backroom.

Outside, though, Hope starts to run, still screaming like a banshee, flames covering her body. Even her hair is on fire. She rolls in the snow to put out the flames. She screams, "Get your Father's old coat off me. I'm on fire! My skin is burning!" I can't help thinking of the witch that shriveled up in "The Wizard of Oz."

We pull at her clothes, but they're not coming off as fast as Hope wants. "Get them off!" she keeps screaming.

"We are! We are!" I scream back.

Pretty soon her clothes loosen and fall off, and Hope yells, "Call an ambulance, Pat! Call one now!"

Pat runs to the phone and calls an ambulance for help. We're told to keep snow on her, that the ambulance is on its way.

Hope starts to grab snow herself to put into her private spot between her breasts. She leans her head back. Her face is wet and cold, and her lips are turning purple. There is no place to touch her that doesn't hurt. We want to help her up, but she screams, "Don't touch me!" She is all sprawled out. It takes all of us kids together to get her up from the snow-covered ground and into the kitchen to wait for the ambulance. Her skin is black and has strings hanging from it.

Hope pulls Pat closer to whisper, "Get some butter from the refrigerator and spread the butter on my chest. It's starting to tighten up."

We have managed to get all her clothing off except for the full-length girdle she always wears under her clothes, and we each take a quarter-pound of oleo and spread it on her chest. She says it feels good and that we must keep her skin soft until the ambulance comes to get her. We try to dress her in a loose housedress. Her hair is breaking off as we wait for help.

When the ambulance comes, they're shocked at how bad the burn is. They talk about a serious infection, how deep the burn is, and about the flesh hanging off her chest. They put gauze over it to hold the skin together. Hope, still crying, kisses us good-bye. We are crying as they take her away.

When Hope arrives at Sandusky Hospital, the emergency staff takes one look at the oleo we kids had spread on her and say, "Well, that is the worst thing you could have done, Hope. The oleo kept your skin cooking. You turned a first-degree burn into a third-degree burn."

My brother Joe calls my father, and Bill comes home. Joe watches us while Hope is in the hospital. In a few days, Bill takes us to see her. She is still in a lot of pain but misses us kids a lot. She has saved her pain pill containers for us — little white paper cups, all stacked up—and some crackers wrapped in plastic.

Doctor Shimon walks down the hall in his long bright white coat. He says, "Good job saving your mom, kids. That oleo treatment was really fast thinking. How did you come up with that?"

I tell the doctor, "Well, Hope said it would keep it all moist. She smelled like popcorn," I add.

Doctor Shimon rubs his chin and says, "Well, kids, I think she looked like pizza and smelled like popcorn. This was a real close call for Hope. We need to celebrate with triple-decker chocolate ice-cream cones."

Denise, Charlie, and I jump around with excitement, thinking how big a triple-decker ice cream cone is. We're excited to be in a hospital, too. A nice nurse takes us down a shiny blue hall to the kitchen, where another friendly woman, who looks like she eats a lot of ice cream herself, makes up three triple-decker ice cream cones for us.

Sitting in the hallway of the hospital, trying not to drip ice cream on the floor, we watch the people come and go. Then someone takes us to wash our hands and back to visit Hope. Tears drip off the end of Hope's nose as she tells us she is fine now. She is taking a pain pill called Darvon and shows us how you can take the pill apart: the bead inside is what kills the pain, and the rest is aspirin.

Bill comes to see Hope. He seems to hate the hospital. He picks up Hope's hand and holds it, looking worried, his clear eyes filling with tears. After their visit, Bill walks slowly to the waiting room. "K-k-kids," he stutters, "we need to help Hope. She, she's ready to come home."

We have to help Hope with her gauze and the special medicine we are supposed to spread on her sore red neck and chest. Hope says, "Well, I'll be back in the saddle in a month, but until then I will be counting on you kids to make the oatmeal and say the rosary without me."

Hope dresses with scarves now. She tucks a scarf into the neck of her dress. Whenever Bill looks at Hope, he gets tears in his eyes. He is grateful that we kids were all home to get her help.

Bill gets Hope's glasses and settles her safe in her reading chair. He kisses her on the forehead, saying, "Hopie, we almost lost you! I would think you would know better then try to light the furnace yourself. I just had Jack check it, and he must have bullshitted me. I told him just last week I smelled fuel and you would think he would understand the seriousness of the problem. You would think he would know his own job. He's to blame for almost wiping out our whole clan."

Bill stands next to Hope's side, saying, "I'm pissed off that a man can tell you a furnace is fixed when he clearly had his head up his ass. This is not okay with me! I would be lost without you! The basement must have been full of fumes, waiting for you to strike a match and ambushing you, for God's sakes. I have no respect for the man." Bill pulls out a Salem cigarette and sits down on the davenport next to Hope's chair.

Hope moves slowly for a long time. "Even the wind from the door being opened hurts me," she whimpers.

Most of the weekend my father tries to make Hope more comfortable. He makes soup for us kids, and we serve Hope on a tray and tell her stories to keep her company so she can sit still. My sisters Marianne, Pat, and Shannon clean the house to make her feel better. Even Ladybird comes in and must want to say thank you if she could talk.

Cleaning Day

I HEAR THE LOUD SCRAPE as Bill's back bumper hits the patch of cement at the end of the driveway and the bumper bounces a little. My father drives slowly. The rearview mirror of his car is held in place with a thin fishing wire to hold it straight for its most important job of getting Bill back and forth from work.

Bill shuts off the engine and reaches over to get his metal lunch pail with a shamrock painted on each end. Wearing a bright smile that lights up the outdoors, he takes off his sunglasses and greets the family waiting for him in a straight line on the porch. Hope has us wait for our father like this to show him how much we appreciate him for supporting us. My father reminds me of a happy leprechaun. He is five foot and eight inches tall and has smiling blue eyes. He pats me on the head when it's my turn to be greeted. He looks each of us in the eye to make sure the girls are not wearing make-up.

Hope is waiting at the end of the line, wearing bright red lipstick, "Evening in Paris" perfume, and a dress that shows her cleavage. Her nylons are held up with garters, and there are little orange pills (she is a diabetic and that is the medicine she takes) attached to her garter belt. She likes it that way because if she forgets her pills she has them right on her. Hope has fixed liver and onions for Bill, so tough that only he could ever eat it. The smell is all through the house. Bill seems to love the burnt flavor of whatever Hope cooks, but I think it is just her company he really loves. I'm happy to be going to the game uptown to escape the meal.

This will be a good Friday night if Hope doesn't drag out all the bills she keeps under their mattress. It is payday! Bill empties the change out of his pocket and calls me to go to Harold's Market and get some peanut brittle, his favorite treat. I stick my head into the kitchen to tell them that Arnold has just stopped by. Bill is waving his hands, yelling, "Hey, how the hell are you, Arnold?" Arnold hugs a huge brown case of tall bottles with "Drury Beer" written on the side of the case. It's put under the table to be drunk up before it has a chance to get warm.

Doctor Shimon drives up. His white car with red velvet inside has doors that open facing each other. Parking in front of the green fire hydrant, Doc slips in through the back door, smiling as he takes off his white coat and lays it over the back of a kitchen chair. "I have been here so much for medical reasons, this feels like home," he says. "Where's the beer, Bill?"

Hope walks across the room, her dress swishing from side to side. Her high heels look almost dangerous as she sits and kicks up her leg. "Erin! Come in here now and get the juke box to work!" She points to the reel-to-reel tape recorder and player in the corner of the room on a small dusty brown table. I walk over to put my finger into the small hole and start to weave the tape through its gears. The hole and gears are too small for my parents even to see, and their fingers won't fit the hole.

"Now get the hell out of here!" they tell me when I've done this job for them. "Take a walk or go eat a bowl of s-s-soup!" Bill stutters. He has a smile on his face, but he means what he says! "Go eat a bowl of soup" is how he says "Get lost!"

"Yes, sir," I answer, fast enough for him to know I'm paying attention. "Is there anything else?"

"No, honey, there isn't. Just a few kind words." Smiling because it will be a good Friday night, I skip out of there.

We kids all wait on the other side of the kitchen door, knowing it will be a party soon. We love that. We stay out of the way of the adults having their fun together, but by going to the back windows we can look in and see what they're doing and spy on them.

Soon the kitchen is full of Hope and Bill's friends. They drink beer and listen to loud music. Hope and Bill dance with their hands behind their backs, and Hope's dress sways back and forth as if she is a cat stalking prey. Yep, it is payday at our house!

My parents have lots of drinking buddies. Someone is always trying to drink someone else "under the table." Everyone is having fun! They often say, "Well, this is just drinking talk!" That means, don't hold me to it in the morning! Jokes and laughing are a big part of their night. Hope and Bill love to talk about the President, too. We spy on them for a while until we lose interest and clean up to go to our football game. The bathroom is on the other side of the kitchen, though, so we have to scoot through the kitchen quickly, not to be seen. Sometimes we put our hands up over our eyes to give the grown ups privacy as we pass through their party.

The next morning, Bill calls upstairs to where we kids all sleep, "Off your ass and on your feet!" We stumble to our feet, ready for the Saturday workday that we hate! But this time is different.

"I have an idea," Bill says, as he blows smoke towards the ceiling. "Today we are going to play a game! I have hidden money in each dirty part of the house, and you can have the money when you clean that part of the house spotless!"

I run to the silverware drawer. I know that this is one place he is usually mad about. It's a mess, as usual. I scream and start to dance around the room. I'm the first to get real money! I start dancing around, holding the money up to the light to tease my father like I'm checking to see if it's real. Charlie goes to the medicine cabinet and finds two quarters hidden in the back of it, but he is moving slower and doesn't seem as happy as I am. He cleans the medicine cabinet and moves to the next place to clean. I see my sisters collecting money from my father. We are running around the house, cleaning and collecting money. This is a pretty fun way to clean house!

Hope stands in the kitchen, saying it is pretty smart of Bill. Pat and Shannon run to the "Monstrosity" cupboard to start cleaning and find a five-dollar bill. The house is humming with joy! We are not having a typical Saturday, for once. We're getting rich while we work! We run from one dirty spot of the house to another, cleaning and cleaning, finding dimes and quarters. This is fun! By noon we are all done cleaning, and each kid has found some money.

I'm on my way to spend my dollar when Bill calls me back into the house. "Not so fast, Erin, you are not excused!"

"Well, sir, may I be excused?"

"Not yet. The garden has to be worked up and the weeds turned under."

I look at him to see if he's joking. He isn't. "But, Bill, that is not fair!"

"No one ever said life would be fair, Erin. Get movin'!"

Angry, I run out the kitchen door and push the screen farther out on my way! Bill wants us to use the old thread spool he has nailed on the door for a knob instead of pushing on the screen, but I don't care. I slam the door behind me, knowing that makes Bill mad, too.

Then I remember that we have a box of clothes in the back room where Ladybird, our dog, sleeps. I run to the back room, empty the box, and find the lime green ice skates I remember that were given to us in July. They're lace-up two-trackers, and they fit perfectly! I put them on and start to walk to the garden.

It's a hot day. The ground is still kind of damp. I think I might just as well make this job fun, and I dance up one row and down the other, turning the soil, throwing my head from side to side the way I've seen skaters do on television. I have a song that I'm singing in my head to keep the beat. My shorts are getting dirty; my blouse buttons are pulling. I look right up to the sun to feel the heat. Dirt and mud fly. Some flies up the back of my knees, but that doesn't stop me. I'm even learning a new dance while doing what I've been told to do.

Yelling with my deep Mae West voice, I come around the corner of the row and spot my father with his big bare belly hanging over his pants. Bill looks like he is going to scream, but he just stands there, watching me, not saying a word. I think I might be in trouble, and I have a reply all ready, but Bill doesn't speak for a long time. He just stands there squinting, blowing cigarette smoke. Finally he says, "You're kind of a smart-ass, aren't you, Erin?"

"No, sir. I'm doing what you told me to do. You didn't say I had to use a hoe."

No response at all. I keep dancing, and soon he starts to smile. "Well, honey, you have ingenuity, don't you?"

Taking off my muddy skates, I pull the dollar out of my now-soaked back pocket. It is wet, but old George Washington is still on it. Hosing down my legs, I watch the hair stand up on them, thinking how good it feels to have made a game out of my father's order. He is always telling me what to do, and I can never answer back. This time I obeyed and disobeyed at the same time.

I run past the hotel and bar to Harold's Market, where I spend half of the money. I know we won't get to clean like this very often—Bill won't have the money—but it sure was fun.

Denise's Bright Idea

HOPE IS IN THE HOSPITAL again. This time she's resting from a heart attack. Joe is in charge of us kids, and the good part of that is that there's no rosary and no oatmeal.

Denise and I play on the Tarzan rope swing that hangs from the apple tree in our backyard. This tree is huge and beautiful. It has two parts to the trunk, and we use one for a tire swing, the other for the Tarzan swing. We love the back yard. Whenever we walk by the swing, we can't help running and flipping upside-down and taking a swing. When it's raining, we can play longer under the shelter of the tree, and it always seems to be waiting for all of us kids to take turns on it. Every day after school we run up and take a swing, even if we have work to do first.

Joe cooks for us. We eat spaghetti for the first three days, then bean soup for the next two days, and then on the weekend my father comes home and makes his famous soup called catch-a-man soup. That is the best except for the big piece of fat in it. We all have to have some fat in each bowl, too, to keep "lubricated," my father says. Bill says if he keeps making catch-a-man soup, someone will love it so much he will marry one of Bill's five daughters. Catch-a-man soup is full of vegetables, with beef cut up in small pieces and a beef bouillon taste. We love it. Usually we have it with homemade bread, but this time it is with saltine crackers and lots of butter, the way Bill likes it. The food is good. Not as good as having Hope at home, but at least we don't have to follow the same rules when she is away.

For instance, when Hope is home she will not allow us to go into other people's houses at all. Hope says, "Kids, we are a big family, and if our kids are in anyone else's house and something gets broken, they will just assume it was one of the Quinlan kids. So always stay outside when you are at someone else's house. Stay in the yard and wait for your friends to come out."

Denise, Charlie, and I are playing on the Tarzan swing. The game we play is to run as fast as we can and throw up our legs, wrap our toes around the rope, and hold on tight with our toes and our hands, hanging upside-down. But this time the rope gets stuck in the tree. We throw sticks at it and even ask Joe to help us get it down, but Joe is too busy getting ready for a baseball game.

Then Denise and I have the great idea of wrapping a rope around a rock and throwing it up high. I wait up in the tree, and Denise throws the rock. It is a hot summer day, and the sun shines in our eyes. The rope catches on the swing, but the rock tumbles down without the rope. The rock has sharp edges, and as it falls down it hits Denise in the mouth and breaks off half of her front tooth. Denise puts her head down, and tears and blood fall on the bare spot in the middle of the ground under the apple tree.

Denise is smart and gets straight A's in school. She is in fifth grade, and I'm in fourth. Denise always has good ideas, but this was not such a good one. Now she's crying. Charlie and I are sorry we let her try to solve the problem, even sadder to see her cry so hard. Denise is older and stronger and smarter then we are, so her crying scares us.

We put our arms around her and try to look inside her mouth for the broken piece of tooth. Denise has a big fat lip already and is getting a purple bruise on her cheeks. We need a big person to look at her mouth. I find the tooth piece on the ground and put it my pocket. If we need to, I think, Charlie and I can put it back in her mouth somehow.

Dickey Roach is coming down the street, dancing and singing. Dickey is a kid who wears his mother's fancy bras and underpants. He has a brush cut hairstyle, but today he has put a pink ribbon around his head and is wearing only his mother's slip and bra over his shorts. What he's singing is not country music, he says. It is called opera. I like the way he sings.

Other kids tease Dickey. They say he is a "queer," but we like him. We also love the real malt machine at his house. Dickey says I'm lucky to get to wear a dress 'cuz I can twirl it any time I want. Sometimes I do just that.

Dickey comes to dance in front of our house. He just wants friends who let him dance and pay attention to him. It never really looks right to see him in heels and women's dresses, but we get used to it. I think he is lonely, and wishes he were a girl.

Charlie and I look around. We only have Dickey to count on for help, so Charlie and I put our arms around Denise and take her to Dickey's house. He never asks anything of us except to watch the show he puts on, which is him in his mom's dresses and high heels. If we watch the show until the end, we always get chocolate malts, made with the big metal three-headed malt machine. We figure he is lucky not to have his parents around the house. Mrs. Roach works as a cashier at a store called Farmer Jack's, and Dickey's house has a lot of food in boxes and treats in packages, not homemade like we have. In the freezer there is ice cream in cartons. Strawberry, chocolate, and vanilla — so many choices of ice cream! We never had malts before we met Dickey. He seems rich to have a malt machine.

Charlie and I have decided that Dickey is kind of an adult because he is three years older, and we think the malt would feel good on Denise's broken tooth and fat lip. All Charlie and I have to do is watch the bra, underpants, nightgown, and high heel show, and we will get malts, too. We owe it to Denise, anyway, because we are sorry we got the Tarzan swing caught up in the tree. We walk with our arms around our sister Denise, who is bent over now, catching blood in her hand from a nosebleed.

Charlie asks, "Dickey, can we come in to watch the show?"

"Sure," he says, singing his answer in opera. "But you have to watch the show before the chocolate malt."

"Well, then, we're not going," I say. "Denise is hurt, and she can't sit through a long show without something cold on her lips and tooth." I'm getting mad at Dickey. "We will go and watch, Dickey, but you have to give us the malts first!" I scream at him — without a song in my voice!

"Okay, but you're breaking the rules." Dickey says.

We help Denise slowly up the stairs of Dickey's parents' apartment. The Roaches live above Dickey's father's plumbing store. His father is always too busy to see Dickey's show. I think he would rather have seen Iris, his wife, wearing her own clothes.

Dickey is a fun kid to hang out with, even if he does look strange in women's clothes and makeup. He sings as he prances around the living room, throwing his shoulder up and down like sexy women on television, wanting a bra strap to drop off his shoulder. Denise, still wiping away tears, drinks her chocolate malt with her dirty feet up, waiting for the fashion show. We have seen it at least fifty times before, which is a lot since we are not allowed to be in other people's homes, but Dickey is always entertaining, and he is worth getting in trouble for.

Today as the show is getting underway, Mr. Roach runs upstairs to the kitchen to get a cold beer to go with his lunch and hears opera music. He bursts into the living room where we are relaxing with our dirty bare feet on the pretty orange-flowered couch, drinking tall chocolate malts with long straws from the frosted metal containers they're made in, watching Dickey do a few nice turns in his mother's bra. Suddenly, as sore as Denise is, she is wishing she had not taken Charlie's and my advice.

Mr. Roach slams down his beer, saying, "I'm goddamn sick of this dressing-up stuff! I won't allow any son of mine to be made a fool of, even if he is the one doing it." When he slams the bottle down, beer spills onto his hairy wrist.

"How can I run a business with a boy who goes around town dressed in his mother's clothing? Huh? Answer me! I have a kid who acts like a queer! Now I know you're not, but what do you suppose the neighbors think of this kind of a stunt?" Wiping up the spilled beer, he adds, "And you kids are not welcome in this house again. It might be you kids putting him up to this behavior!"

"Yes, sir," we say.

Dickey tells his father that we asked him to put on the show. Mr. Roach gets Denise a dishrag with ice in it for her face and sends us all home. He makes us pour the malts down the drain before we leave.

So, no more malts. (We can, however, still jump on the trampoline built into the ground in Dickey's yard.). Denise is sore. I'm sorry. Charlie acts sad. We all walk home and decide we should show Joe, our brother, the broken tooth.

Later we play with Dickey Roach again, but from then on he just jumps for us on the trampoline in his mother's bras and lacy underpants. He takes off one piece of clothing at a time while jumping. But there are no more malts, so we don't go to his house as often. We are the Quinlan kids, and we have learned that if we are in someone else's house, we will be blamed if something goes wrong. Hope was right about that.

Carsonville Hotel Fight

HOPE BARTENDS FOR HER FRIEND Lena and sometimes helps clean and get the hotel rooms ready for the next guests. The rooms have fancy green shag carpet on the floor. All the beds are doubles. (Two people fit just right.) The lights in the rooms are small and are on the walls, not hanging down from the ceiling in the middle of the room like ours at home. There are black light switches and frosted glass cups over the bulbs.

The rooms smell like frying grease from the kitchen below. Lena cooks most food in hot grease and serves it nice and shiny.

She is a short woman with a pointed nose and eyes that kind of bug out a little. She wears pink high-heeled shoes with lots of feathers on the front straps and long flowing nightdresses, even in the daytime, with matching robes. Her neckline matches the shoes — feathers on it. She has lots of matching shoes with feathers. I wish I had outfits like that, and I'm sure Dickey Roach does, too. Lena's bulldog lies in the back doorway, so all the guests have to step over him to get in. The dog picks up his eyelids, showing bloodshot eyes, but never moves out of the way.

Lena starts her day by serving the hotel guests a nice breakfast of eggs, potatoes, and toast, talking nonstop about her coffee as she fills and refills their cups. When she catches us kids running past the bar, she grabs us to come in and earn some money. She is generous. Charlie burns her papers for cash or sometimes a box of candy bars. The candy bars are kind of stale but still taste good.

Hope is Lena's only bartender, but she is a good one. When Charlie and I walk home from a baseball game in the summer, we love to sit outside the bar on the painted, slanted cement porch with green pillars and listen to the music from inside. The jukebox is going loud, and it seems like a fun place to be.

Hope is bartending one night when she and Lena get into a huge fight. Lena shuts Hope off from drinking, and Hope walks out, saying she will never, ever return. Then Lena says there is money missing out of the till. Now Hope is an honest loving hard-working mother who doesn't deserve this treatment. She might drink while working, but never would she steal. The fight goes on for months. Hope is not allowed to walk into the Carsonville Hotel.

She misses the stories, the dancing, and most of all her friend. She seems almost lost without her special friend. But after months of rumors about Hope being dishonest, rumors started by Lena, Hope gets mad and decides she will pay Lena back.

First she hires some kids in the neighborhood to put rotten eggs in the air conditioner outside the back of the hotel in the alley. The fans are going, and the smell is sucked into the hotel and bar. A lot of people run out, and Lena is forced to buy a new air conditioner.

The feud gets stronger. In anger, Lena keeps telling people bad things about our family, and Hope is hurt by Lena's lies. The Carsonville Hotel is no longer Hope's playground. She cries at night, missing her friends. Finally Lena tells people that my father is not faithful to Hope, and that is the last straw.

We have a brick pile in our side yard with orange bricks piled up in a square. I get up one night and see Hope in the yard, getting a brick. I go out to see her pulling on her nightgown, and ask, "Hope, what you are going to do?"

"None of your business, Erin," she says. "This is war!" She brings the brick into the house and writes in big clear letters "HOPE" and waits for the bar to close that night. Then she walks up to the front of the hotel and throws the brick with her name on it through the window. It is one of those big picture windows, and the glass flies everywhere.

About an hour later, the police come to our house. One officer is carrying an orange brick in one hand and holding a police stick in the other. Lena gave the police the brick. I'm kind of nervous because I'm not sure what they will do with Hope now. Her name is on the brick! But Hope is not afraid at all.

Lena flies down the street, her robe flowing, screaming, "Arrest her, arrest her, she did it! Well, Hopie, you have outsmarted yourself this time! I hope you rot in jail! We know she put her name on the brick — arrest her!"

Hope stands on the porch, watching Lena run to accuse her, and politely asks the policemen to come in. They have smirks on their faces as they show Hope the brick, telling her it sure doesn't look too good for her. They say they have hard evidence and know she threw the brick.

Hope, smiling, says, "Surely, gentlemen, you don't think I would be stupid enough to put my name on a brick! What kind of fool do you take me for?"

"But, Hope, it's obvious! It's your handwriting, Hope!"

She smiles, saying to the officer, "You have never seen me write on brick! Now please, I need to get some sleep."

The policeman stands there with the brick in his hand, looking at Hope, and then he climbs back into the police car, mumbling about how the brick matches the ones we have piled up in the yard.

"Good night, Officer," Hope yells from the porch.

On Friday night the next week, my brother Brian and his wife Susie come home for the weekend to see Hope and Bill. The reel-to-reel plays Johnny Cash, and longneck beer bottles cover the counter (for us kids to clean up in the morning). Bill is singing. (He never stutters when he sings.) Everyone seems to be having a good time.

After drinking most of the night, Hope and Bill go to bed, but Brian and Susie decide to go to the Carsonville Hotel, thinking Hope will never know. Hope does know, of course. When they come home they see that Hope has written on the dining room mirror, where it is sure not to be missed, in red lipstick, in large letters, "ET TOO BRUTUS?" Brian, smiling, puts his arm around Susie, guiding her to the upstairs bedroom, but I think he gets the point.

Then one day when Hope is walking past the hotel to go to Harold's Market, Lena comes out of the bar and says, "Hi, Hope." Hope smiles back. Lena invites Hope into the hotel for a cold draft, and Hope walks back into the hotel. She decides this fight that the whole town got involved in has gone on long enough. The old worn oak floors seem to welcome her back.

Cannonball

THE WINDOWS ARE STEAMING, crying from the heat. I see their tears running down the glass. My bangs stick to my eyebrows. I hate canning! It is stupid to have chores every day! I want to do fun stuff like swimming. My friends all know how to swim, but I haven't learned yet. "Hope, can we finish canning peaches tomorrow and go to O'Connell's pond today, please?" I beg.

"Hold your horses, Erin. The pond isn't going anywhere. We're going to get this job done — a dozen jars to add hot syrup to — and then we're good to go!" My bare feet stick to the floor all the way to the stove to get more syrup. "Believe me, Erin, you will be grateful," Hope tells me. When the first snow flies, you will eat the best peach cobbler in town!"

I pour in the hot sugar water, tapping my knife up and down the inside of the jar to make sure the syrup makes it all the way to the bottom getting the air bubbles out. "Come on, Hope, please? Can't we finish up tomorrow? We've put in a hard day's work already."

"Erin, you don't know what a day's work is. No, we can't finish up later. You need to put the syrup in now. I gave you the easiest job, as it is. Now get moving!" She taps me on the back of my head with her last words.

"Mr. O'Connell says that if we have an adult with us, we can use the pond that has just been re-dug. Can we go today?"

"Okay, let's kick it into gear," she agrees. "I would love to go for a swim." Hope stops what she is doing for a minute and looks like she's thinking about her own childhood. "When I was a little girl," she says, "I was a great swimmer. We used to swim in a gravel pit, and I'm pretty good."

"Hope, would you teach me to swim?" I beg, hands joined as in prayer. "All my friends know how. It would be fun to surprise them with a cannonball sometime and just swim to shore. That would be great! You don't even have to have bathing suits, really. Just underpants are good enough. No one cares."

"Well, I'm sure as hell not going in without a suit. I don't care how far back from the road it is!" Hope looks everywhere for her swimsuit. Finally she yells, "I'm wearing my black suit. We're on our way to do the cannonball, Erin!"

Hope stands in front of us, showing off. "I look pretty good for a fifty-year-old woman who's given birth to twelve kids."

"You look prettier then any other mother in town!"

"Come on kids, let's get out there before the pond cools down. The sun is going fast."

Our dog Ladybird is at Hope's side, watching her every move. Charlie runs to his friend's house to borrow an old bike for Hope. She walks up and down, smiling at the bike, and starts to laugh. "Oh, no you don't! I'm not riding to the pond! I haven't ridden since I was your age, Erin. Yeah, about ten, I guess – that's almost forty years ago." She says she won't, but she gets on the bike. "Steady me, kids! I'm going to tip over!" Denise and I hold onto the seat and walk fast on both sides of her. Hope lets out a scream as she starts going faster. "Come on kids, don't let go! Keep up!" I'm running as fast as I can, and so is Denise. "Let go, let go, I'm on my way now!" Hope screams this time. "This is great!"

There she goes, headed for a tree on the side of the road. "Watch out, Hope!" we all scream. She turns to hear us and hits the tree. Her head snaps back, eyes rolling, and she falls off. Then her head is in her hands, and she's laughing so hard she's crying. "I don't know why in the hell anyone would plant a tree next to a sidewalk," she says. She just keeps laughing. "Okay, Denise you take the bike," she says at last. "I've enjoyed as much of this as I can stand."

The water is calm, pink from the sunset, and small ripples roll toward the high grass at the edge. I slip off my shorts; I can't wait to wade in.

Hope dives off the huge rock. Swimming, face calm, she smiles up to the sun as it sets on a perfect day. "This is living! Why in the hell are you kids standing in the muck? I couldn't stand being in muck. You gotta start swimming." I look straight ahead, past the weeds, where Hope reaches out her hands to us saying, "Come on, Erin, Denise, and Charlie, you need to get away from that edge. Even the frogs are croaking! You're probably standing on their heads."

I hear my friends splashing loudly, laughing, on the other side of the pond. The older kids are diving, and everyone is having fun. I want to be with them. I wish Ladybird would show us how to swim; she is not afraid. I glide my hands in front of me as my bare chest hits the water. Ladybird swims up to me, and I think to myself, "Come on, Erin, just do what Ladybird does."

Hope takes my hands and shows me how to do the dog paddle. I'm staying up and not afraid at all. Hope does the breaststroke and pushes far away from me. I can hear the splashing in the distance as the big kids do the cannonball.

I just paddle around for a while. I love it! This is my first time really swimming, and I'm pretty proud of myself. We're all having fun. Hope shows us both "the dead woman's float" and the "dead man's float," with "woman" facing up, "man" facing down. We stay on as the moon replaces the sun. It is not cold. It is beautiful. When Hope dives, her face comes out of the water first, cheekbones facing the man in the moon.

I feel ready, all of a sudden! I climb out of the water and run as fast as I can to the other side of the pond. I run up the rock, look both ways, and tuck my legs under my bare chest. My wet hair is dripping down my back. I close my eyes and jump. The sound of me hitting the water makes a loud splash. "It's a cannonball!" Denise screams. "Erin can do a cannonball!" I dog paddle to the edge and climb out. Hope is clapping for me. So are all the kids. I feel like a movie star. Everyone is doing cannonballs now, and I do another one myself. I'm not afraid at all. Then we have to go.

Hope and Ladybird shake off. Wrapped only in a yellow striped towel from the Breeze soapbox, Hope says, "It's almost dusk, and I'm sure as hell not walking home in a cold wet suit. No one will see me. We'll just have to take the back way instead of Main Street."

Tired and happy, Hope gives us safety tips, like, always tread water until someone comes to get you if you have gone overboard in a boat. We don't have a boat, but it sounds like a good idea.

Souls in Shoeboxes

Fifth grade is out early today. Hope had been running for the town council and had painted "Vote Hope" and "There is Hope for Carsonville" on the curb. She thought she would be able to make some good changes in the town. She was not elected, but the paint stays on the curbs way past the election, and I see it every day on my way to and from school. Today I feel pure excitement as I hit the first step of the porch.

The door is unlocked, and Hope is home alone, taking a bath. Midnight our cat is meowing hard for her. I run through the dining room on the gray-planked floors, hoping not to get another splinter. This room has a simple dining table, large enough to seat us all on the holidays when the big kids are all home. A huge mirror hangs over the "Monstrosity" (an old piece of furniture we use to hold most everything), with junk hanging out of its drawers.

Midnight has climbed up on the back of Hope's chair. When Midnight meows it sounds like she is saying "HO-O-O-PE!" She calls Hope's name as if she is mourning her death. Hope has not died, but to Midnight it seems like it every time Hope leaves the room, and sometimes when Hope cries, Midnight wipes her tears with his paws. I pet Midnight, calming her down.

Running to the kitchen, I see the bathroom door closed, but I hear splashing on the other side of the door. "Hope, are you still in the bathroom? Can I talk to you?"

"Have at it, honey," Hope replies with a deep sigh. "You have kind of a captive audience here."

"Today at school," I begin, "some kids said I was adopted. Am I? The big kids call Denise, Charlie and me 'the three little pigs.' I'm kind of mixed up about our names. Bill can't say some names, so he gives us different ones." It seemed to me that Hope had a lot to explain.

"Now why in the hell would they say you're adopted? Who would be dumb enough to adopt twelve damn kids?"

"I guess they think it's because we call you and Bill by your first names."

"Well, honey, most people don't have as much imagination as your father and I. They go through life doing what everyone else expects them to do. Your father and I are not average: we think for ourselves. I didn't want all of you kids calling us Mommy and Daddy because we wanted to raise you as individuals. We were afraid that with twelve kids we might have a household out of control." There is a pause, then — "Well, Erin, I'm going to dry off now and come out of the bathroom."

The door opens, and out comes the smell of baby powder as Hope sprinkles some in her black flats (to soak up the sweat) and up her clean legs and between her legs instead of putting on underpants. Next she runs her hands through her wet hair, pushing it back away from her face. Finally comes a splash of baby oil and a palm full of make-up to dip her fingers into for the finished look. With lipstick she puts three colored dots on each cheek, rubbing them in with an upward motion. "Where in the hell is my girdle, Erin?" she asks.

"Right there," I reply, pointing.

"Back to your question," she finally says. "We have twelve kids because I wanted twelve kids, and so did your father. It's no one else's business how many kids we have! On our wedding night, I told your father I believed there were shoeboxes in closets in heaven, full of souls waiting to be born. I needed to try to empty the boxes and give the souls a life with us. Your father agreed to give the souls a home. Erin, you were one soul waiting to be born. I have spent my lifetime trying to get souls out of shoeboxes and give them a good life with us. We always have enough, don't we? So why does some do-gooder say we should limit our love? That is where you kids came from. Now your father says, 'I asked for a drink, she turned on the fire hydrant.' Well, we're a proud Irish family who don't need to do as the Jones do!"

Hope slips on her full-size girdle and does the row of eye-hooks one by one. "Now I have a new shape," she says with a smile. She slips her slightly worn blue paisley dress over her girdle. Content with her look, she smiles at herself in the mirror. "Erin, Bill loves you kids very much. Your father just wasn't raised in a family that showed their feelings. And he stutters, so he doesn't use unnecessary words when he talks."

"I know," I reply. "A knuckle in the head usually says it all for Bill."

Hope looks disappointed, "Erin, you will never disrespect your father in front of me. He is a good man, and he works as a truck driver in 20-degree weather for this family, providing a life for us. He does the very best he can. He drives 100 miles just to be with us on the weekends."

"I'm sorry, Hope, I don't mean to be disrespectful. But I do like him best when he is drinking and singing. Why doesn't he stutter when he sings, Hope?"

"Well, that is God giving him a break," she says, smiling at me. She moves past me to close the white painted bathroom door. "Erin, we love you kids, and we're doing the best we can! We brought your souls to life!"

I stand up, ramming my hands deep in my pockets and say, "Hope, I think now I know why shoes don't come in shoeboxes at our house!"

Good Friday

SITTING ON THE DAVENPORT, looking out the window, I say to Denise, "What is so good about Good Friday? We still have to do all of our chores, and then we have to say the rosary with Hope." I move closer to Denise and Charlie on the davenport, wishing we could play outdoors.

Hope's arms are folded, and her coffee cup full of red wine sits on the edge of the coffee table. "This will be a reminder for you kids of how much Jesus suffered for our sins," Hope says as she takes a swig of wine. Sliding our butts off the davenport, we look at each other, knowing we don't have a choice. Today Hope is going to show us how to pray in a more serious way. I guess because Hope is sorry for her sins, we kids have to get on our knees to show God we are all sorry for his Son hanging on the cross, and I'm pretty sure she's drinking red wine because Jesus drank red wine at the last supper.

Hope takes the rosary down from the praying hands on the wall and makes the sign of the cross, kissing the cross on the rosary before she says, "Glory be to the Father and Son and the Holy Spirit." Then to us, "We are to pray for Jesus on the cross, thinking only of him from twelve noon until three o'clock. I'm not sure, but I think someone in our house needs to be prayed for." It can't be me, I think. I know I have not done anything bad.

My knees are bony, so they wobble from side to side. Charlie is smiling because he can hear our friends playing baseball just outside the window. The rosary is white and glows in Hope's hands. Hope leans over to pour some more wine into her coffee cup.

When the rosary is all done—five decades, with ten prayers on each, not counting the small beads on the cross—Hope puts it back up on the wall for safekeeping, wrapping it around the praying hands. She tightens her slightly wine-stained top lip and says, "Now, kids, I want you to think about Jesus and nothing but until three o'clock! In silence! Because at three o'clock he was done suffering. Look straight ahead, no smiling! This is serious."

I start to think about what Jesus wore on the cross. How come that cloth never came off him? How come his hair is so long? I wonder if he was ever mad, or if Jesus ever had to say the rosary? Did his mother drink wine? I'm not sure what to think about Jesus, but I do know you can't even chew gum during the time from noon until three on Good Friday. We are to feel sorry for our sins for the whole three hours.

Suddenly there is a crash! Glass flies through our paper curtains, cold air rushes in, and a baseball lands on the living room floor. Now Hope is on her knees, and the rest of us are on our feet! The paper curtains are ripped down, and a baseball is lying straight in front of Hope. She reaches over to pick it up.

She seems relieved that it's not a rock from Mary, the mother of Jesus, but she's kind of shaken up and scared. She picks up the ball and says, "I think this is a good sign from God, kids. He is proud of you for praying on your knees. You're not like other kids, out playing baseball on Good Friday!" Hope stops and pours herself another drink.

Charlie and I start to giggle because we know who is out there and that Dennis is the best batter we have on our team. We think he might even have done it on purpose, which is funnier yet. Joe, tired from kneeling, leans over to give us each a quick smack on the back of the head.

"Stop laughing!" my sister Pat says. "This is not funny! It's Good Friday, and windows are expensive to fix, Erin! We can't hide it from Bill, either, because the paper curtains are ripped down! So we have to let Hope soften him up with a drink before we tell him." Pat shakes her head. "Well, at least it's not that cold outside. It's only raining, not snowing."

That night Bill pulls into the driveway slowly, as usual, his bumper hitting the curb. He opens his smoked-filled car, smiling. He wears his red plaid wool CPO jacket over his work clothes and carries his metal lunch pail. Standing on the porch, waiting for him to walk by and give his approval, we are happy to see him and kind of excited to see what will happen with the broken window that we didn't break (for a change) but a neighbor kid did.

"How about a drink?" Hope asks brightly.

"Yeah, Hopie, I will do just that," Bill says with a smile. Hope goes with Bill into the kitchen and closes the door. We listen, and it isn't long before we hear Bill yell, "Those little sons-of-bitches!" He is really mad!

I look at Charlie and say, "Well, you better hope Greg is as good a runner as he is a batter!"

Bill comes out of the kitchen hiking up his jeans by his big belt buckle, pulling the belt tighter across his belly. "Let me see this broken window!" He stands looking at the broken glass still sticking out of the edge of the window frame.

"Can you fix it, Bill?" I ask.

"Hell, yes, Erin, I can fix it. But that's not the point. Why was that little son-of-a-bitch playing baseball facing a house?"

"I don't know, Bill," I say with a quiver in my voice.

Hope stands with her hands behind her back, swaying back and forth. "The kids didn't do it, Bill. They were praying on their knees! I'm sure it was an accident, anyway. But it sure scared the hell out of me!"

Hope reaches over to Bill, slides his CPO jacket off and says, "Honey, we can fix it in the morning. It's not that big of a deal, is it?"

"I guess not." He takes a swig of his Tudor Ale beer. "I'll go to McPherson Hardware tomorrow and get the glass and glaze. Kids, find my putty knife!" Bill rubs his smooth face with fingers stained yellow from smoking.

Hope puts her arms around Bill and guides him clear of us kids to drink with her in the kitchen. "It's Holy Saturday tomorrow, Bill. Let's not worry tonight!" Hope pulls out another cold Tudor Ale and hands it to Bill.

Saturday morning Bill takes Charlie up to McPherson's and gets the supplies and teaches Charlie to fix a window. The rest of us color eggs for Easter morning after church.

Sunday morning is Easter, and it is great! We girls were all given Easter bonnets this year. They're pastel straw and have soft wide ribbons on them that go around the hats and tie under our chins. We're proud to go to church as a family. We load into Bill's green 1967 Mercury and go to church stacked on top of each other in layers, the Quinlan way. I walk into St. Mary's Church feeling like we have earned a good Easter Sunday. Mrs. O'Mara plays the organ and sings, "Jesus Christ has risen today!" I love that song. It's a happy song.

After church we come home where the big kids have hidden three dozen eggs for us to find. Whoever finds the most gets the eight-inch-tall hollow chocolate rabbit with candies for eyes. Sometimes the big kids help one of us little kids win. This year it is Charlie who finds the most eggs. Charlie gives me the rabbit's ears and Denise the rest of the head.

We are all happy. We sit as a family at the dining room table eating ham, scalloped potatoes, cucumbers in vinegar, hot homemade buns with butter, corn, and lots of deviled eggs. (I think we eat deviled eggs because we hate the devil!) Bill is at one end of the table, and Hope is at the other. It is Easter, all right! We all laugh while eating, feeling closer to Jesus. We understand what

Jesus has done for our sins. Bill, putting more horseradish on his ham, flips the fork upside-down to put ham in his mouth and says, "Praying on your knees is your mother's idea because the boys are in Vietnam. It won't hurt you kids in the least!"

Stepping Out

Hope is wearing a black dress with a big rhinestone pin on the neckline. The pin holds down a filmy scarf that covers the burn scars on her neck. With her red lipstick, ruby red blush, matching red nails (short), her lingering scent of "Evening in Paris" perfume, and her stiletto black heels, she's the most beautiful woman in our town.

Hope has a convenient job now, cleaning the post office just down the street. She gets paid in cash, so she feels she has money to spend on herself occasionally, barring any disasters. When she takes ten dollars and puts it in the cleavage of her bra, she calls it "mad money". She says, "I need the money so I don't go mad!"

Dressing up in fancy dresses she gets from Goodwill is something Hope likes to do, but my favorite dress of hers was store-bought for my brother Mike's wedding. It is a beautiful white dress with big black polka dots. Hope wears it with her freshly dyed hair, short bangs, smooth finish of make-up, and bright red lips. Her well-shaped legs show just enough of who she is — more then just a mother: a beautiful woman, too.

Tonight Hope wears black high heels, stilettos, with a thin strap on the ankle. She has just gotten them. She dabs "Evening in Paris" behind her ears and inside her elbows and stands looking in the mirror on the dining room wall at her hair and the fit of her dress. She seems satisfied with what she sees. She is ready to go.

Denise, Charlie and I skid across the kitchen linoleum to get to the dining room to watch her do the finishing touches, amazed at how beautiful she has become right in front of our eyes. We circle her like locusts, admiring everything about her. I watch as she puts on her fake fur coat and fur hat to match. (The hat has a small lace veil in front that can go up or down.) Hope gives one last glance into the mirror. She is going out on the town.

"So," I ask, "Where are you going, Hope?"

She looks into the mirror and smiles, saying in a calm but stern voice, "None of your goddamn business." I know not to ever ask that question again.

Not a Movie Star

"HEY, DENISE, LOOK AT that nice pretty new car in front of Greg Dennis's house. I bet it's his aunt from out of town who comes once a year to see Greg's mom! She is so pretty! She wears short dresses with high heels and pink lipstick and her hair in a net. She doesn't have any kids. Is that why she doesn't wear a tent dress?" I ask.

"No, you idiot! Hope wears a tent dress because she's had twelve kids. She dresses so no one will see her belly!"

"Well, I think she looks nice like that!"

Denise smiles as she says, "I think she wears tent dresses at home because they're cooler, too, and she doesn't have to wear underpants."

"I still wear them," I say.

"I know, you idiot, and you don't just shoot powder up your dress to cool off, either, now do you?"

"No, I don't. Let's get closer and see what Greg's aunt is wearing. I'll name her Miss Marlene, because that's a movie star name, and she looks like one." Close together, Denise and I move slowly and curiously toward Greg's house to see what Miss Marlene, the movie star, is wearing this time.

The shiny black car is in front of Greg's house. Yep, that is a movie star's car, all right! I'm sure of it. We look inside to see an all-black seat but no Miss Marlene. She must already be inside her sister's house.

Just then Dickey Roach comes by, dressed in his mother's nightdress, singing opera, and we go to jump on the trampoline with him. Dickey has made up a new song that is a mix of country and opera so it's not too bad to listen to. We play jump-on-the-flagpole over and over again. We laugh with

Dickey and ask him to show us his mom's make-up. "Bring it out to us, Dickey. Last time we went into your house, we got in deep trouble!" Dickey brings the entire make-up bag and we put our make-up on like Miss Marlene, the movie star.

"Dickey, guess what! There's a real movie star in our town with a fancy shiny black car with doors that open in the same direction. It's so pretty, Dickey. You have to see it!" I explain with pure excitement. "Hey, let's go show her our make-up and see if she thinks we look good? Do you want to?"

"No, that's a stupid idea," Denise says before Dickey can answer. "Let's just spy on her and wait for her to come out of the Dennis house!"

We creep cautiously down the street to show Dickey the movie star we've named Marlene. No car!

"She's gone!" I yell. "We don't even get to see what fancy clothes she had on!" I am so sorry I missed her, I start kicking stones.

"Wait, Erin! I think I saw that black car in front of Connelly's house yesterday. Did it have dark windows?"

"Yes, it did!"

"Did it have really shiny windows with a black metal piece hanging over the windshield?"

"Yes."

"It had a man in it, not a woman!" Dickey sings the news with great joy— he did get to see the car! "Let's go to Connelly's house and see if it's there!"

I get excited again. "We never have shiny cars in this town, and we know everyone!"

Charlie comes running up to Denise and me and tells us he has a fun game idea. "Let's trip the cars that come into town with a rope across the street. We can put it up when they try to come across."

"No! I don't think so, Charlie. We have an adventure here, and you can come or not, but you will have to shut up if you are part of our spy club!"

"Okay, that sounds f-f-fun, Erin," Charlie says, stuttering. He is embarrassed.

"Don't be embarrassed, Charlie, we know you stutter! Right, Dickey?"

"Yeah. We don't care how you talk. We're all friends, and we have a mystery to figure out! Erin thinks it is a movie star named Marlene, and I think it is a man dressed in women's clothing," Dickey states.

"No, Dickey, you are the only boy who dresses in women's clothing. It's a woman."

We head over to the next street to see if there is anything unusual, but — no luck. I think, "Hey, let's forget about it and play red rover, red rover at our house!"

"Okay, let's," Denise agrees.

We cut through Connelly's yard like we always do, and the car is now in front of our house! We get excited to see the movie star and find out if it's a man or Miss Marlene! We run to the front yard and stand there staring at the car with the little sun protector over the windshield. It is beautiful, all right!

The four of us are standing in the side yard talking about the beautiful black car when the window comes down. I strain my neck to see who is in the car, my heart beating faster and faster. I just know I will be right! It will be Marlene, the movie star! I start to edge closer to the car as my brother Joe comes out of the house and calls us to come in and have peanut butter and jelly sandwiches. Joe is watching us — Pat, Shannon, Denise, Charlie and me — because Hope has taken a road trip to see our father down in Pontiac.

Joe yells, "You kids get your butts in this house now!" He is a good babysitter but not a friendly one.

I look at Joe and say, "You made the movie star, Marlene, disappear."

"I don't care, Erin. Get in the house!"

"Joe, when you came out the front door, the black car took off." I climb sadly up the cement steps to the house, knowing that Miss Marlene will never come back. We never get to see movie stars in Carsonville! Joe is standing there looking like a big brother who does not want to watch kids at all. He is seventeen and wants to be with girls.

Denise, Charlie, and I eat our lunch and go back out with our friends. Dickey is waiting on the porch for us to get done eating. I follow the others down the street. It's a hot day, but it rained the day before, and there is still dew in the high grass in our yard.

Another thing our babysitter has not done yet: mow the grass! After playing for about an hour, we see the car again, and this time we are determined not to let it get away.

The car stops in the sunlight. It has light dew on the trunk and a lot of chrome. We all stand still, and the window comes down. It is just an old man! I am so disappointed!

"Hey, kids, do you know where this street is?" he asks us. His hair is grey, and his face has a smooth calm look to it, kind of like a dead man. He does not smile. He looks older than my father. He runs his hand through his hair as if he's hot. I go over to the car window with Denise and Charlie to see the map.

It's a homemade map with lots of red roads drawn on it, not a real map like the one at school. I'm not scared at all until he moves the map, and then I see that his ding-dong is standing straight up. It's big. His pants are down to his ankles, and he's moving his hands up and down on his ding-dong with a smile on his face.

We kids just stare. We don't know what the map says at all. We stand there for a minute and then say, " Sorry, mister, we can't help you! We're just kids!" And we run off.

We aren't far from home so we run down to our house where Joe is just coming out the front door. I tell Joe what the man said to us. "His pants were around his feet, and he was moving his hands up and down! What was he doing, Joe?"

"How in the hell do I know?" Joe stretches his neck out angrily.

I want to know what direction the car is going, so I run out and see it moving slowly down our street. Looking for my friends, I bet. I point it out to Joe, and he starts swearing and running after it. "You son-of-a-bitch!" he yells as he chases the car down the street.

I am disappointed that I saw only the ding-dong of an old man instead of a real movie star. But Joe comes back and tells us kids we did really good to leave the car and not talk to the man. He was a very sick man and could have stolen us, Joe says. "That is why you have to have a babysitter, even if he is not always nice to you, because he makes sure you are safe. That is my job!" He gives us each a little smack on the head.

Hope comes home on Sunday night, pleased at how well we all handled the situation. She keeps her eyes open in case the old man in the black car returns, but he doesn't. I don't think much about the old man. I am mostly sad that I didn't get to see Marlene, the movie star!

The Exercise Club

IN THE SUMMER CHARLIE and I play spud and red rover, look for pop bottles, and sometimes find ways to make extra money. I want to start an exercise club to make money, so I call Charlie from downstairs to ask him to help me get one started.

Charlie pulls up blue gym shorts against his golden tan. The teachers let us kids take from the lost and found anything not claimed at the end of the year. That's where Charlie got these gym shorts.

Charlie stutters, "Hey, Erin, the exercise club we t-t-talked about last night is a good idea! We teach our friends to look like Jack Lalane, and all we really need is a dog. I think we could use Ladybird and a folding chair. Jack Lalane bends his knees and points his toes, with his arms always straight on the back of the chair. But one problem is, I don't have black shorts, only faded blue gym shorts."

"Figure it out, Charlie," I say. "I'm working on my own stuff. I know how to climb a tree, but I have never taught anyone else how to do it. By ten o'clock this morning you better have your part figured out. Then we'll both walk around town with a canning jar and collect the money for the club. We'll say the class starts at twelve o'clock today."

"Let's ask D-d-dickey Roach," Charlie stutters. "He always has money, and we'll tell him that he can't wear his mother's clothes this time, but afterwards he can do a little dance for us for our break time. He has lots of money. The other d-d-day I saw his father give him two dollars for cutting the lawn. And they hardly have a lawn. Now that is spoiled," Charlie mumbles under his breath. "He m-must have some of that money left."

I see some old cigarette butts on the corner and kick them over to Charlie. "You don't smoke, Erin," Charlie says, making a face.

"Oh, yes, I do, but only butts! I don't like the lipstick, but they're kind of fun to smoke. Sometimes you can taste mint and your mouth feels hot. It kind of burns."

Charlie says, "Well, next time you and Karen go and smoke old butts, c-c-can I come and see how it tastes?"

"No, it's a best girlfriend thing, and you are just my little brother. Besides, when you and I get in a fight, you would tell Hope I have tried smoking. If you ever tell, Charlie, I will never be your best friend again! I will just say" (pinching his back) "'Charlie is lying, Hope.' Come on, Charlie, who else can we get to join the club? I don't care about smoking. It's stupid. I really only did it once." I smirk with my fingers behind my back, crossing them because I'm not telling the truth.

"I knew you were making that up, Erin. No one in fifth grade smokes. It's just for mothers and fathers."

Charlie is wiggling around, and I know he has to go to the bathroom. "Charlie, just pee in the backyard," I yell, turning my head the other way so I can't see anything.

"Okay, Erin, I'm done now," Charlie says.

"Sucker!" I yell. "Now if you tell Hope I smoked, I will say you peed in the yard!"

"Erin, you are not my best friend any more! You are always t-tricking me!" Charlie yells.

"I'm the trickster!" I yell, running across the street to the other side with my ponytail swinging all the way around the back of my head. Then I stop and yell to Charlie, "Hey, we need to get to O'Connell Pond now and stop fooling around. Why don't you ask all the kids that are swimming if they want to join our club? It might help your stuttering to practice talking more instead of me talking for you." We run past a few more houses and see four bikes at the pond. When we get near the water's edge, we yell to our friends to come and join our club. We will make O'Connell Pond be part of the exercise! It's only twenty-five cents to join.

Our friends seem excited. They dry off and follow us on their bikes to the county garage. Charlie and I are proud to have two dollars in our canning jar. "Well, then! Let's get them all tired out, and then take a break and go and spend the money!" I'm thinking out loud.

Charlie has ideas of his own. "Part of the exercise is to climb the wall of the county building and jump off, just missing the pile of b-b-bricks. At the end of the class, if you are strong enough to jump over the bricks to get to the grass, then you will get a 'Jack Lalane award.' We'll write out awards like they do in school, but it won't be w-w-words. It'll be a picture of Jack Lalane with his chair. Or if you're a girl, you get a picture of a girl climbing a t-t-tree," Charlie says to me.

It is noon, and we have eight kids who want to join. Charlie is all set up with his Jack Lalane chair.

"One, two, three, four!" Charlie yells. "Point your toes. And bend your knees. This will make your knees stronger so you can stand longer." Wow, we are feeling pretty smart! I do my exercise in the back row, watching to see who is there and who is not. I feel like a rich kid, for sure!

Next I take the girls to the backyard to show them how to climb a tree without letting anyone see their underpants and how to swing upside-down and not hit their heads on the worn dirt spot under the swing. Charlie and I use the tire swing and the Tarzan rope to teach the class tricks we have taught ourselves. Karen Fagan is good at tree climbing.

Soon parents start calling out their back doors. It's time for the kids to go home and eat.

I say, "We will see you after lunch," and Charlie and I run as fast as we can, with the money in my fist, to Harold's Market. We split the money in front of the store, standing with our backs to the sun so we can see better. Mildred, with her stiff tight lips, follows us around the store, positive the Quinlan kids don't have any money. But we do! Charlie buys a Black Cow sucker and Orange Nesbit pop. I have to have a candy bar called Big Moe (it is all coconut striped like a rainbow), one Mellow Cup, and a candy necklace. Walking away with our candy, we spot our friends returning.

"Oh no, Charlie! Karen and Joel are back! What do we do?"

Thinking fast, Charlie says, "Well, it's snack time!" I give my candy necklace to Karen. Joel asks if he can pick Charlie's Black Cow sucker. Charlie and I climb up the plum tree and across the roof to hide and eat the rest.

While we are eating our well-deserved treats, we hear a loud scream coming from the backyard. It is Joel, holding onto his leg, his face soaked with tears. His hands are shaking, dirty fingers pointing to his shin. Joel had climbed the twenty-foot county building and jumped off, falling in the brick pile and breaking his leg.

I tell Charlie, "Well, Jack, I guess you better tell Hope what we've done."

Joel's mother is crying as she whisks Joel out of the brick pile, her arms loaded with his pain. Glaring at us kids, she demands, "Where is Hope?" Joel's mom is mad because no one was watching her son. We tell her that no one ever watches us in our family after the age of nine.

When she hears what happened, Hope says, "That kid must have a screw loose to climb a twenty-foot-high building and jump off the roof! Now that kid was a real idiot! I'm going back to the bar, so call me if the leg is actually broken."

Charlie and I pull Joel around in our wagon for the rest of the summer to make up for the broken leg.

Shotgun

Hope stands at the bottom of the stairs and yells, "Joe, Pat, Shannon, Denise, Erin, and Charlie! Hit the deck!" I have to start moving my feet around on the floor while my body is still in bed so she'll hear the noise and think I'm up. I don't want to drag my thin lanky body out of bed today at all.

Looking at myself in the mirror, I take the pink tape off my bangs and brush my auburn hair. (The tape is supposed to hold my bangs down during the night. My sisters taught me that.) Smoothing the lumps in my ponytail, I put spit on my finger to get the sleep out of my eyes. Hope stands waiting at the bottom of the stairs.

Most mornings start out the same. First we say the rosary, and then we eat hot oatmeal, often with hot homemade bread right out of the oven. The hot fresh bread smell comes from the kitchen now. Hope has been baking, wearing an apron over her worn, red and white flowered tent dress. She smiles with wisdom, a hymn under her breath, as if she is singing privately to the gods. "Today, Erin, you and Charlie and I are taking a road trip to see your father."

My father lives in Pontiac, and we live in Carsonville. In the 1960s, even before the riots in Detroit, my parents decided Pontiac was becoming unsafe, so my father moved the family to the small town of Carsonville. Bill, my father, drives home almost every weekend to be with us. It's a 2-hour trip if he's driving it. When Hope drives to Pontiac, that trip becomes a 5-hour adventure. Hope doesn't always have a car, but this is 1964, and we are able to afford one for her that actually runs well enough to get to Pontiac. Hope enjoys the break from the other four kids, and they kind of fend for themselves. I love these Friday trips to my father's apartment in Pontiac.

I run back up the stairs, taking three steps at a time with my long legs, and pack what Hope calls my "hillbilly Samsonite," a paper bag from the local IGA. It feels fancy to take extra clean underpants and a t-shirt and just go. I even love the printing on the outside of the bag. It seems important to me.

Packed and ready, I yell out, "Shotgun!" This means I get to sit in the front seat, mix drinks for Hope, and hear her great stories. Charlie can stand on the back floor of the car to listen; he doesn't have to sit way back in the seat. The sun is out, and the roads are clear. It is a good day for a trip.

After driving for about an hour, Hope glances in the rearview mirror (for police) and announces it is time for lunch. We kids always have the same packed lunch: Spam and mustard on homemade white bread. The bread is so thick, it is always fun to try to eat it. Hope's lunch is Popov vodka and Faygo Diet Frosh. She is diabetic.

Hope is a storyteller. She loves to tell us about her childhood and how hard it was. She even tells us scary stories to keep the trip interesting. Hope is an exciting storyteller, and we hang onto her every word. She looks us in the eyes from time to time and stays with her audience, even if they're only eight and nine years old.

Soon we're done with the sandwiches. Hope has her mixed drink. "Riding shotgun is a serious job, Erin," she reminds me. "Don't worry about the police coming towards us, honey. They can't see if I'm drinking. It's the ones behind us — they can see the shadow of me tipping my drink."

We take back roads because Hope says the other roads have too much traffic and those people are not having as much fun as we are. That's true. This trip gets more fun as it goes on.

We are stopping about every hour and going into a bar. Charlie and I love it. We can have either a pop or chips. Today seems to be a celebration of some sort because Hope is drinking more then normal. At one stop, Charlie and I wait in the car, and while we're waiting we play around with the car's lighter, daring each other to put our thumbs on the hot rings and push down on the lighter so we will be burnt brother and sister. It hurts! We are both pretty burnt. We unlock the car door and go to show Hope what we have done and tell her that it really hurts. Hope is very upset and doesn't let us play in the car any more, so we are able to go in the bar again with her at the next stop.

The next bar is dark and smoky, with barn wood walls and red light fixtures. I can feel the music as well as hear it. Hank Williams is on the jukebox, singing a song about being lonesome. Some people are slow dancing, and some are sitting on tall stools at the bar, laughing. One man looks like he is sleeping at the bar. Hope gives us each a dime to play two songs on the jukebox. Charlie and I dance to a song called "Bat Man." It's a song that has its own dance to it. You make a mask with your fingers over your eyes, and you run your fingers up your arm to make it look like you are dressing to be Bat Man. We stay at that bar the longest, and it starts to get dark outside.

Hope is still drinking and her friends are all around her — four people, all amazed at how talented she is. I'm standing next to her when she recites one of her favorite poems: "There are strange things done, in the midnight sun, for the men who toiled for Gold. Their Arctic trails, have their secret tales, that would make your blood run cold." Charlie and I keep dancing on the old wood dance floor. We know we are supposed to go to our father's, but we would not be having as much fun there as we are dancing in a dark bar and having burnt thumbs and being full of pop and chips. When we get to Pontiac, Hope and Bill will be together, and we will be on our own.

Hope stumbles when we help her out the back door of the bar, and I watch in amazement. She doesn't even look like our mother now. She still looks pretty, but her curly auburn hair is flyaway-looking, and her red lipstick is all worn off. Hope's face is still soft, but she smells strange, and her eyes have changed. They look distant. She seems restless, like she feels she has stayed too long.

It's dark now, and she is not telling stories any more. She wants us to be quiet so she can concentrate on her driving. I look out the car window and see the fins on the back of the car, and I think maybe, if this ride is scary, we will just fly home on the wings of this car.

We are fine until she pulls out onto the dirt road. She drives on the edge of the road for a while, then she's okay for a few minutes, and then we go off to the other side of the road. It's scary! But she tells me, "Erin, if I start to go into the ditch, don't scream. It will make me nervous. Just bite your hand instead of screaming."

Charlie and I are so scared we're both biting our hands. This is not good! I'm the oldest and figure she will listen to me, so I beg her to go back to the dark bar and ask for help. Hope says, "Erin, honey, I'm just tired. I promise, I won't go in the ditch anymore."

Dirt is flying all over from the tires, and I start crying. I'm afraid I won't get to see my father, today or ever. So I choose not to bite my hand any more. I want Hope to be afraid for us, and I scream, "I'm afraid, Hope! Go back to the bar and get some big person to help us!"

Hope stops the car. She says, "Erin, we can just walk for a while, and it will be fine." We do that, holding her soft loving hands, walking up and down on the side of the road with the wind blowing in our faces. I have no jacket, and it's getting cold outside. I wonder why Hope can't walk straight. I'm confused. We were having so much fun! Why is she wrecking this? I wonder. We keep walking, Charlie on one side and me on the other. What she says is hard to understand, too. She is trying to tell me that she is late for my father and needs to get on the road. Even after we beg her not to drive, she gets back behind the wheel of her dusty black car with white and black fins on the back, and on we go. The ride is still scary. I'm afraid all the way to my father's apartment.

When we finally get there, my father yells," Hope, what in the hell could you be thinking? You're drunk!" This is not the first time this has happened, but Bill just puts his arms around Hope and winks at me, holding her shoulders straight, saying, "Kids, give us some time alone."

I think, Hope was not celebrating; she is mourning my brother Butch's death. Hope has told me that drinking kind of takes the edge off life. Some of the sharp edges hurt her a lot.

We stay with Bill at his apartment, and Charlie and I play a game called "Black Jack." It's a game we made up. It's where you jump over huge bushes, yelling, "Black Jack!" (Black Jack is our favorite kind of candy.) You try to see who can jump the highest. We love to explore my father's apartment, too. My father named it the "Bat Cave" because it is dark and lonesome without his family. I look for bats with Charlie sometimes, in case one could be hanging upside-down in a closet.

Hope and Bill kiss in front of us, so I know he isn't mad any more. They make dinner and go to bed early after the reel-to-reel plays country songs. We don't miss our friends in Carsonville. When we get home, we tell them we were in the big city learning new games.

New Shoes

HOPE IS SITTING BACK, looking out the window with a drink in her hand.

"Okay, we've got a lot to accomplish before your father gets home. I want to get the cinnamon buns going, and then size you kids up for shoes! It's almost time to go back to school."

Oh, no, not shoes! I love going barefoot and washing my feet off with the hose at night! And then there's the problem of the way Hope buys shoes for us.

"Hey, Hope, I know! Why don't Charlie and I go with you and pick out our own shoes?"

"No, Erin. This is not a job for kids."

"A lot of my friends go to try on shoes and see what fits them just right!" I say, but, feeling disrespectful, I look away when I say it.

"That's ridiculous!" Hope says. "Why would anyone listen to a kid on what kind of shoes to buy? That is pure nonsense, Erin. You're a kid, for God's sakes!"

Grabbing a broom, I start to sweep the kitchen floor, staying in the kitchen to see if I can change her mind. The linoleum has red and black lines, each square going in a different direction. "But, Hope, we would like the shoes more if we picked them out!" I tell her.

"Who in the hell cares if you like your shoes, Erin? They're shoes, for God's sakes."

"Please, Hope, I'm almost eleven years old, and last year I wore shiny pink shoes all year, and everyone made fun of me."

"Well, then, they weren't friends, were they?"

Hanging my head down, I mumble, "No, I guess not. Maybe you could just take one kid at a time?"

"Hell, no! I'm not wasting my time that way. It's fourteen miles round-trip! And I might end up hitchhiking. I don't like imposing on my friends, and I can't walk home carrying six pairs of shoes. Hell, it would be Christmas before the job was done if I had to take you kids one at a time!"

Hope mixes powdered milk to pour over her homemade bread. "Erin, this year is no different. You're lucky to have shoes. Now hold the dustpan for me while I sweep up the flour. Can you smell the cinnamon?" Hope smiles.

"Yes, ma'am, cinnamon rolls are great. But I'm just afraid of getting pink shoes again this year. I'm almost eleven, and I think I should be able to pick out my own shoes."

Hope tucks her bottom lip under her slight overbite and sighs. "Erin, people in hell want ice water."

She hasn't convinced me. "I just want those red tennis shoes that have the red ball on them, Hope! They're called Keds! My friend Karen Fagan has a pair."

"Well, Erin, I don't give a good goddamn what Karen Fagan has or doesn't have. I'm in charge here! When the work is all done, we will eat cinnamon rolls, and then you will lay out the paper grocery bags like we always do, and I will draw your feet!"

Sitting at the table, I look at Denise over the cinnamon rolls, and whisper, "We will be the laughing stock again!"

Denise smiles, saying, "Well, Hope doesn't have money to get special shoes, Erin."

"I know, but every year we look stupid. I know I could run faster if I had Keds."

Charlie pipes up, "Erin, you're already a ghost runner for baseball, so that makes you the fastest on the team. If you had Keds, it could slow you down."

"Hope just doesn't care," I complain. "Remember last year when she laid the bags across the kitchen floor and drew our feet? Well, she couldn't see well enough, and she made mine too small. I was in pain the whole year!"

"I know, Erin. But this year you might get lucky! Last year Shannon had those blue fuzzy shoes that Elvis sang about, remember?"

"Well, one year I got pink tap shoes. I clopped down the hall like a horse. Everyone could always tell I was coming."

I get up from the table, pulling my hair back, and start to look for six A&P bags to spread out on the kitchen floor. They stretch across the entire floor as I line them up side by side.

Hope yells, "Erin, you have to find a pencil too!" When she's ready, I'm ready. We stand in a straight line side by side.

Hope gets down on her knees. Her glasses keep sliding off her nose as she starts to draw around our bare feet. It tickles! She grabs my ankle. "Stand still now," she warns, "or you'll get shoes that don't fit again." Hope traces my feet, then writes "Erin" in big letters across the picture. I slide back out of the way, sticking my tongue out behind her back. "Come on, kids," she says to hurry the rest. "I don't have all day."

Shannon, with a frown on her face, says, "I hate this, too, Hope."

Charlie steps on the paper and asks, "Hope, do you think I could have a pair of black shoes that tie?"

Hope doesn't answer either of them. She pulls at her dress to make a pad to kneel on, then looks up and comments to the whole group of us, "How in the hell do you think I know what you kids are getting until I see what's on sale?"

Charlie rubs his brush cut and stutters, "I know, Hope, but l-l-last year I had a pair of penny loafers. I think those are for big people."

"For Christ's sakes, Charlie, I do the best I can! Do you kids think I like walking into the shoe store with six kids' feet drawn on rolled-up paper grocery bags? Already, I have to match the shoes to the feet. Then I have to hitchhike home with all those goddamn shoes. It's economics! No, it's not my favorite time either!" Standing up with the pencil behind her ear, she stalks out of the room, mad!

"We're sorry, Hope! We will be happy with whatever you get us."

Hope pulls the pencil out from behind her ear, saying, "I'll ask Bobby if he can drive me this time. I'm in no mood to hitch a ride or discuss this any further."

Hope has the last word. All we can do is wait to see what we get.

When Hope returns from her shopping trip, all the shoes are dropped on the front porch for us to sort out. Pat and Shannon stack them, and everybody comes running to see what they're stuck with. We all step forward to get the shoes that are in the place of our bare feet drawings. I'm afraid to look down to see what's mine.

First I look to see what Charlie got—black lace-up shoes just like he wanted. No pennies fit in those shoes. Pat and Shannon get matching shoes, in style, with buckles. I look down farther but can't see what Denise got.

There are already tears in my eyes. I know the kids in school will laugh at me! As I feel Hope's eyes on me and step forward; my foot bumps into red tennis shoes, and I scream out loud! "Yippee!" They look like Keds! I wipe the tears from my cheeks. Hope picks the red shoes up, saying, "The man at the store said, 'These tennis shoes are for ghost runners and are faster than Keds.'" I put them on, tie the white laces, and start to run as fast as I can.

Mr. Jones

I RUN ACROSS THE STREET, calling Hope's name. She is standing in front of the Carsonville Hotel. Next to her is a man holding his hand over where his eye should be. Hope holds him by the other hand. His head hangs down, and blood is running out from behind his hand. He smells like he has been drinking a lot of beer.

"Hold still," Hope says to the bleeding man. "We will get you some help. Get some ice, Lena!" she screams. "Call an ambulance! We have a serious problem here." Hope nudges the man and asks him, "What is your name, sir? Who are you here with? You're not from Carsonville, I know, but we need to get your driver's license to see who to call." He says his name is Jones.

Mr. Jones is bleeding over the edge of the concrete steps, blood falling on his shoes one drop at a time. His green shirt is full of fresh wet blood, and his nose looks flat. He is screaming, crying, shaking. I'm afraid he will take out his pain on Hope, and she is just trying to help him! "Go home, kids!" she orders us. "Get Bill!"

My father comes right away. He and Hope put Mr. Jones in Bill's car and drive him to the hospital. Bill drives fast. He treats Mr. Jones as if he is a younger brother, I think, as I stand in the driveway of the bar, watching the car drive away. I'm pretty scared because I know you can't just put an eye back into a person's head.

Lena calls us kids into the bar and sits us down at a table. She brings us grape pops and tells us, "Mr. Jones will be fine! There's a good doctor in Sandusky."

Leaning towards her, Charlie and I ask, "But will he be blind?"

Lena looks down at her pack of cigarettes and pulls one out without answering. She walks over to a friend, tapping on his shoulder. He pulls out a shiny lighter to light her cigarette for her, while she holds back her long flowing chiffon robe so it won't catch fire. She thanks the man with a smile and a pretend kiss. Walking back to our table, she says, "Hmm, will he be blind, Erin? Well, that's a good question. But it's an adult problem, and you're a kid. So drink up, you guys, and if you want to help Mr. Jones, I suggest you clean out his car."

Charlie and I finish our pops and find the car behind the bar. It's a square brown car with a window missing. The back seat is full of clothes and all kinds of old stuff. We play in the car for a while, pretending to be able to drive. I'm eleven, curious about what it would be like to drive. We're still messing around when the car door opens suddenly. It's Lena, and she looks mad.

"Kids, you need to stop goofing around and clean this car out! Here are some cleaners and paper towels."

I open my palms to show her the quarters we have found in the car. "Can we keep these, Lena?"

"No, you can't! That man lives in his car, and he uses the change to do his laundry at the laundromat." She leaves us to our work.

I have a great idea. "Charlie, why not keep the money and do his laundry for him? Do you want to?"

"Keen idea, Erin! I've got it! We'll pretend we took his clothes to the laundromat, but we can do it at our house and keep the money. Hope won't even know. Hope is gone, and he'll have a clean car and his laundry all done!"

We start cleaning the windows to get off the yellow stains, putting the quarters on the floor until we're done. Charlie and I hurry to surprise Hope when she gets home.

A few hours later Hope comes home with Mr. Jones, who has a round white bandage on his eye. She helps him into our living room and lets him stay on the couch for the rest of the day. Hope is always bringing home stray people in trouble. She makes soup for Mr. Jones and keeps ice in plastic wrap on him. He shakes all of the time. Hope tells him that she will bring his car around to the driveway and park it so he won't have to worry about anyone climbing through the missing window or anything.

"Charlie," Hope yells, "come and watch Mr. Jones! He's taking some medicine for pain, and he doesn't really even know us, so he might try to get away. Don't let him get off of the couch, not even to go to the bathroom. He could fall. We're going to let him stay until he can get around better."

Hope drives the brown car all the way up the driveway so my father can still fit his car in behind it. When she comes back inside to check on Mr. Jones, she tells us how nice and clean the car is. "Where are all of his clothes?" she asks.

I smile and say. "Well, he usually goes to the laundromat, Lena told us, so we just took some quarters off the floor of his car, and his clothes are in the dryer now. We knew you would want us to help! Right?"

Hope walks over to the dryer opening the door, "Erin, you've really done it this time! Have you spent the money yet?"

"No, ma'am, we have not. We were waiting to fold the clothes first."

Hope holds out her hand for the quarters we think we have earned. Shaking her head, she says, "In the first place, what in the hell were you thinking to charge a blind man to help him? Did I teach you that? Did I take a few quarters when I drove him to the hospital with Bill and he bled on my dress? Did I take a few quarters when I spent my own money to get him a cold draft beer?"

"No ma'am, you didn't."

"It's just not what you do, Erin. You don't make a profit on someone else's pain! I'm ashamed of you!"

"Well, we cleaned the car too, Hope!" Wishing she wouldn't be so disappointed in us, I say, "We were trying to help him! I think he will be glad."

"No you were not thinking about helping, Erin. You were thinking of yourselves! That is exactly what you were doing. Erin, in this life you need to think of those less fortunate. Like Hank Williams says, 'Help your brother along the road no matter where he starts, for the God that made you made him too!' You will return that money to the car and fold his clothes and put them in a hillbilly "Samsonite" (a paper bag), and then you will never forget this as long as you shall live, so help me God. We have so many blessings, and we are meant to share them, not take advantage of people in trouble."

"I know you're right, Hope. I'm sorry! We just didn't think it was such a big deal. We figured he would be happy, and that would be that."

"It doesn't matter if he even knows. You know right from wrong! You give from your heart, Erin."

Hope makes a nice dinner for Mr. Jones, packing up some of our home-canned food for him, too. He seems to be almost happy he got hurt. He gets to see how a real family works. Mr. Jones stays with us for about three days and is happy to have his laundry done. He can only see out of one eye, but he's not blind.

As he is leaving, he pats Charlie and me on the head, saying. "You're good kids. Thanks for cleaning out my car. You did a nice job." As he starts out the door, he reaches into his pocket and gets out four dimes, two for each of us. He thanks Hope. Bill reaches out to shake his hand. They all seem happy.

Mr. Jones stops on the way out the door and says, "Bill, you have a pretty nice family here. Any man would be proud to have such a life."

Bill replies, "You know, you're right. This old gal is a good cook, too!" He reaches his arm around Hope. She looks back, smiling.

Cheating Boo Boo

ELEANOR IS A FRIEND HOPE met while bartending. She is a tall unhappy woman who wears her soft brown hair all back out of her face. She comes to spend time with Hope because she can tell Hope her problems. Hope says she is a lost soul. Hope is a good listener.

Eleanor had a child late in life, a little girl who is a "slow learner." Eleanor and her daughter visit our house a lot near the holidays. Her husband works a lot of overtime so she likes to watch our big family work and spend time together. Since she is an only child herself, with no parents living, we are her replacement family.

It is Thanksgiving, Hope is humming in the kitchen, and the floor is slick with flour and butter. Pat, Shannon, Denise, and I are all helping to bake cherry pies, my very favorite! Hope doesn't seem to worry about money at Thanksgiving like she does at Christmas time. Food is something we can always make from scratch. Hope says, "Thanksgiving Day is my kind of holiday because it is about being grateful, and I always have so much to be grateful for." She believes that God's gifts to us are meant to be shared, and that is what the holiday is all about.

She rolls out the piecrusts and puts them in her special glass pie plates that she says heat more evenly than metal. She tells us, "Girls, never roll a piecrust over and over. That makes it tough. Pay attention and try to only do it once." Then we help make the filling.

Baking pies is just one of the fun things to get done before Thanksgiving dinner. We also need to peel ten pounds of potatoes and soak them in cold water, clean the cranberries, boil the beans for baked beans, and start cutting the gizzards into small pieces to be sautéed with onion and butter to make the stuffing. Hope spreads oil and salt all over the turkey while we wait for the hot buns to come out of the oven for breakfast. (On holidays we get cocoa and hot buns instead of oatmeal.) Then all that's left to do is make the slaw and cook the cranberries.

Hope tells us about timing, how we need to make sure everything is hot at the same time. That is the trick to a good meal. Hope makes everything special for this holiday meal.

Bill will not be home for a while yet, and Hope has kids finishing up the peeling of potatoes because her friend Eleanor has just stopped by. Eleanor has a man's face, I think. She's wearing Capri pants with a white shirt. Hope says, "She doesn't like men, for some reason, but to each his own! She's my friend." Hope and Eleanor are drinking buddies. Eleanor's husband lives down in Pontiac, like Bill, so she has to bring Boo Boo with her whenever she comes over. Boo Boo (her real name is Renee) is in third grade. Hope tells us to be good to her. She says, "Kids, I don't think Boo Boo is dealing with a full deck."

Our reel-to-reel is on in the background, playing country music, like Roger Miller. Hope's full-length apron is covered with flour. Her hair still has bobby pins in it, in small pin curls, and she has no makeup on. She has been up since five o'clock. It is now twelve noon.

"Time for a drink?" asks Eleanor brightly.

Hope says, "Well, let me get the beans out of the oven and the turkey in. It takes a long time to cook a twenty-three pound bird." Eleanor folds her long arms. "Hopie, I need a drink!"

Hope looks across the room at her and says, "Hold on, Eleanor! I need to finish the meal first! "

Our part of getting the meal ready is finished and now we kids have to go around to find poor people and ask them to join us for Thanksgiving dinner. This part of the day is not fun for us. Denise, Charlie, and I walk around town looking for poor people and feeling stupid. One old man is peeing into a jar in his front yard when we walk up. We say, "Just wash your hands and come by at five o'clock, okay?" We return home at last with a count of how many poor old people promised to come to dinner. Usually they bring friends too, and Hope loves that. "The more the merrier, kids!" she always says.

Hope seems pleased with the count today and wants to get Boo Boo out of her hair, so she pulls me closer to tell a secret in my ear. "Erin, why don't you take Boo Boo into the kitchen and cut half of a pie? You kids can share it."

"Wow, you're kidding, right?" I ask, doing a little dance!

"No, Erin, I want to rest and have a beer with Eleanor, and Boo Boo is hanging all over her. We need time alone now. You can cut a big piece of pie for the three of you to share, and then you kids can play."

I'm in fifth grade and don't like playing with a third-grader who talks slow and mostly just stares at me with big brown eyes, but I know to do what I'm told. Running to the kitchen, I tell Charlie the news. I get out the sharp knife and start to cut the cherry pie — my favorite pie! This day could not be better!

I cut half of a pie into only two pieces, though, not three. I figure that Boo Boo is not as smart as we are and will not know that she is supposed to get a piece of pie. We leave the other half of the pie for my sisters.

But Boo Boo is smarter than we thought. She's actually smart enough go to her mom. She runs into the living room, crying, tugging at her mom's arm. She cries, "I didn't get any pie! They ate it all!"

Hope asks Boo Boo, "What happened?"

Boo Boo says again, "I didn't get any pie! Everybody is mean to me! Charlie and Erin ate pie in front of me and didn't share!" Boo Boo stands in front of her mom and Hope as she tells her sad story, giving Hope those big sad cow looks I hate, only this time tears are falling as she talks.

Hope looks at Eleanor and says, "I will talk to the kids. There might be a mistake!" Hope excuses herself and flies into the kitchen. She's on a rampage, madder then I have ever seen her. "What could you kids possibly have been thinking, cheating a little retarded girl? I did not raise kids to do a thing like this!"

I said, "Hope, we weren't trying to cheat her," I say. "We gave her a piece— she just couldn't reach it."

"Run that by me one more time!" Hope sounds like she's daring me, but not in fun at all.

"Yeah, Hope," I'll try once more, "we were planning on sharing it! I swear we were!"

Charlie starts to stutter. "Erin, this is your f-f-fault. You are greedy!"

Hope walks out of the kitchen for one minute and then comes running back. She goes right to the counter where the pies are and grabs them one by one, throwing them on the floor, smashing her favorite glass pans, one pie after another. She smashes six pies in front of our eyes, then yells, "Now clean it up, and don't ever cheat anyone again! We don't cheat people!"

Charlie and I stand there in shock, then finally bend down and start cleaning up the mess. Later, the whole family is mad at me for cheating Boo Boo and wrecking Thanksgiving dinner.

The poor people who come to dinner don't seem to miss the pies. They're happy to have a hot homemade meal, made with love from Hope. I glare at Boo Boo a few times during dinner, but I don't let Hope catch me.

Dead Man's Curve

IT IS LABOR DAY OF 1968. Hope is standing at the back door, watching us put one hundred jars of fresh new tomatoes on the counter—a whole day's canning. "Wow, one hundred quarts, kids! That is good for five bushels of tomatoes. No waste at all. I guess he gave us a good count this year." Charlie opens the back door and lets cool air into the kitchen so the jars can seal.

"Now clean this place up, girls." Hope goes to the back door, making sure it's open far enough, then screams, "Oh my God, look! It's your brother Joe!"

There stands my brother Joe smiling at all of us. He comes through the green screen door with his dark blue hat in his hand, and Hope starts to cry. She hugs Joe as hard as she can, her shoulders moving up and down as she leans into his strong twenty-year-old chest and sobs. Joe's Adam's apple is even bigger than it used to be, I think.

We are all jumping around, happy to see Joe. He looks sharp in his uniform! It is all blue and has creases up the sleeves. Even the back of his shirt is pleated. His name reads "Quinlan" on a gold pin. His shoes are shiny, and we try to see our reflections in them. I'm happy and excited to see Joe walk through that kitchen door, but he looks thin, with sharp features to his face.

After admitting how good it feels to be home and see us kids, Joe lets Hope whisk him off to the Carsonville Hotel for a nice draft beer. Hope walks arm and arm up Main Street with her son, the Marine. I don't remember ever seeing her prouder.

Later, Charlie and I are making macaroni and tomatoes for dinner when Hope comes in and says, "Kids, we are going to the Applegate Inn in a few minutes. Get your hair combed. Tonight we will celebrate. Joe is home safe from Vietnam!" Charlie and I grab our jackets and jump into the back seat of our 1958 Chevy Impala. It is getting late.

Hope is driving to the Applegate, and Joe will drive on the way back home. She tells him to be careful of the big curve called "Dead Man's Curve" when he is driving. Joe just laughs out loud at the name. Joe is not afraid of anything.

We all walk into the Applegate Inn and sit at the table with Joe in his "dress blues," as he calls them. I think to myself, "Wow, they're beautiful and his brass buttons are shiny!"

Jill, the bartender, comes to the table and asks, "What will you have?" She's smiling at all of us, especially Joe. Jill is single. She's about thirty but still loves to flirt with young boys like Joe. She says she loves a man in uniform. Jill is one of Hope's friends, and Charlie has a crush on her, with her high French twist and her purple eye shadow with white eyeliner. She says, with a special kind of smile on her face, "It's kind of late for ten- and eleven-year-olds, but this does look like a time to celebrate."

Hope says, "How about a vodka and tonic for each of us and orange pop for the kids." Joe looks around at the bar, feeling good about being home from the war.

Soon a man walks up and calls to Joe, "Hey, you! Jarhead!"

I lean over to Charlie and whisper, "He doesn't look like a jarhead to me. Why would a total stranger say that?" We spent all morning canning, and I know just what a jar looks like. We filled one hundred jars today!

"That's what they call Marines, you idiot!" Charlie says.

"That's stupid," I say.

Hope and Joe are talking about the Marines and how bad their food is. Hope wants to know what the war is really like. Joe says, "Well, Hope, at night when we sleep, we tie ourselves to trees on the hillsides so we don't fall into enemy lines."

Hope, with a tear on her cheek, gulps her drink and waves her empty glass to Jill the bartender. "Well, how do you find the gooks?" she asks Joe.

"You walk point," he says, sitting up straighter as he remembers.

"Well, what is that?"

"Well," Joe says, "you have a knife called a bayonet hooked onto the end of your gun, and you walk into the dark with the knife pointing into the dark, back and forth, and you're scared to death because sometimes you stab someone. I hate walking point, Hope, but everyone has to do it. It's the most dangerous job of all. Sometimes it's punishment, too, for falling asleep during watch, which is the worse thing you can possibly do. The Marines need to get their sleep, so when you're on watch you have to stay awake until your shift is over. You smoke to stay awake, putting your fingers around the paper part of the cigarette so when you hit that part of the cigarette it will burn you and wake you up."

Joe's voice gets shaky. "Hope, I was shot one time, so close that it put a hole in my shirt. But I wasn't hurt, and I knew then and there that my family saying the rosary was what saved my life. I want another vodka, Hope. This is getting deep."

Hope waves another empty glass. Jill brings them two highballs each this time.

"We pray a lot and go to Mass out in the field, but no confessions — which I kind of like," he says with a little laugh. "You get used to the food rations, but they sure don't taste like home. Nothing out there is like home. We're all scared out there, Hope. That's how it is."

Hope gets up to go to the bathroom and stumbles, hanging onto the backs of the barstools.

Joe looks at Charlie and me and says, "Hey, let's get some barbeque chips to go with your Nesbit orange pop! It's not every day you kids get to hear war stories! But don't tell your friends these stories, okay? They might get scared."

The front door of the bar opens, and four large tough motorcycle guys come into the bar. They have long beards and chains that hold their wallets next to their pants and hankies on their heads under their helmets. Someone calls them "Harley hoggers." I think that is a good name for them. The hoggers start playing pool. As our stories go on, so do theirs, but they're not having as much fun as we are with our jarhead, Joe.

Joe gives Charlie and me each a quarter to play the jukebox, and we play the unicorn song and sing along. Joe plays Hank Williams and seems a little more relaxed after four drinks. (Charlie and I love to count them.) Then I hear one hogger yell at another, "You son-of-a-bitch! That was a scratch!" He takes his pool stick and slams it down on the side of the pool table. As the stick breaks, it makes a loud CRACK! like a gunshot.

Joe hears the loud bang, and in one second he is lying flat under the table. He looks like he's going to do push-ups, and he's shaking like he's just seen something the rest of us did not see. Hope puts her head under the table partway to talk to Joe, but he will not come up and sit down in his chair again right away.

I ask Hope, "Hope, why is Joe under the table?"

"Well, kids, Joe has been places that can't even be explained to us. He lives in another world, where you don't know where your enemy is or what form they take."

I say, "Yeah, Hope, but this is the Applegate Inn, and we come here with you all of the time."

"Erin, Joe is a combat Marine. That noise made him think he was back in the jungle."

Finally Joe climbs back out from under the table. He starts ordering shots. Jill is counting, "One thousand one, one thousand two, one thousand three," pouring liquor while she counts. As Joe starts doing shots, the stories flow from his mouth. We hear about kids just six and seven years old who will run up to you with a hand grenade in their pockets and blow away whole platoons of Marines, so you could not even trust a first-grader. Wow!

Another fight breaks out. They knock over the extra chairs at our table, and once again Joe is under the table — not afraid, just doing what he is trained to do when he hears loud noises. A Marine in his beautiful dress blues, he goes for cover.

This time Hope says, "Joe, you need to get some rest. You've been through enough tonight." She tucks her hand into the crook of his muscular arm, and they walk proudly, arm and arm, out the door of the bar. Charlie and I hook our arms together like theirs and walk behind them. Looking up to Joe and wanting to be like him is easy. He is our hero.

It's dark now, and Joe is driving. The car is quiet until Hope says, "Joe, be careful! That is Dead Man's Curve right ahead of you."

As he steers around "Dead Man Curve," Joe laughs louder than I have ever heard him laugh.

New Dresses

THE FALL AFTER JOE comes home, I'm in sixth grade. My teacher is Mrs. Hurt, a woman who never smiles or laughs. Every year I hear she is retiring, but every year on the first day of school she is standing in the hall, wringing her hands and sticking a tissue up her sleeve for later in the day. She seems to look through kids in sixth grade as if they were all young criminals. Her hair is short. (To me it looks like frog fur, even if there is no such thing.) She has lots of wrinkles and wears no makeup.

It is the morning of the first day of school. Mrs. Hurt has asked me to be the safety patrol person today.

I roll my toothbrush around in a tiny cone of baking soda in the palm of my hand. Brushing my teeth is the last thing I do before leaving the house, ready for a big day. Then I run across the fields, my legs bare, hairy, and full of bruises, my dress soon covered with "pickers" that scratch my knees as I run. Ladybird runs by my side, keeping up with me. I can't be late! If I am, someone else will get to be the safety patrol person!

Hot steam is shooting out of the radiator in the school hallway. It looks like a train running. I'm always afraid it will burn my arms when I walk by.

Mrs. Hurt is waiting at the first door to the left. The light green and white checked floors show her reflection, arms folded in disappointment. "You're late, Erin," she says in a fake whisper. I'm five minutes late even though I ran all the way in my new red tennis shoes. "You only get one chance, Erin," she says, as she drinks her coffee out of a cup brought from home. Her eyes shift down. "Aren't you cold?" she asks, pointing to my bare legs.

"No, ma'am. I ran as fast as I could. I'm actually hot."

Shaking her head, she says, "You should have socks on!"

"I was in a hurry this morning, Mrs. Hurt." I wiggle my shoulder to get my safety belt on correctly.

"This is a serious job, Erin. If you don't do the job right, someone could be hit by a car and die," she says, pulling on my belt to get it straight. The safety belt glows in the dark so cars will be able to see me. It doesn't matter how small you are: the driver can see the belt.

I'm really not looking forward to sixth grade. Some of the older kids say Mrs. Hurt slaps at least one kid every year for acting up. Mrs. Hurt wants the kids to be afraid of her. I try not to think about the slapping. I'm putting my safety belt on, proud to be given a chance to lay down the law to other kids.

The wind is blowing my dress up, and I can see all the pickers sticking to it. Here comes the first group of kids, laughing and pushing each other. They've no idea how dangerous this is in the middle on a one-lane, paved road!

"Stop!" I yell. "This is not a game! I need to walk you across the street."

Some of the kids are in tenth grade, but this is my street until 8:30 a.m. today. I walk them across and hold the little ones' hands and keep everyone safe. I love this job! No money but a lot of respect — at least I think so. And September, the first month of school, is an important time to be so responsible.

Mrs. Hurt thinks I'm the best and calls me the Lieutenant of the safety patrol. I'm second in command, Mrs. Hurt says, next to her. For now she is the Captain.

(Later I end the year as Captain of the safety patrol, and Mrs. Hurt gives me a yellow parka that says SAFETY PATROL on it in large letters, along with a certificate with my name on it. As she hands it to me she says, "Erin, we got off to a rough start, but I'm proud of you!" I'm proud of myself too. I squeeze her hand and say, "I knew if you would just give me a chance I would do a good job!")

In a month or so Mrs. Hurt actually starts to like me. One day I'm late getting out of school when she calls me into her office.

"Erin, come by my house tonight. I have a few dresses I want to give you. My granddaughter is fourteen and a little bigger then you, so they should fit."

I look down at the floor. I hate "hand-me-down" dresses from people I know. But if her granddaughter doesn't live in Carsonville, maybe no one will find out, I think to myself. I lean over to get my books and ask, "What time, Mrs. Hurt? After supper?"

"Yes, that would be good, Erin," she replies with a half-smile.

I run home to do my chores and don't let Hope know where I'm going after supper. I don't think she would approve. Hope is a proud woman who doesn't like adults telling our family what we are missing in life, like socks and warm clothes.

I run to Mrs. Hurt's house, and she greets me at the door. I feel funny being at a teacher's house, especially a teacher no one else likes. But Mrs. Hurt has given me a chance to prove myself, and we have become friends.

"Come in, Erin," she says grandly, as if I'm holding up a long line.

Mrs. Hurt's living room has two candy dishes, a loud television blaring the news, and lots of dust. The carpet is not worn. I sit on her davenport and notice that it smells sweet, as if she put perfume on it just before I arrived. I look around and see books everywhere on dusty old shelves and magazines spread out on the table, some of them stained with coffee rings from her cup. I wonder if Mrs. Hurt is going to give me a math problem to prove myself to her before she gives me the dresses. The test turns out to be worse than that.

Mrs. Hurt has decided I should try the dresses on in front of her so she can see if they're a proper fit. I have never worn a proper-fitting dress, ever! Not knowing what she is looking for, I say, "Okay." She tells me to go into her bedroom and take off my clothes and put one of the dresses on.

I get up slowly, excusing myself to walk past her to get to the back bedroom. In the bedroom there is a white bedspread that touches the floor and has bumps all over it. I crouch down on the floor on the other side of the bed to take my own dress off. It is hard to take off a dress almost lying down not to be seen, but I'm afraid Mrs. Hurt will walk in and see that I'm not wearing a slip and that there are holes in my underpants. She is my teacher, a stranger. As I struggle with my clothes behind the bed, she does walk in.

"Erin, what are you doing getting dressed on the floor? Stand up!"

I get up slowly with tears in my eyes. I feel ashamed, half-dressed, knowing I should not be here at her house without permission. Now she is going to know personal things about my family, and Hope doesn't like people knowing our business.

I stand up and say, "I'm sorry. I can't get undressed here, and I don't belong here."

She has the same kind of three-foot ruler in her hands that she holds in our classroom at school. She looks at me and says, "Erin, kneel down! I want to measure the dress on you and make sure it hits the floor when you kneel."

I say, "Mrs. Hurt, I want the dresses, but not this bad. I'm used to people just dropping off bags of clothes on our porch, not me having to get undressed in front of them. It doesn't feel right." I look away, but I know what I feel. "If these dresses don't fit right, they won't be the first. But if you need to see me put them on in front of you, I don't need them that bad."

Mrs. Hurt says, "Erin, I already know your family is poor. I'm just trying to help you out!"

I walk with long strides to Mrs. Hurt's side of the room, taking all four dresses and draping them over my bent arm. "Mrs. Hurt, if I can leave now with the dresses, you are helping me out, but if I need to undress in front of you so you can see just how poor we really are, I don't want them, no matter how pretty they are or how proper they fit." Standing first on one foot, then the other, I wait for her response.

Looking out the bedroom window with her yardstick in hand, she says, "I'm sorry, Erin. I did not realize how uncomfortable you were. Take the dresses. It is getting late, and I don't want you to get in trouble at home."

I hug the dresses to my chest and run home, stopping once under a streetlight to have a look at them. One is purple and green plaid with a pointed collar. Another has a small print of yellow daisies. The third is all bright blue, but my favorite is the burnt orange with small orange squares on big pockets in front and even brighter trim. I am so excited! No one will know where the dresses came from.

Whenever I wear the dresses to school, I wonder what Mrs. Hurt is thinking about me. I feel like she is trying to be good to me, but she really did make me feel poorer and more out of place with her kind gift. I wonder what her granddaughter had to do to get the dresses. I bet she just went to the store and tried them on over a new slip, new underpants, and matching socks. I don't have those things, but I think I have more love in my family than my lonely old teacher.

Mrs. Hurt never gives me any more clothes, and that's fine with me. I take care of the dresses she gave me, hanging them carefully in my closet. They're softer than my other dresses—they don't even get wrinkles in them.

I feel like a rich girl wearing them. Hope doesn't even notice.

Babysitting

WE ARE PUTTING AWAY three cases of dented canned goods with no labels on the cans when the telephone rings. The cans without labels are the best-priced foods in the store, real bargains, and at mealtime it is always a surprise to see what comes out of the cans. It is Hope on the telephone. She is working at the courthouse in Sandusky and excited to have found another way to help someone in need.

"Erin, a new family has just moved into town and needs a babysitter to watch their kids, Grace and Rick. You go down there and offer to do it." I waltz down the street to the address I'm given to help my new neighbors.

I knock on the door, introduce myself to the parents as Hope told me to do, and offer to watch the kids for free, as a trial run, so they can get some groceries in Port Huron. Eager to take me up on Hope's kind offer, they grab their coats and leave me behind. I'm babysitting the kids for a few hours. Hope always says, "Erin, you help your brother along the road no matter where he starts." My "brother" is anyone who needs help, not just family.

Later, when the parents still aren't back, I make dinner for Grace and Rick — the last box of macaroni and cheese in the cupboard. Washing up the dishes, I realize that the sink doesn't have a drain. I'm hungry and eat some candy from the refrigerator, caramel candies called Ayds. I eat the whole box. There is nothing else for me to eat.

Within half an hour, I can feel myself getting kind of jumpy. My heart is racing faster and faster, and I have more energy than normal. I keep the kids up an hour past their bedtime because I need the company but finally put them down about 9:30. As for me, I just can't fall asleep, no matter what.

Restless, I go through the "Monstrosity" in the dining room (like our, at home) to see if there are any games. The last drawer is full of papers. They start falling out, and I reach into the drawer to push them back. Dirty pictures of nude women fall out. I wonder if the women in the pictures are cold with no clothes on. Then I find a white-and-black swirl-handled gun. Now I don't even want to sleep. I'm kind of afraid.

I'm sitting in the big orange chair, the middle of the cushion sinking down, resting my arm on a burnt spot on the chair's arm. I stare at the clock. Three o'clock in the morning, and they're not home yet. I stare at the gun, wondering if Grace and Rick's father has ever shot anyone.

The next morning at home, no one seems to notice that I haven't come home from my babysitting job until Hope calls the kids downstairs to pray, one by one. When I don't come downstairs, Hope asks the others where I am, and Joe says, "Well, she went to a special job you told her to go to and hasn't been home since."

Hope gives Joe the rosary and starts down the street to the house where I'm babysitting. She pounds on the door with an open hand, yelling, "Erin, open this goddamn door!"

I glance at the clock—it's 7:45. Running to open the unlocked door, I'm relieved to see Hope. Still in her nightgown, she has a look of disbelief in her eyes. She is wearing no makeup, and her hand is red from pounding on the door so hard. "Erin, have you been here since yesterday?" she asks.

I say, "Yes, ma'am. I did what you told me to do."

"Where did they say they were going?" .

"Well, the man said 'out for a while,' and the mom said 'for groceries, in Port Huron.'"

"Where are the kids?" Hope asks.

"Sleeping," I answer. "There's not even milk for their breakfast!"

Hope seems more concerned about me than about breakfast for the kids. Shaking her head, she says, "Well, kids can eat cereal without milk. Just do what you can do. And when the parents come home, don't say anything to them."

About three o'clock in the afternoon, the parents finally come home, without a single bag of groceries. I don't say anything but just leave as I was told to do and go find Hope at the bar.

"Yeah, and they were so busy they forgot the groceries," I tell Hope.

"What?" Hope exclaims.

"Yep, that's right. They were too busy to get food for their kids." Hope is stomping, calves shaking as she stomps, hands going through her hair by now, pulling the hair at the same spot. She's mad and ready to tell these people a few things.

Remembering the gun, I say, "Hope, they've a gun in there! What if the man shoots you?"

"Erin, you only die when your time comes. When the good Lord wants you, he will take you. It might be his time, however," she says with a kind of smile. "I won't be the judge and jury on this one. He will, however, know how I feel!"

As we arrive at the strangers' house together, I beg Hope to calm down. She pounds on the door. It takes a long time before anyone answers. Then standing before Hope are the mom and dad.

Hope steps through the door uninvited and says, " I think going for groceries and being gone for one and a half days is taking advantage of us."

The man starts to explain that it took longer then expected, but Hope looks pointedly at the kitchen table, saying, "Where is the food you went for? Or was it all a lie just to get a free babysitter? You are an opportunist, my friend, and there's no room for your kind in this town!" She turns away in complete disgust, saying, "Don't ever ask for Erin or any of my kids to babysit for you again!" She slams the door behind us so hard the curtain rod jumps off.

On our way home I say, "Hope, when it comes to dying, how do we know when our number is up?"

Hope kind of slows down and tells me that the "angel of death comes."

I'm picturing an angel with the black-and-white handled gun shooting me. "Hope, what if you are not ready to die when the angel of death comes for you?"

"Erin, this is not the time to talk to me," Hope says, but she slows down her pace to add, "I'm a fatalist. I believe you have free will but that you are predestined to die at a certain time and place. God gives us choices, but He knows what we will choose to do before we choose it. It's hard to understand, Erin, but we are all accountable for whatever we do."

It's a lot to think about.

Taking the E

I'M LEANING AGAINST THE DOOR to the gym with my hair pulled back in a tight ponytail, waiting to meet the teacher for my first day of gym class. Weighing ninety-two pounds, standing five foot seven inches, I stand in front of Mr. Scholdick.

"Quinlan, do thirty push-ups and keep your body straight!" he barks.

I get to my knees to do girls' push-ups, only to hear him yell louder, "Quinlan, there are no such things as girls' push-ups! That is sissy stuff!"

I hate him. He is mean, and he tries to make us into little Marines. His brush cut smells of Brill Cream. He has a tight jaw, and his eyes, set too close together, are blue with red veins showing in the whites. When he yells (which is always), the veins on his neck stand out in huge lumps. He wears freshly polished combat boots, even with shorts, and when he first met our class of skinny shiny-faced seventh graders, he made it a point to yell our last names at us. Until then we were just kids!

Mr. Scholdick rules the shiny gym floor. Carsonville's school gym has a red line that goes all around the floor a few feet from the walls. A few feet closer to the center there is a wide black line. We have about three feet to run between the red and the black lines.

Mr. Scholdick runs alongside me, screaming. My wornout shoes feel loose, but I don't dare slow down to retie them. I'm sweating and feel a strange tightness in my chest but tell myself to keep moving. "Quinlan, if you slow down, you are getting an E today!" he yells. I'm the fastest runner in my class, but he is never happy with my time. He thinks all of our times should be better so we can get the President's award. Speeding back up to my old pace, I learn for the first time that running is harder then it looks.

Mr. Scholdick is so mean! I wish Hope could see how he treats our class; she would not put up with it. When our twelve laps are over, we stand at attention in front of him.

"Quinlan! You better make this class shine today! That was just a warmup. Now we are moving to the outside. Quinlan, I'm putting you up in the front to keep pace with me! If you slow down, it's an E. If you stop, it's an E. What will it be today, Quinlan?"

I give Mr. Scholdick a dirty look and run in the opposite direction. Running across the football field, with mud splashing up to the middle of my calves, I pound through each and every mud hole, not caring at all how wet and dirty I get. I need to prove to myself that I'm not afraid. My throat is dry, as if I've had dust for breakfast. I hear my heart beating loudly in my ears. My legs feel disconnected from my body.

Glancing back, I see him coming to yell again, but I can't move faster or take my focus off the goal post I have it in my mind to reach before he bothers me. No, he is here! This time he just throws a disgusted look my way as passes me without saying a word.

The next day I act excited about running so he will not pick on me, but the football field is muddy and unforgiving. "Quinlan, you just slowed down, and that's an E!"

"I never slowed down! I just kept running." I'm still running now, and so is he, right next to me.

"Oh, there is another slowing down! Another E! Wow, Quinlan, you have two E's and you've just started." The end of the run gave me four E's, He seems to enjoy the fact that he has power over me, but I won't give in. I will ignore his meanness!

At the end of the run, turning a corner, I accidentally bump his side. "Quinlan, come into the office. I want to show you something!" Leaning over his desk, covered with volleyballs, basketballs, old rims, a white phone, and a coffee cup half full of cold coffee with a film over the surface, I stand ready to see the grade book. "Erin Quinlan, E, E, E, E. Four E's in a row."

I look at it, saying, "Wow, as hard as I run, I still get four E's?"

He closes the small brown grade book and says, "Yes, ma'am. That is what you have earned!"

I say, "Okay."

"Okay, sir!" he corrects me.

Looking up to the ceiling, I say, "Okay, sir," then, "I'm tired. I want to go take a shower."

"Excused! Yes, Quinlan, you may!"

On Monday morning I go to gym class ready to run again, but then I stand there thinking. Well, he hates me and I can't run fast enough for him. If I slow down or stop, I get an E. So I might just as well sit the class out. I take off my street shoes, knowing the rules oh-so-well, and wait for roll call, standing in my street clothes with a smile on my face.

Mr. Scholdick comes to the front of the class. "Erin, what are you doing?" he says in his normal gruff voice.

"Well," I say with confidence (loud enough for the class to hear), "I'm just here to take an E!"

"That is ridiculous! You are going to run today!"

"No, I'm not! I'm taking an E!"

He tells the rest of the class to get running, that he wants to talk to me alone. We walk back into his messy office with old equipment thrown around, and he sits down behind his desk. "Erin, if you do this, you will fail gym class!"

"I know. But you made up the game, Mr. Scholdick. You are trying to break me. Well, instead of running and getting E's for not being fast enough or for slowing down, I'm not going to run for you at all. I'll just take one E and not even get dressed!"

I walk out of his office feeling proud of myself for standing up to him. Back in the gym, I sit in the bleachers, watching him hassle other girls. He doesn't want girls in gym class at all, so he's trying to make us cry to prove that we are not as good as boys. I watch the class, relieved not to be screamed at or spit at (accidentally) when he yells. Shortly, two more girls join me.

When gym class is over he says to me, "Quinlan, if you don't get dressed now, I will show you who is boss. I'll send you to the office." I stand up with pride in my fast-beating heart, ready to go to the office.

Down the long hall with lockers on one side and a window that follows me as far as I need to walk, as if the sun is on my side, I sling my shoulders forward to climb a set of ten steps that lead to the principal's office. Someone's mom is filling in for the regular secretary and says, "Hi, Erin. Are you in trouble?"

"No, not really. Well, maybe. I'm not sure."

The office door opens. The principal is a friendly man about my father's age. He pushes his glasses down on his nose, looking over them at me. "Say, you've never been here before! What seems to be the problem?"

Explaining to the principal that Mr. Scholdick makes me run faster than anyone else and is always screaming in my face, I feel a sense of relief. I would not have gone to the office to tattle, but Mr. Scholdick sent me here, so now it's his problem. My parents will be mad if I come home with all of these E's, and it isn't fair.

The principal places a hairy-knuckled hand on my shoulder, "Erin, trust me on this. You will be treated with respect tomorrow. If not, come back to see me. You have gotten your last E."

The next day while we're shooting baskets, Mr. Scholdick says to me, "Quinlan, maybe I was a little hard on you."

Another basket is shot. I pick up the ball, throwing it at the ceiling. "You're just a mean man who doesn't like girls in your gym class," I say to him and walk out.

I wait for my report card. I get a B-minus in Physical Education. I don't have Mr. Scholdick for a teacher again. I think he went back to the Marines where he belonged.

The Abandoned House Game

THE DISHES ARE DONE, the dishrag in the sink, and Hope grabs a bottle of wine and puts it in a paper bag. We take back roads to the fields outside town where there are lots of old houses that have not been lived in for a long time. We pull into a driveway mostly covered over with high grass. There is a pathway through the grass to a beautiful front door.

It is dusk, and the moon has a smile on his face. Hope has us walk around the outside of the house first to make sure the roof is not sagging. It isn't. Then we are shinnied up through a broken window, and we open the front door from the inside to let Hope in.

Hope traces her finger around the pretty cut-glass window in the door. The design shows the shape of a peacock.

"Something is not right on this one, kids," she says. "No one would leave a house this beautiful." She shrugs her shoulders. "Well, let's take a look." She opens the glass door wider. It has a beautiful lace curtain.

Hope goes over to one of the windows where broken glass has fallen on the floor and finds a small bit of blood on the glass. "Nope, this is no place to play our game tonight, kids. Whoever left this house left in a hurry or was threatened in some way." But then she shrugs her shoulders, saying, "Well, what the hell! We're here — we might just as well look around. Maybe we can figure it out."

We stand in the living room, looking up at what Hope calls the cove ceiling. It is white with fancy carving on it. Attractive green paint (it still looks fresh) covers the walls. The room has a stunning rug in the middle of the floor, with a big red rose on the middle. There is cat fur in the corner, but no cat.

"Look over there, Hope," I say in a whisper. "It's a bookshelf, and they left some books." There are three books of poems. One is Robert Frost, one has a cover too faded to read, but the last one is Hope's favorite—Robert Service.

Picking up the book, she says, "No one in his or her right mind would have left Robert Service." She thumbs through the pages, smiles, and puts the book back on the dust-filled shelf. Then, taking a swig of wine, she reaches back for the book and pulls it out a second time, saying, "Robert didn't deserve to be abandoned!" She tucks him under her arm.

The room is clean, but there are lots of broken things. There is even a big hole in the bathroom door and one in the bedroom door too. Some of the drywall is torn right off the wall.

"Let's go upstairs, Erin, and see if we can figure this one out," Hope says.

I run up the stairs, touching the banister all the way. It is shiny, with a fancy knob at the top and bottom.

"Listen, Hope! There's a strange sound behind this door. It sounds like hornets hitting the window glass." I try to get the door open, but it is locked.

"No use, Erin," Hope says. "You can see the broken key in the keyhole."

Charlie opens the next door and screams when a huge hangman's noose swings down from the dark.

"That's some kind of a joke, Charlie. It's not real. Say, this is getting to be a pretty good mystery, isn't it?" Hope asks, taking another swig of her wine.

"I don't like this house, Hope," I say. We usually try to guess what happened to the people who abandoned the house, and we all get to yell out ideas, pick the kids' names, wonder what they were like. But this place feels scary. What if the man killed his wife by the broken window? What if he hung her? "I don't like it at all! Let's go!"

Charlie jumps in front of me, saying, "Erin, that's stupid! We are going to figure this out. I don't care how many kids and what their names were. I want to know who killed who!"

Hope starts to laugh, "This is Carsonville, and no one killed anyone, but there was some definite pain here. Let's go to the back room and see if there are more clues."

The last door is opened. There are broken pictures on the floor, all turned upside-down. There is a pile of clothes in a basket. "It doesn't make sense," I say to Charlie. "Maybe he killed her for not getting the laundry done!" I'm laughing as I run out of the room.

"It's not funny, Erin," Hope calls after me. "You're crazy to think these aren't all clues for someone to figure out."

"Let's go downstairs, Charlie," I say. "This place is giving me the heebie-jeebies."

Hope follows us downstairs. After poking through the other rooms a while, we find her standing by the kitchen sink, looking out the window. "Well," she says, "they had three kids living here. Look! They used to draw lines on the cellar door to keep track of their growth. Look—Martha, Alice, and Bob. Not much imagination." Hope rubs her arms in their winter coat sleeves. "I think we need to leave now," she says. "This place is giving me the willies, too."

She drains the last drop of wine, puts down her empty wine bottle and says to us, "There are trapped spirits in this place, and I have been feeling them since we first got here. It's the 'razor's edge.' I don't like it. We are disturbing something here. Come on." Then, "Look at that lipstick rolling out on the floor from the bathroom!"

I scream, "I'm with you all the way, Hope!"

Charlie steps out from behind the bathroom door, laughing. "Erin, that was m-me, you idiot!"

Hope says, "It doesn't take a genius to figure out what happened here. Really, it doesn't. A jealous husband went into a rage when he found his wife had left him for another man. He smashed all she loved, except for the front door, just in case they did get back together. He tried to lure her back with the perfect front door and her books of poetry. But she would have been hung had she returned. I thank the good Lord she was smart enough to know not to return. Look at the holes in the walls! He was a madman! I'm glad she got away."

This is a clear case of not being able to judge a book by its cover, I think. We talk about the abandoned house for days. My friends at school love the story. They think my mother would be a fun mother to have.

Sleepover

"COME ON, ERIN, ONE MORE TIME," Denise urges. She is helping me practice my prayers to recite to Hope. We lie face-to-face on Saturday morning, knees touching, with the green wool army blanket pulled over our shoulders. The heat from the blanket kisses my face as I try to get the words right. We have to memorize our prayers to be allowed to go to a sleepover.

Memorizing is important to be a good Catholic. I have learned the Act of Contrition, Hail Mary, Our Father, and the Apostles' Creed. Denise is really good at poetry, like Robert Service, but I am better at prayers. Prayers are shorter than poems.

Hope does not really like us to spend the night at other kids' houses. Bring them here, she says, but really, I want to leave this house and giggle all night at Karen's house. She is the first in seventh grade to start her period and tell me about how it feels. The wallpaper at Karen's house is full of flowerpots and pretty vases. Her mom irons all day, wearing a bathing suit and smoking Chesterfields, leaving smears of red lipstick on every butt, and the butts fill her gold metal ashtray stand next to the ironing board. What I think of as a "jag-wire cat" stretches over the top of the ashtray. After dinner we kids scrape the plates, clear the table, and sneak butts in our pockets for later, when we have an excuse to go outside to burn the trash.

Karen calls her mother Mom. (Her real name is Beverly.) Her mother has sharp features and a laugh like a hyena's when she is on the phone with one of her girlfriends. (The phone cord stretches across the kitchen so she can cook dinner and talk at the same time.) She dances and loves loud music with a beat. Buddy Holly is one of her favorites. She shows us new steps we can do at the next dance, and the wood floors are perfect for dancing.

Music from the radio is always a surprise. When a good song comes on, we run to the radio and squash our ears up to the small speaker to hear every word, and we are allowed to move our hips, too. Karen's mom doesn't care. We can't even touch our hips at our house. Or lie on our side to look at them. Hope says, "That is not necessary." But Karen's mom lets us tie up our t-shirts to show our belly buttons.

Sometimes Karen's mom takes us to the roller rink and skates with us. Her laugh can be heard from one end of the building to the other. I wish I had a mom who would skate and smoke and dance. Karen's mom even helps the kids with their homework. When Karen's brothers and sister are home, we all have fun together. The mom grabs her oldest son and makes him dance until her tassels in her shoes are too tired to move any more.

They are a nice family. They don't go to church, but it doesn't seem to matter. Karen's mom gives us Girl Scout cookies and milk after school, and when we eat supper there, after school or on a snow day, she puts a loaf of store-bought bread on the table and breaks the bread apart instead of cutting it. Hope says she is pretending it is the Last Supper. Hope never wants to tear bread. She says it is a lot of work to make bread and that bread is not meant to be torn by the handful. "If she would've baked her own bread," Hope says, "she would not've destroyed it like that."

Karen's father seems crabby. He's called "Curly," with his one curl in front of his bald head after he takes his hat off, and I have never seen him except in a dirty white t-shirt, with a Blue Ribbon beer in his hand. Curly works at the county garage (where we dare each other to jump off the roof). His work boots have black oil on the toes from spreading it on the county roads. He carries a small cup around all the time and spits tobacco into it. Hope and Bill really like Curley and say he is a "good Joe." I don't think the mothers have met.

As much as I like sleeping over at Karen's, tonight I want to have Karen spend the night with us at our house. We are both excited, and she is expecting my call and answers right away. I hear her dad yell from another room, "Is that a Quinlan kid?"

"Yes, sir," Karen replies. Then she says to me, "Just a minute" and lays the phone down.

I listen hard, and I can hear her in the next room crying, " No, Dad, please don't say that! Please! She is my best friend!"

Her dad gets on the phone and asks, "Which Quinlan are you?"

I say, "Erin," while Hope is yelling from behind me, " Well, is Karen coming or not? I need to know how much corn to put on!"

The phone is silent again for a while, and then Karen's dad gets back on. "Erin, no, it won't work. I know your mom and dad, and they are good people, but living next to the bar — well I gotta tell ya, I got a problem with it. I'm sorry, honey, but Karen is not allowed to spend the night."

As I start to hang up the phone, Hope grabs it from me. " Hi, Curly! How are you doing?" She listens and then taps the phone on her shoulder as she thinks. "What do you mean, Curly? We're your friends! You've worked with Bill, and you know we are honest, hard-working people!"

Curly is still troubled about our living next to the Carsonville Hotel. He says, "but really, the fact that you live next to the Carsonville Hotel - an uninvited drunk could wander into your home Hope." Hope listens closely and has an answer to everything he says. "First of all they wouldn't be uninvited! Curly, I am disappointed in you. You of all people! I would not expect this kind of behavior. You're our friend."

Curly has a suggestion, but Hope rejects it. "No, Curly, that won't work. This is not easy on me, but Erin will not come to your house. You live next to the railroad tracks! And besides, Curly, it is like this: if you feel we are not good enough to take care of Karen, why would I send over Erin to your house? I am disappointed in you as a person. You know damn well we would not let anything happen to Karen, but one excuse is as good as the next." She hangs up the phone.

"Can Karen come, Hope?"

"Not tonight Erin. She has lots of homework and needs her rest."

Running up the stairs, I want to cry.

Denise is sitting on the bed. "What in the hell are you crying about?" She is in eighth grade now and loves to swear.

"I just wanted Karen to come and spend the night! I worked so hard at learning the Apostles' Creed, and now she can't come because her dad doesn't think this is a safe place to spend the night!"

"I'm glad," Denise says. "We're already crowded enough without you having your dumb friends sleeping with us. Karen is nice, but she's too boy-crazy. I heard she smokes, too. Does she?"

"Yes, she does, but only with me," I answer in a snotty voice.

"I hope you are lying, Erin. I know you are!"

"Denise, Karen has started her period, and I want to know what it's like. She was going to give me the details."

Denise says, "Erin, you wear a belt with a pad, and it's stupid, and you have sharp pains. Anything more than that, she is just making up. You can't talk all night about that!"

Climbing out of bed to reach up and turn out the light that hangs off the wallpaper of wild roses, I let out a yell, then run back across the dark room where the street lights shine through and jump into bed, landing on Denise, who screams and kicks me over to my own side. We don't really need to have friends sleep over. We are best friends.

St. Patrick's Day

"Pocahontas" is what they call me at school. My hair is long, and I usually wear it in braids unless there is a holiday. For those special times I curl it in rags, taking the long hair and twisting it up in small rag strips as I go, bangs taped down with special pink tape so they won't spring up in the night. When I take it down, it is a perfect spiral curl.

Tomorrow I want to look perfect. My sister-in-law, Suzie, came up for the weekend with my brother Brian. They're in love and just got married about a year ago. Suzie loves to bring us kids surprises, and this time it was long dresses for Denise and me for St. Patrick's Day. Suzie hands the two matching dresses to Denise and me and tells us they are "Granny dresses." I have never seen a dress this long in my life! It looks like something Mary Ingalls would wear. It has an empire waist, with a small amount of lace that ties in the back and hangs down, and the material is a print of small green leaves and red flowers on a white background.

"Why are you giving us dresses, Suzie?"

"They're the newest rage in Detroit, and I thought it would be fun to see you and Denise do your hair up and surprise your friends this St. Patrick's Day."

I'm not sure we can wear these kinds of dresses to school, though. No one has worn anything this long before to find out if it's allowed. Girls in our town are wearing "mini" dresses, and teachers are sending them home from school because the dresses are too short. In our school, if dresses are no more than three inches above the knee, you can wear them. But this long?

Denise grabs her dress, which is even longer than mine. "I've heard of these dresses! They're called 'maxi' dresses, and they're more popular than 'minis.' Hey, come on, Erin! Let's see if they fit!"

I run to the stairs and kiss the banister like it's a man.

"Oh, please God, make them fit us perfect!" Denise yells out, while we undress in our pretend apartment and throw our old clothes into our pretend kitchen area. "I know they have to fit! Please!"

Denise has hers on in seconds, and it looks great. She twirls in front of the mirror. "Yea! They both look good," she announces as I'm still adjusting mine.

"Denise, we can wear matching white tennis shoes, do our hair in rags tonight, and then we will be the prettiest in our junior high class tomorrow. I can't wait, Denise! I can't wait! This will fix that little brat, Debbie, for always pointing out the clothes she has given us when she walks down the hall. I hate to have her pass me in the hall. Last time she pointed at me, I undid her bra from the back as she walked by."

"Oh, sure, Erin," Denise smiles. "I bet you couldn't even reach it, then to do it that fast. I doubt it, Erin."

"Oh, ask her then, Denise! But no one will know where these dresses came from. The kids might even think we have rich relatives in the city, like some kids do, or rich grandparents."

I can twirl this long dress, and when I walk you can't even see the tennis shoes. Standing in front of the mirror, I can see my eyes are getting to look darker brown, eyelashes longer. My bone structure is like Hope's. I wish I had her pretty slanted eyes; instead I just have her little ball on the end of my nose.

Denise and I take a shower together, planning the day ahead. Later, lying in bed and watching out the window onto Main Street, I hear the older kids playing spud and mother-may-I. I'd like to be playing, too, but nothing is more important tonight than getting my hair set just right and laying out my dress for tomorrow. I lay out pale blue underpants next to the dress and fall asleep. In my sleep I'm walking into school in my new granny dress, the prettiest girl in seventh grade.

In the morning, I see that the dress is still there, but Denise is in a bad mood. Her hair is still wet. "And it's St. Patrick Day, Denise! I can't believe it's almost time to get dressed, and my hair is still wet!" My own feels damp, too.

From downstairs, Hope yells out, "Rise and shine, ladies! It is St. Patrick's Day, and breakfast is hot cocoa and homemade buns."

I can't believe my ears. We usually have to have oatmeal on school days because it "sticks to our ribs,' but today the big commercial kettle on the stove is half-full of hot cocoa, and I can smell the chocolate from the doorway of the kitchen. Dipping the cocoa out with a cup, I sit down with my sisters and brothers, and we spread the hot buns with soft oleo.

Finally Denise and I can't wait any longer for our hair to dry. We take the rags out and comb our curls. Perfect! The hair is dry, dresses on, and today we will show that old Debbie that we have our own store to shop at now. I can't wait! Hope is excited for us, too.

We walk to school as always, this time with big smiles on our faces.

My first class is home economics. Mrs. Birch is taking roll call with her book when she looks up at me. What, no smile? I say, "I'm here!" She has looked up at the sound of my voice without noticing my new dress. She finishes her job, saying we are going to learn how to hem a skirt today.

I'm smiling at the other girls in class, and my close friends are saying I look pretty, like Laura Ingalls. Then, out of nowhere, Mrs. Birch says, "You need to come outside in the hall with me, Erin."

"Okay, Mrs. Birch."

Outside the classroom, she says, "Erin, it's not that you don't look pretty today, because you do, but I'm afraid I will have to send you to the office for the principal to decide if this is 'proper dress.'"

I twirl in my dress, saying, "You're kidding, right? This is a little St. Patrick's Day joke, like an April Fool's Day joke, right?"

"No, I'm afraid not," Mrs. Birch says, as she looks closer at the pattern in the dress. "What a shame a dress like that is dangerous to wear in school," she sighs.

Just then I see Denise being taken to the office for her dress, too. She has tears in her eyes. I yell out, "Denise, don't worry, this place is stupid! We can't be in real trouble. This is some kind of joke!"

When we get around the corner, we see Hope sitting in the office. "Hope, what are you doing here? Is someone hurt?" I ask, concerned.

"No, Erin, this is a principal who likes looking up young girls' dresses, so he is kicking you and Denise out of school. He called me to ask me to come and get you. He wants me to make you change your pretty dresses, but actually I'm here to say, come home. You don't have to go back to school today at all. This is ridiculous! It is really about a dirty old man that wants to look at legs! I will walk you home, but I think we should just all have some fun making chicken stew and baking pies. I'm pretty sure I can teach you more than your home economic teacher can."

Mr. Die seems to be upset as he opens the office door, saying, "Well, to tell you the truth, this is to assure that you don't trip on the stairs of this old building, but if Hope wants to give you a day off to celebrate St. Patrick's Day, well, you're her children, and who am I to argue with her?"

Denise and I don't change our clothes all day. Our hair is still pretty curly. After baking pies all day like Laura Ingalls would have, we go to see our friends in town after school. I usually do learn more from Hope than any schoolteacher.

The Broom Dance

IN WHAT SEEMS LIKE much less than twelve months, it is St. Patrick's Day again. It is dim twilight, and the moon is out when my sister Denise gets the call from Hope. "Kids, get up and come to the bar. We are dancing tonight, and we want you kids here right away!"

I smile at Denise and ask, "What should we wear, Denise?" We can't do our dancing in long dresses!

She says, "Call Charlie! We need to hurry, Hope said."

I make the call, "Charlie, it's time to go to the Carsonville Hotel. They want us to dance."

Charlie is excited, too, and doesn't hesitate. We are to be part of the entertainment tonight! We comb our hair, brush our teeth, and grab the broom, making excited, nervous conversation as we fly around the house.

The porch of the bar is a long slanted slab of cement and has eight porch poles on it, their ancient-looking paint peeling away in long curls. Inside, the bar is green and brick and has an old warped oak floor, slanted and slippery. There is a pool table and shuffleboard. I can hear loud Celtic music. It is the Clancy Brothers, an Irish band, and everyone seems to be happy, clapping to the rhythm. One man has his knee on the chair as he claps his hands. Men are raising their glasses, cigarettes are falling out of the ashtrays still burning, and jiggers of whisky from Lena are being passed around. Beer is flowing — some onto the floor. I have never seen everyone so happy. Even the women are drinking green beer. The bar is smoky, but I can see Bill across the room doing an Irish jig as Hope stands by clapping her hands.

I stand by the door, waiting for my turn to dance. At last my father throws a broom at me. He has a smile on his face. "Erin, this is your song, honey." It is my favorite, performed by the Clancy Brothers. I take the broom with great pride and start dancing from the door on into the room.

In this dance you move the broom from between your legs and kick as high as you can. The faster music, the faster you go — and soon you are throwing the broom between your legs with more and more distance in each throw. Then there is a time when you take the broom, hold onto both ends and jump over it, again and again, without letting go of either end. The jumps get higher and higher, and soon you are doing it from behind your back. Moving the broom from the back to the front is the hardest part. It is like limbo, but you are hanging onto both ends of the broom. The music gets louder and faster, the tempo building.

I'm sweating and enjoying this dance to the -nth degree! I glance across the room to see my sister in the dining room, facing me, doing the same dance, dressed in a ruffled green dress that she has been saving for St. Patrick's Day. I'm wearing a pair of jeans and a green blouse with a white collar. Charlie is waiting to take his turn whenever one of us gets worn out. He is our backup man. I need him first, and he grabs the broom and starts to do an Irish jig we also learned that goes with the broom dance.

The crowd is getting excited and drinking more and more. They're respectful with us kids but truly enjoy the whole dance they're witnessing. We are thrilled to be invited to the bar. It is a private place for adults, and we are rarely allowed inside, but Bill and Hope have many good times in the Carsonville Hotel, and it is a fun-loving place to be.

When the dance is over, we are given "the look" from Hope. It's her "Kids, one more, and then you have to be out of here; it is already 11:00, and kids are not allowed after 9:00 o'clock" look.

The music begins and I proudly grab the broom again. This is my chance to shine as a dancer, so I do. My father (whom I love, especially when he is drinking) stands proudly by my side, and I can tell he loves me. Bill always says, "We are an Irish Clan." We are proud to be Irish.

When the dancing is over and we get "the look" again, it is time to go home. Sadly we walk out onto the porch and wipe the sweat from our brows and begin to discuss our dancing.

Denise says, "Erin, you hogged the broom for three dances, and Charlie only got one."

Charlie and I decide to mess around instead of going home. Denise keeps us in line, for the most part, and now she says we are pushing our luck by not going right home to bed, but we don't care. We are going to sneak out tonight.

Eddie, my boyfriend and the only kid in town with a car, told us where there is a bottle of Ripple in a ditch outside town. Charlie and I jump into his car (which we are not allowed to be in) and start to look for the bottle of wine. It is getting dark, and we know we are disobeying Hope and Bill, but I figure we will be back before they get home from the Carsonville Hotel, since they will be at the bar until 2:00 a.m.

But this night is different. Bill gets drunk and calls to have us come "walk" him home. (We actually kind of push him from the back, down the sidewalk and up the steps.) This time Denise does what she is told and never mentions that Charlie and I are still gone. She figures we are safe, because Bill and Hope are drunk and will not notice we are missing. She takes off Bill's boots and makes him goulash. Meanwhile, Charlie and I take the back way home and then climb up the plum tree and slowly crawl across the roof and into the window.

Surprise! Hope is standing under the light as I turn it on. I scream, "My God, Hope, what are you doing in our bedroom?"

She looks at me and says, "Erin, get undressed and get to bed."

I plead with her, "Please let me explain, Hope!" But there is no explanation allowed. She gives me a cold, cold stare and repeats what she has just said. I beg her to punish me but not to tell my father. Hope just says, "Go to bed, Erin. It's late!"

The next morning, I wake up knowing I have to go downstairs and face the music. I think how disappointed my father will be, and I come around the kitchen corner expecting to be told to go for a switch. I start to explain where I was last night, but Hope interrupts. She asks me, "Erin, did you have a good time dancing last night?"

I say, "Yes, Hope, it was wonderful to dance like that!"

Hope says, "I bet you were tired and went right to bed?"

I smile and say, "Yes, ma'am, I was tired!"

Hope never told Bill how Charlie and I broke the rules and stayed out until 2:00 a.m. without permission. Or so we think. With Hope and Bill, we're never sure.

One Eyed Jack

Dinner is over, and Hope is sitting in the kitchen at the gray Formica table with the wide metal rim around its edge. Usually the table is covered with a plastic tablecloth, but not tonight. Hope, with her slanted eyes ("Eyes are the windows to the soul," Hope says), has a smile on her face as she hands me a deck of cards.

Leaning forward, her large breasts touching the table, she says, "Shuffle the cards, Erin. I want only your luck on the cards. I don't want to have anyone else's fortune here but yours." She says this with a serious tone in her voice.

While I shuffle the cards, Hope gets up and turns off the light in the living room. I start to think this is a pretty big deal. Sliding back into her chair, she gets her serious look back, saying, "Erin, do you remember me telling you that my mother ran a boarding house?"

"Yes, I do remember," I reply.

"She took in boarders in the bedrooms of our house and made their meals for them," Hope began. "Then, after the boarders ate dinner at night, my mother, May, would go down to the river where the gypsies camped, giving them whatever leftover food the boarders did not eat. She became friends with the gypsies, and they shared with her stories of mysteries of the land. May was interested and learned a lot from these stories.

"The gypsies shared their belief of spirits living alongside us as we live our lives, spirits we are not able to see, taking care of their unfinished business," Hope goes on as she keeps her hands outreached to gather up the cards. "May enjoyed sitting on the bank of the river, visiting, letting her feet dangle in the water at the edge of the bank. It was there she learned she was pregnant. She heard the news first from the gypsies instead of from her doctor. May must have felt a blush to have four women's hands rubbing her belly, their eyes closed, nodding to say, 'Yes, dear, this is the truth!'

"Shelia was the wisest of the women; she did most of the medical treatments with herbs and spices. 'Next winter, you will be giving birth to a baby girl,' Shelia said as she put some awful cream on May's forehead. 'It is a girl for sure. A beautiful healthy baby girl!'

"That baby was me," Hope smiles, "born on February 4, 1919. I think Sheila liked May because she spent almost two years there on the riverbank. Not in the coldest time of the year, though: they moved inside old buildings to wait to return in the spring."

Hope says, "My mother told me this story, Erin, and it is the truth. She said that the baby girl named Hope would have a special gift of telling fortunes. It would be passed down to the youngest girl in the family, and that is you, Erin. The gypsies also said I would be able to have the ability to know things no one else knew."

"What do you mean, Hope?"

"Well, it's hard to explain, Erin. Sometimes I get a feeling about things before they actually happen. It comes in handy in raising kids, for sure! One time I was in the Umbrella Inn in Keego Harbor and heard a siren. I ran out of the bar, saw an ambulance passing, and I felt a sharp pain in my chest. I knew that one of my kids was hurt. I just knew it. I jumped into my car to follow. When we got to the hospital, I was in a panic. They asked my name, and I said, 'Hope Quinlan.'"

"The nurse said, 'Yes, we have your son, Mike Quinlan. He has been in a horrible motorcycle accident. His bike rode up over a car. He's lucky to be alive! His eye is open with a slit. He is one lucky man. He is in surgery now, and you can wait here for him.'

"I was standing there when Mike was rolled out of surgery. As they were making up his bed, I stood by with tears in my eyes." Hope says with a smile, "Now, Erin, there is no way I would call that just woman's intuition! I had to trust my intuition, for sure, but much goes on in this world that we don't understand. These messages come from somewhere."

Hope leans back into her chair, saying, "Sometimes, Erin, when I'm worried, I get my answers in dreams."

I stretch my wrist out to reach for the cards. "Okay, Hope, I'm ready to learn now." I think, so I will be able to tell fortunes, but why would a 15-year-old girl need to tell fortunes, and who would believe me anyway? But I listen respectfully to Hope.

"Honey, it is time for me to show you," Hope says in a whisper.

I would rather be getting ready for the dance at school, but it is clear from Hope's bottle of red wine and her old coffee cup that we are going to have a totally different kind of evening. It won't be me dancing with Eddie Davis after the basketball game but me and mother and the cards at our kitchen table.

Leaning forward again with her breasts against the table, Hope hands me the cards. Shuffling them now, my knees bouncing slightly under the table, I try returning them to her.

"No, I can't touch the cards, Erin. This is your fortune. Now, split the cards into three piles towards your heart."

Rolling my eyes, I do as she says.

"Now, let's get a preview of what the fortune will be from the three cards showing. If more than one of the cards is red, it will be in your favor, but if they're all black cards, well, we need to go further into the fortune to see exactly what is going on." The cards are all black, so we go on further. Hope tells me the rules of telling fortunes. "First and foremost, don't ever accept money for this. And remember, this is a gift not to be used for evil doings."

I spread the cards seven across and make seven rows. It is fun to see what shows up. If two cards touch each other when I lay them out, Hope asks, "Honey, are they friends or foes?" I'm not sure. I just keep spreading the cards while glancing now and then at the clock.

Wow, this will change many of my thoughts about playing cards! We are not allowed to play cards because my Grandfather Hank was a gambler and lost everything they owned. Since then, my Grandmother May and Hope don't believe in cards, except for fortune telling.

Strangely enough, the cards seem to be taking on their own character traits. I can actually see that if a jack has only one eye, he must not be trusted. The worse jack of all is the jack of spades. The king of spades is strong, powerful, but also not to be trusted. (We don't have any real kings in Carsonville, Hope assures me.) The hearts are full of love, and a queen of hearts is the best you can get. She is like a mother: she loves all that are attached to her. Soon I start not liking the spades at all. They seem mean and unfriendly.

"The clubs don't have much going for them," Hope says. "Carsonville has a lot of clubs living in it. They're dull normal."

This is crazy! These cards seem to be making sense! I wish I could have one sip of Hope's wine so I could see how everything will tie together. The phone rings. I get up, sneak a swig of wine from Hope's bottle, and pour a little in a glass for myself. Hope pretends not to see.

Now we are getting to the good stuff. Hope, tapping her finger on the table, says, "What falls to the floor comes to your door, Erin."

"Everything that falls on the floor, from now on, comes to my door? How will that work?" I ask.

"If you see an ace of spades fall on the floor, well, that is the death card. But don't tell anyone that if you're telling their fortune. Just stop the fortune telling. If it's a queen of hearts, well, all goodness comes from her. She represents love and family and has enough love to pass on to others. Hazel, your Godmother, is like a Queen of Hearts.

"Look at the faces of the cards. You will be able to see what they want you to know. Always pause" (and she stopped talking for a second) "and look into the eyes of the person across from you. The eyes will give you the answers you need to add to what the card is saying. Remember, Erin, nothing is more interesting to anyone than hearing their own story. So watch how comfortable they're sitting. Are they at ease? If not, well, you might just have something. Dig deeper. Don't move the cards. Keep them in the positions they had when you laid them out on the table."

Sitting back, pushing the cards towards me as she enjoys her fourth refill, Hope says, "Erin, you will learn best by telling me my fortune. See if you can read me!"

I can only read what four glasses of red wine do for her. That information alone is a lot to absorb. I push the cards back at her saying, "Hope, I need more time to think about all of this. Why don't you tell me whom I will marry? Will it be Eddie Davis?"

Hope closes up the bottle with the metal cap, saying, "Erin, you will not marry Eddie. I don't need to read the cards to know this. Eddie has a problem keeping his pants on. If I were to read your fortune, I would say he is a one-eyed jack. You would be barefoot and pregnant while he ran around on you, Erin. I don't have the cards to show you, but he is not bright enough, either. No, he is not a keeper! Black cards surround him; he will have lots of struggles with honesty. His old man was a charmer, and I enjoyed having a drink with him, but he had the same problem."

Sliding a one-eyed jack in front of me, she says, "Memorize it, honey. That is your future with Eddie. He is a nice kid, but watch out for the one-eyed jacks. They look good, but they always have their eyes on someone else instead of you. Don't marry one, no matter what."

With her pants twisted a little sideways, she walks across to the kitchen, saying, "Erin, that's it for tonight. My wine went a little faster than usual, so I'm going to turn in now. I will tell you this, honey. You will have whatever you choose to work for in life, but no free rides."

Looking at the clock, I realize it is late, but maybe I can still catch one dance with Eddie. I ask Hope, "Well, do you want to do this more some other time?"

"Yes, Erin, you have a lot to learn. We will do it again some other night. For now, I'm turning in. I have enjoyed as much as I can stand!"

I jump up. "Hope, would it be okay if I still went to the dance? I'm sure Eddie is lonely waiting for me."

Hope is already in her bedroom but hears me through the door. "Sure, Erin, now would be a prefect night to see your one-eyed jack. Be home right after the dance, though."

Running up the stairs, I take every other step. I put on my pretty new corduroy pants that Denise made for me in home economics class. Eddie says he likes the way they fit.

I run to the school. Pushing the long metal handle of the gym door, I stand in the dim light from the hall, looking for Eddie. I know he must have been lonely waiting for me on the bleachers. He loves to dance but just with me.

My head is full of information and light from the wine I was able to sneak. Thoughts crowd in on me. I'm now looking on the ground for cards from the neighbors that might have fallen on the floor. ("Coming to my door" did not sound like it would be good.)

Eddie is sitting up in the bleachers, kissing a girl, his hands up her white blouse, her bra hanging slightly below the edge of her blouse. Her bra is lace.

My heart is beating fast, and my face feels hot. This is a new game. Eddie is out doing what boys do when their girlfriends are not around. I feel betrayed. I walk up the bleachers at an angle, not to let him feel the breeze of air rushing beside him. I move as silently as I can to get closer. I want to let him know that even if he is in the dark, I'm not. My palms are wet. Eddie picks up his head for air and sees me standing only six inches away. My heart is broken, not just beating fast. I look at Eddie, hot tears hitting my face, jumping off my high cheekbones for a break from the burning. Jan stands up, pulls at her skirt, reaches her right hand up the back of her blouse to refasten her lace bra and moves out of my way. I give her a glare but am not interested in her.

I stick out my own chest to make him realize he is never going to get a chance to put his hands up my blouse, yelling, "You are a one-eyed jack! You will always have your eye on someone else! You are not trustworthy! You bastard!"

Eddie looks white and clammy. His hands still adjusting to being outside Jan's blouse, he moves them to his crotch to adjust his newfound friend. With his messed-up hair, he smells of Ambush perfume mixed with his Hi-karate cologne. "Erin, you have lost your mind now!" he yells back at me. "What in the hell are you even talking about? What in the hell is a one-eyed jack?"

I whisper in a low grumble, "Look in the mirror, you son-of-a-bitch! I have learned a lot tonight! I'm breaking up with you! You are a one-eyed jack! I just did not see it until now!"

The music seems to have stopped. My girlfriends are coming around, trying to get me to walk away and forget Eddie. I feel betrayed, but at least from now on I will be able to recognize a one-eyed jack.

I walk home directly under the streetlights. Light dances on the hundreds of June bugs gathered beneath on the sidewalk. It is too creepy just walking on them, so I do the teaberry shuffle all the way home.

Getting My License

It is my sixteenth birthday. The rosary has been said, the oatmeal eaten. I get dressed quickly, excited about spending time alone with Hope and getting my driver's license.

Sliding down the stairs with my cold bare feet, I see Hope waiting for me. She reaches out to give me a hug and plants a kiss on the forehead. "Erin," she says, "what do you want for your birthday dinner?"

I always ask for the same thing, spaghetti and cherry pie. Hope hands me my birthday card. It has a one-dollar bill in it, and the card is signed "love, Bill and Hope." I grab the dollar and leave the card on the table. Leaning over Bill as he sits smoking, I kind of hug his arm. (Bill doesn't show his feelings much or say "I love you," but you just know he does.) Birthdays are something of a big deal in our family.

I plan to drive my father's green 1967 Mercury (his "pride and joy") to the State Police station to take my driver's test on this December 4, 1972. I climb in the car feet first, with small bits of snow sticking to my white tennis shoes. I have not had much practice because Bill doesn't let me drive, and I've only had a little practice with Hope.

Bill's car is important to him. The ashtray is overflowing with Salem cigarettes, smoked down to the butt and bent slightly, and the car smells heavy with smoke, while the windshield is stained yellow with nicotine. But I'm grateful to be behind the wheel.

Hope says, "Erin, we will be taking a little side trip first, to get you some practice." I feel important spending time with Hope. She is exciting and very different from my friends' mothers. This time she doesn't make a drink for the trip because we are on our way to the State Police Post in Sandusky, Michigan.

At last we arrive. I love this building! It is two stories tall, brick, with vines growing up the side of the building and a beautiful oak tree standing by it, as if to protect us all. I'm so excited I'm not watching where I'm driving. I turn my head to look, but the wheel doesn't turn fast enough. Crash! I hit a blue State Police car, crushing its passenger door. I scream loudly, "Oh my God! What in the hell are we going to do, Hope? I think I'm going to throw up! I'll go to jail now for sure!"

Hope leans forward, pauses, and looks both ways. Her eyes light up with a crazy look, and she says, "Punch it now, Erin! Yes, Erin, punch it now!"

I look at Hope, shocked. "No Hope, I'll get in trouble. Hope! We're at the police station! There are cops everywhere!"

Hope just says, "Trust me! I know there are police everywhere. Just get the hell out of here!"

Scared to death, but knowing Hope will handle it if we get caught, I punch it, hitting the gas pedal. We jerk around corners, practically on two wheels, until we reach the graveyard, where Hope tells me to stop at last.

I can't even think. I pull under a tree and close my eyes, leaning my head back on the headrest. Gradually my brain starts to work again.

"Hope!" I snap at her. "That is a hit-and-run, isn't it? Isn't that against the law? I'm going to go to jail at sixteen! Why did I listen to you? What were you thinking?" I gather my thoughts again, apologizing to Hope but still upset.

"It's fine, Erin. You are overreacting. Sit tight." Hope reaches under the seat. "Erin, forget about it."

"Oh, sure, Hope, why not? Yes, of course! I would love to forget I just hit a police car and I don't have a license yet, and now I might never get one. Yeah, Hope, I have lots of time now, because I'm not going back."

"Oh, yes you are, Erin, believe me." Hope has it all figured out. "They will never, ever catch on that it was you. First of all, they're not that smart, and this is way too obvious for them. Police don't think like that. They're rubbing the smashed side of the car, sure, but by the time we get back it will be fine. No one would have the guts to go back to the scene of an accident to get a driver's license! Nope, it is right under their noses, but they will not catch it. Trust me."

Hope has pulled a bottle out from under her seat, and now she says she is going to tell me a story that will get my mind off the accident. Leaning against the car door, she starts out by saying, "I might have told you this before, but perhaps you were not old enough to realize the significance of it." She scratches her back on the doorknob and starts her story about the devil coming to earth and visiting her father, Hank.

"Hank was a gambler, and gambling is wrong. The devil appeared without a ticket on a train my grandfather, Hank, was riding. Hank was dealing cards, playing poker for money, and this stranger came and sat down at the table to play. Hank said later that he had a red cast to his eyes. Well, my grandfather dealt him in.

"The devil spoke with a drawl that did not sound like anything Hank had ever heard. He was a handsome man, but his skin had a gray shadow to it. He was talking about the lure of gambling. 'I'm telling you, Hank, this is your game!' he said. He even knew my father's name, you see. Hank became suspicious but kept dealing the devil in."

"'How do you know my name, sir?' Hank asked.

"'Oh, I must have picked it up from one of the guys in the next car. They were talking about you, saying you would sell your soul to be the best poker player in the land! Is that true, Hank?'

"Hank laughed, saying, 'I don't know what in the hell they're even talking about! I'm already the best in the land!'

"The devil said, 'Well, deal me in for one more hand. I have an appointment in a few minutes.' After that hand of cards, the devil said, 'Well, Hank, you sure are the best in the land. I fold.' As he threw his cards on the table, one card fell on the floor. Hank remembered that what falls on the floor comes to your door, so he put his head under the table. Hank saw a queen of diamonds card turn into an ace of spades before his own eyes. He knew at that moment that he was playing cards with the devil. He reached over closer to pull up the man's pant leg to see hooves instead of feet. When Hank lifted his head, the devil was gone. Hank was left with only the ace of spades in his hand, the devil's calling card.

"Hank, who was more a gambler than a drinker, ordered a double scotch on the rocks. He never spoke of it again except to me that night when he came home. I was about eleven years old, Erin. The devil himself had played cards with Hank." Hope stopped the story, pausing to give me a cold stare. "Hank disappeared a few years later and was never heard of again. Maybe he did sell his soul to the devil!"

I usually enjoy Hope's interesting stories, but today I have my mind on getting my license (though I don't know when I'm ever going to get to use Bill's car again). I don't want to go back to the police station, but after feeling like I have just played cards with the devil, I figure I'm getting off easy, even if I have left the scene of an accident. Hope says cops by nature are not smart. Trusting everything my mother says, as usual, I get up my courage to go back for the driving test, feeling like an already hardened criminal with a long prison record.

We drive back to the police station. I feel guilty for what I have done. I hate having to drive back to the scene of the accident, and my fear shows. The policeman says, "Don't worry, Erin. This will not be difficult at all." He assumes that the test is what frightens me.

I never mention during the test drive that the car we passed in the parking lot is the one I hit an hour before. Hope has a way of making adventures out of terrible situations. I just hope things will all work out this time. I take the test by driving around with the policeman. He seems friendly enough (and doesn't recognize Hope). He asks a few questions about driving, and he keeps nodding, adjusting his seat to back out of the sun.

When the driver's test is over, I park next to the smashed-up police car and jump out of Bill's 1967 Mercury, which is not as pretty as it once was. The policeman smiles and says, "Job well done, Erin! You have passed! You are a good driver. Do you drive much?"

I smile, saying, "Well, today is the most I have driven in a while."

He adjusts his hat in the mirror as he leaves the car. "Well, you seem pretty confident." He hands me a small green sheet of paper.

Thanking him, I drive to the Secretary of State's office. I'm now a wheelman!

On Monday I stand in the hot lunch line at school, talking to my friends, telling them about getting my license on Saturday. My friends crack up laughing, saying, "Erin, there is no way that could have happened! No mom would ever do that!" I realize they would not believe that my grandfather Hank had played cards with the devil, either. I just say that Hope is not like any other mom.

"You are such a storyteller!" Nancy laughs out loud. "You are such an interesting friend, Erin. I'm glad you moved here. Every day is a new story with you!"

Hope gets a kick out of the story, too. She is not upset at all. My father (who refers to his kids as "the goddamn kids") doesn't see the same humor in it. He loves his car, now with a bent-in bumper and a splash of blue paint on it.

I'm happy and relieved. I'm not in jail, and I have my license. Having a driver's license is important at Oleo Acres—to escape!

Charlie Gets to Drive

Hope and Bill are retired now. We live in the country, and Charlie and I have extra chores to do. Hope and Bill plan to make the extra money they need to get by right here on the farm. We have four sheep and about one hundred chickens. The chickens just walk the farmyard, but the sheep have to be taken in and out of the barn.

To go with the farm, Hope and Bill have just gotten a 1971 white Ford pickup truck. The truck shines. It has nice smooth seats in a black and white tweed pattern, and the inside roof is black. I have never ridden in a truck before. It's exciting.

Hope swings open the back door (the handle, made from a spool of thread, nailed on). The sides of her black flats pull away from her swollen feet, and the black dye on her shoes runs onto her feet. She yells out the back door, "Charlie and Erin, get ready! We're going to Sandusky! Her toes are slightly blue from her tight cast."

Hope has an egg business now. Today, on our way to Sandusky to buy more hens, she will deliver eggs to neighbors' homes and a couple of stores.

Hope yells, "Hurry up, Erin and Charlie! I need to be the first one there to pick out nice healthy-looking ones."

Hope will also be teaching Charlie how to drive today, kind of against his will. I think Charlie is scared and excited at the same time. Hope picked this day for Charlie's driving lesson because she has a broken leg. As for me, I jump into the truck without a care in the world.

Hope shows Charlie how to use the stick shift, and soon we are all heading down the road to buy new chickens, with Hope driving by using the clutch and the stick on the floor while Charlie pushes the gas pedal. I watch the fields of wheat out the window, wondering about the point of a clutch and gearshift. Driving is complicated any time, but Hope seems to be in pain today with her broken leg, and she needs our help.

"Charlie, keep the speed low until we get past the house," Hope says. "Your father is watching out the window, so I'll steer until then. Then, when I think you can handle it, we'll trade places, and I'll have a drink. But not yet! I want to make sure you can drive."

Soon we arrive at Ed and Alice's Bar on the main street of Sandusky. Climbing out of the truck, we remind Hope that we need to get to the farm early to get the best chickens. Hope says, "Kids, don't worry. If we get the chickens too early, we'll just have to go right home, or they might jump out of the truck."

"Hope, do you mean we didn't bring any cages?" Charlie asks.

Hope says, "Well, I forgot the cages, but we can put them in the front seat with us. They're small, and anyway, we're only getting six chickens."

"Hope, I don't see how we can do this," Charlie says, shaking his head.

Hope grits her teeth. "Damn it, Charlie, it is not an impossible situation! We will have one drink here and think it over!"

I look at Charlie. He is concerned, and I know he thinks my father is going to be upset with this whole deal. I tell him, "Charlie, we're the kids, she's the adult. Hope will figure it out — don't worry!"

Ed and Alice's Bar smells like grilled hamburgers and steamed buns. Hope has personal friends here and loves visiting with the owners. (She has also been a bartender for them in the past.) Ed is always grumpy, but Alice smiles and has a high giggle when she hears a joke that we can't understand. She also has a beautiful white streak going right through her hair. Ed runs the grill, and he is not happy to have to walk over to the table and write on the small green pad.

We always order the same thing: three cheeseburgers with extra mustard and pickles. Ed asks us if we want pop, and we say, "No sir." We don't want to push our luck with spending the money we're not even sure Hope has. Hope orders herself a draft beer in a tall frosted glass, very pretty to look at.

Soon Arnold comes in, one of Hope's many friends. He smiles and winks at Charlie and me. Hope asks him to join her.

We are now getting ready to eat. He orders two Nesbit orange pops for us. Smiling at each other, we are happy that he stopped by. He and Hope spend several hours ordering drafts and sharing jokes while Charlie and I enjoy the music and being in town with Hope. At last, though Charlie wants to go get the banty hens. He also wants to take over the driving, figuring it might be a good idea.

"One for the road!" Arnold says to Hope. (I have heard that a few times.) Then he moves away from the table and sits down at the bar to visit someone else.

It is still daylight. Charlie and Hope get into the truck, and Hope works the clutch while Charlie works the stick shift and gas. Hope has explained to us that with a cast on her leg we could not get into any real trouble with Charlie helping to drive because it can't be helped. We make it to the farmer's house, and the farmer suggests we not put the banty hens into the cab of the truck. Instead he gives us a small metal cage for the hens, and we load them into the back, safe and sound. Then Charlie leaps out of the truck, follows the farmer to the barn and gives him the money Hope has given him for the hens. The deal is done, and we are on our way home.

Hope is feeling so good about the bargain she got on the hens she says, "Hey, kids, let's stop at a grocery store and get a candy bar."

We drive back into town. Hope gives us fifty cents and sends us to the grocery store while she goes next door to a Michigan Liquor store. After we are back on the road for a while, she pulls out a small flat bottle of clear liquid. Charlie glances at the bottle and says, "Hope, I think I'm good enough to drive."

Hope says, "Charlie, I agree. Let's give it a whirl."

Hope moves over to let Charlie drive, taking a swig from her flat booze bottle. She says she needs to have a few drinks today because her broken leg itches and she is in pain. Alcohol always makes Hope feel better.

After Charlie has been driving for a while, Hope finishes her bottle and throws it out the window of the truck, and just then a police car appears behind us. Hope is watching in the mirror and sees the policeman go to the ditch to pick up the small flat booze bottle she has just thrown out. He puts it in his police car and drives up behind us with his lights flashing.

Charlie and I are scared to death, both of us thinking Charlie might end up in jail. The police car seemed to have come out of nowhere. (I can usually spot them.)

The officer pulls us over, and Charlie explains that he has to drive because Hope has a broken leg. The officer says, "I didn't pull you over for the driving. I pulled you over for littering. Ma'am, is this your empty pint bottle?"

"No, sir," Hope says, "I only drink from fifths!"

He is not happy, but we are only a mile from home, so he says he'll let us go if Hope promises never to litter again. She gives her word, we wait for the police car to leave first, and then we take off. Charlie is feeling pretty good about his driving, but Hope has to take the wheel now because we are almost back at the farm where Bill is waiting for us.

It is when Hope tries to switch back into the driver's seat that the truck goes out of control. That white Ford truck flies! It veers sharply to the side of the road, hitting a mailbox, sailing over the railroad tracks and landing in the ditch. I'm hanging onto my mother's hand, and Charlie screaming at the top of his lungs. Dirt is flying. Somehow the banty hens have disappeared. The noisy cage fell out about a mile back, and the hens are nowhere to be seen.

Hope, biting her bottom lip, motions to a farmer passing by. He stops and tries to pull us out backwards, but Hope has the gear in forward. The farmer smiles, shakes his head and says, "Hopie, I can't take the competition!"

"Hope, let's just walk home. We're only about a h-h-half of a mile away." Charlie stutters.

We gather up the chickens and walk home. Charlie and I carry the cage, and Hope tells us how nice the farm is going to be with Bill finally getting his dream of being a "gentlemen farmer." I guess a gentleman's farm is where the kids do most of the work.

Orville is Mean

Palms, Michigan, is a great place to live. We have one downtown building which is post office, grocery store and gas station, all rolled into one. It is easy to find whatever you need. Lots of good people, as Hope says. The farmers will plow our driveway for free. They'll pull us out of the ditch and till up our land when we need it done. There is only one dishonest man in Palms, and his name is Orville.

Orville drives around with fresh-cut beef, some wrapped and some unwrapped, in the bed of his old black Ford pickup. The driver's side door is covered with his spit-out chewing tobacco. He has big overalls with yellow stained long johns showing underneath and a hat with big orange flaps that cover his ears in the fall.

It is time to take our lambs and sheep to the auction, and Orville stands in our kitchen with pig shit on his boots, only the top clip hooked. Uninvited, he walked into our house. Hope dislikes the pig farmer on sight. He smells bad and looks dirty. He has brown marks on both sides of his mouth from chew, and he wipes it off on his long john sleeves. "Hey," he says, "do you want me to take the sheep to that there auction?" He throws another plug in his cheek. "I hear you don't got no truck! Joe Victor says that you guys are in a bind and need my services." My parents had told Joe, our land contract holder, that they needed a farmer to pick up our sheep for the auction in Ubly.

Bill extends his hand to shake as Orville is still wiping his off on his big overalls. "Yes-s-s," Bill stutters. "I'm looking for an honest man to deliver my sheep to the Ubly Auction for a good price. What do you charge?"

Taking off his orange hat to scratch his head, Orville replies, "I usually charge twenty-five dollars for a load of animals, but I see you only have four sheep, so I guess ten dollars would cover the gas." Tobacco is leaking from the side of his mouth.

"Ten dollars sounds like a good deal to me, but how will I know how much you get for the sheep?"

"Well, it should bring you about fifty dollars per sheep," Orville chomps out. "They write checks, so you don't have to worry about being cheated."

"It's a deal, Orville!" Bill nods. "I have no way to transport four sheep, and if you are going for other farmers I think this is a good way to go." Bill pulls up his loose jeans and asks Orville, "About where do you farm?"

"Up the way a few miles." Orville starts to point, not knowing directions.

"Ten dollars?" Bill says to Orville. He reaches into his wallet (or purse, as he calls it).

Hope stands up and says, "Bill, Orville has a reputation of ripping off farmers. He has the checks from the auction made out to him!"

Bill gives Hope a look. "Hope, let me handle this one! I think I know an honest man when I see one!"

Looking right through Orville as if he isn't there, Hope says, "Bill, he does the transportation so cheap because he steals the money by having the checks made out to him! He is not our man, Bill!"

"Shut up, Hope! I will handle this! We don't have much choice here. We don't have a way of taking the sheep ourselves, and this is a good price!"

Hope sits back in her green painted rocker. "I don't agree with you at all, Bill," she answers, the volume of her voice increasing. "Erin!" (She yells as if I'm next door at a neighbor's house.) "Get me a basin, now!"

"What is a basin?" I respond quickly.

"Get a large bowl then, and put in hot water and soap, and bring me a hand towel."

Moving as if I'm going to be part of some strange experiment, I get the bowl, soap and water from the bright orange bathroom. "Please, Hope, don't wash Orville's face!" I mumble under my breath so Orville can't hear me. "He is dirty, but you can't just wash the tobacco-stained face of a stranger, Hope!" I say as I squeeze her hand.

Throwing her head back with a wild laugh, she says, "No, I'm not going to wash Orville's face, although it could use it! I'm Pontius Pilate! I'm washing my hands of this whole deal your father is doing!"

Hope takes the metal bowl out of my hands and proceeds to wash her hands slowly. She pours water from a vase and makes a dramatic display of her hand-washing, like Pontius Pilate in the Bible when Christ is brought in front of him to be condemned. Pontius doesn't believe that Christ is guilty of any sins, so he washes his hands in public, refusing to be responsible for Christ's death.

At last Hope dabs her fingers with a towel, drying between each finger. Bill, smoking a cigarette and getting madder and madder, stands up, pulls a ten-dollar bill out of what he calls his purse and hands it over to Orville. Orville leaves without another word.

Bill tells Charlie to ride along to help unload the sheep. Charlie is getting one hundred dollars for his summer's work on Oleo Acres to buy school clothes, so he goes along and stands in line with the two sheep he is responsible for while Orville takes the others to another line. Charlie gets his check made out to him and waits for Orville, but Orville is nowhere to be seen, and neither is his truck. He has left Charlie at the auction, taking our money with him.

Charlie hitchhikes home with the news, arriving home at two in the morning with his check folded in half. Hope and Bill are asleep.

"Erin, w-w-wake up! We got ripped off! Orville t-took Bill's check!" Charlie stutters, pulling on my blanket, letting the heat out.

I wake up, turning on the light to see Charlie's shadow standing over my bed, his strong jaw line moving as he takes a drag off his cigarette. "Wait a minute, Hop Sing," I interrupt. "What are you doing smoking?"

"Don't worry about it, Erin. It's none of your business. I just started, and when I hitched home, a stranger offered me one to keep me warm. It's my life, and you are not the b-b-boss of me!" He leans against the doorway of my bedroom. "I'm not Hop Sing, either!" he goes on. I could use a little respect, actually. I've d-d-decided to join the Army, too." He struggles to get out the words. "I want out of this one-horse town! I'm done being told what to do and doing chores before I even go to school."

"See if I care, Charlie! Suit yourself."

Charlie flicks his hot ash on my bedroom floor. "I'm also going to st-start using my real name, P-p-paul. Charlie is a kid nickname. I'm P-p-paul!"

"Well, great, Paul-Charlie-Hop-Sing. Get the hell out of my bedroom! I waited for you to come home because I was worried about you. But you're busy smoking and becoming a man, so get your ass out of my room!" Then I remember to be curious. "What happened with Orville, anyway?"

Charlie flicks another hot ash. "Well, I guess old Pontius Pilate was right!" he says. "He dropped me off in front of an auctioneer and said he would come back for me. W-well, he took the big sheep, and he never c-c-came back. I waited until d-dark, and he never came. I asked around. He'd left hours before. He took the sheep, got the ch-check made out to him, then split.

"He is an old b-b-bastard, Erin. He has a bad reputation. The f-farmer that picked me up said he rips people off by cheating on the meat he sells, also. He is short on the p-p-pounds on a quarter of beef. This man said you have to weigh it all yourself," Charlie says, stroking another cigarette out of a pack from his pocket.

"Well, that is pretty far out, how Hope seems to be able to judge a man by his cover!" I say in amazement, getting out of bed to see what brand of cigarettes Charlie smokes.

"I'll just give Hope and Bill my check, Erin. I don't really need school clothes. The army will give me new clothes when I join."

"Charlie or Paul, first of all, you're only sixteen years old. You can't join until you are seventeen unless Hope and Bill sign for you."

"Well, they signed for Mike and Brian and Joe. They believe in the service, Erin. They'll sign, believe me."

"So get back to what happened with Orville. If I ever see Hope washing her hands like Pontius Pilate again, I'm gonna pay attention! She does have ESP, doesn't she?"

"I'm not sure what it is!" Charlie shrugs his shoulders. "I'm freezing from hitchhiking all the way home!"

Next morning the yell comes from the bottom of the staircase, "Off your ass and on your feet!" It's Bill's wake-up call to us.

I hurry downstairs with Charlie so as not to miss the details about how Orville tricked a sixteen-year-old boy and his father out of a hundred dollars. I can tell Bill is disappointed in Orville and in his own judgment. Hope rocks back and forth in her painted rocker, listening to the story. Finally she stands up and says, "Bill, you got suckered!"

Bill just keeps the cloud of smoke going over his head. "Well, I guess you were right about that son-of-a-bitch," he admits.

"Bill, you know, of all the problems we have ever had, I like my financial problems the most," Hope says. She gets to her feet and goes to the stove to fry up potatoes and eggs for breakfast.

Bill doesn't have much more to say. After waiting for his chance to speak, Charlie says, "Hope, you can have my check for my sheep."

"Charlie, I wouldn't dream of it! I would not do that in my wildest dreams! You have worked all summer for that money, and it is yours!"

Bill smokes and thinks quietly for the rest of day.

Fitting In

FROM THE SMALL TOWN of Carsonville, where we knew everyone, we had moved out into the country near Palms, Michigan, where Hope and Bill are trying to have a new beginning. Palms is a very small town, also in the "Thumb," about thirty minutes from Carsonville. Hope calls our farm "Polack Hill." It's not much more than a few rolling hills and a two-story white house with black shutters that has "seen better days." My older brothers and sisters bought the place to help Hope and Bill when his retirement came earlier than expected. They thought it would give him something to do with his time and other things to think about besides not having his job any more. The farm cost four thousand dollars.

The farm is old and needs a lot of work. "Oleo Acres—one of the cheaper spreads" is printed in old English writing on a wood framed sign hanging on our porch. There are four bedrooms upstairs and no heat except for a potbelly stove in the kitchen. When we moved in, my sisters-in-law wallpapered the kitchen with orange and yellow chickens and potbelly stoves. The wallpaper seems to fit the house. But it's hard for me to get adjusted to this new small town after living in Carsonville since I was in first grade.

In Palms we can't go home for lunch or see our old friends. We have to take a bus to school, and the ride takes a half hour. In the beginning, we miss the bus a few times, and after that, to motivate us to get up on time, Hope and Bill make the punishment for missing the bus washing all the downstairs walls.

At school, Mrs. Jaffe is in charge of the lunch program. Hope has everything all set up for us, so we go to the office to get free lunch tickets, and

I answer questions about where we live, our address, and how many kids are in the family. Well, we had twelve, but now there are only three at home, I say. I try to sit up straight, as I know this is an important meeting.

Mrs. Jaffe says, "Well, you kids can take the tickets and come back once a month to get new ones." She reaches over her desk to hand them to me. "One for each," she says. I take my ticket and thank her. It is almost lunchtime, and it will be fun to stand in line with all of my new friends.

Nancy has saved me a spot in line. "Hey, Quinlan, come and stand with us!" she yells across the cafeteria. I run with excitement to be a part of the gang, my orange ticket wrapped around my finger, held tight. The cafeteria is hot and steamy. As I come around the corner, the big woman with a black hairnet and a white apron on that makes her look like a butcher is testing stuff. The line is long, but who cares? Free food! It is exciting just to see what the choices are. I'm not used to choices or to chocolate milk with my meals. I know I'm lucky to have new friends so quickly after moving to a new school, and hot lunch is just about more than I could have asked for.

One person away, I notice that Nancy's ticket is light blue. I think, well, maybe hers is last month's and she just did not use all of the punches on the lunch ticket. I wait to see what will happen when she presents an old card. No, that is not it. Mrs. Carver is smiling at Nancy as she punches the ticket and asking how her mother is. Nancy moves on to pick up her tray.

I'm next and proudly hold out my orange ticket with the word "FREE" written on it, turning it over to show my name. Mrs. Carver is a lunchroom helper. She looks at me over her glasses saying, "Where did you get this ticket?"

I say, "The principal gave it to me. Why, is it dated the wrong date?"

"No, it is for free!"

I smile, taking the ticket back, saying, "Yes, I know. Hope set it up for us. It is a special program."

Mrs. Carver excuses herself and goes back to the office while we all wait in line for her. Kids are yelling, "Quinlan, you are holding up the line! Get moving!"

I just say, "Well, I guess she has to go to the bathroom!" In my heart I feel that the whole world now knows I'm getting lunch for free. I didn't know my ticket would be a different color than my friends' tickets. I want to grab it back and walk home. But I don't do that. I wait.

Mrs. Carver comes back quickly and says, "Well, I guess it's okay. Move forward!"

I get my food and sit with Nancy. Nancy asks, "Quinlan, why do you have an orange ticket when we all have light blue?"

I hold my ticket up to the light and tell her, "Well, Hope didn't want the hassle of always having to get us hot lunch tickets, so she got a whole year in advance! I guess Mrs. Carver was not aware that a person could have that kind of money." I sit up straight and eat my hamburger patty and corn and delicious lemon desert.

Every time we have a new woman at school taking lunch tickets, she looks me up and down as if to say, Hey you must be poor! Moving to a new town is hard, and to be a little different from other teens is even harder.

Sleeping with the Chickens

THE FIRST TIME BABY chicks arrive at Oleo Acres, Denise and Charlie and I are all excited, not realizing yet what it is going to be like to actually "sleep with the chickens," as the expression goes. The chicks are cute as hell, so small they keep tipping over on their feet from their own weight. The downy soft feathers make them my instant friends.

Bill sits at the kitchen table on a small white painted oak chair, his entire inheritance from his parents' estate. He picks up each and every chick and examines it as if it is from outer space — for good health, I guess. In his practical way, he says to the three of us, "Kids, this is going to be a real money-maker!"

Hope, nodding in agreement, says, "Yep, kids, this is how we are going to make it through the next few years — raising chickens. It will be easy."

The chicks arrive in large boxes with holes on top and the words 'Fragile - Livestock' on the outside. 'Livestock'...isn't that for bigger animals, I wonder?

The potbelly stove is roaring, and the room is hotter than normal as we take out each baby and hold it. Charlie says, "Hey, let's name them all, Erin."

"I don't think we can even tell them apart," I say doubtfully.

These new little baby chickens will need a nice warm place to live in our house. That would be my bedroom closet, I'm thinking to myself, since we've already discussed this ahead of time. Hey, maybe I can negotiate and get some heat into my room. Going to a new school in my junior year and smelling like chickens! Charlie has one over me this time, for sure.

"Erin, get the special lights, feeders, water bottles, and, most important of all, we need to have the heaters to keep these chickens really warm," Bill says, with his cigarette hanging and bobbing up and down when he talks, like we're all in an old John Wayne movie.

"But, Bill, does it really have to be in our closet? Really! We're going to look like hillbillies, and my friends will know when they spend the night here! Isn't there a way out of this?" I look down at my feet, wishing I were back in my dream, dancing all night.

Hope, with her special drink in hand, assures me that the plan is normal. "Erin," she tells me, "you are so damn lucky not to be sharing your bed with your sister any more! What are a few chickens in the closet? And you get to hear music at night now, with your radio. Small chickens don't make much noise!"

Tears running to the corners of my eyes, I have to agree.

Bill, a man of pride and conviction, standing with his hands on my shoulders, looks me in the face and says, "Erin, no one ever said that life was fair."

Scrunching down to get away from his grip, I look up at this man who has few options in his own life, and as our eyes meet I think, Hell, let's get the chickens and name them and hope like hell they like country music! My social life, as I know it, is over. My feathered friends are now my roommates.

I take down the freeze-dried clothes from the clothesline in my room and move the line to the bedroom next to mine to make more room to get ready for the chickens. Our old farmhouse has four bedrooms upstairs, two of which we don't use except for hanging clothes to dry — or not dry. Hope has put up clotheslines in those rooms so we will have freeze-dried clothes. This is a tried-and-true method, except for the fact that we start out with stiff frozen clothes every morning and have to get warmed up around the potbelly stove, thawing our clothes from stiff to just damp.

Rubbing my face in disbelief, I wonder if maybe the heat from the chickens will help dry the clothes. Hey, maybe my new roommates will actually raise my quality of life on Oleo Acres!

Bill is bending over with a screwdriver hanging out of his old Wrangler jeans pocket, putting together the heat lamp at just the right height so the chicks will stay warm but not get burned. I glance into his pale blue eyes and realize that this is not what he expected from his retirement. I think what I would do if I were cheated out of retirement at his age. Feeling guilty now for only thinking of myself before, I reach over and pick up a baby chick. Bill, bouncing a cigarette as if it is trying to escape his lips, says, "They're kind of cute, aren't they? And they'll be outdoors on their own in the spring."

He steps back and looks at me seriously. "Erin, you could use a little education on this one. This is a brooder house. We don't have a brooder hen to keep the babies warm, so the lights have to keep the closet heated to a constant 101 degrees. If the heat isn't constant, the babies will climb on top of each other and suffocate."

I get it, Bill. We just build a brooder house in my closet. Yep, it sounds like it will be a lot of fun – for the chicks!

With his weather-beaten hands holding onto the walls for support, Bill yells downstairs to Hope, "We're in business, honey!" He means that they have solved their latest problem, how to make a living for a few more years before his social security starts.

Waking up in this house is like no other experience in my life. I climb out of bed every day, looking at the stain on my ceiling, trying to see if it is the shape of a face of someone I know. This part isn't unusual. The new part is that there are now a hundred baby chickens in my bedroom closet.

It is a huge closet, and my clothes hang over the little babies' heads. Thank God, the chicks can't reach my clothes! But their smell can. When I wake up, I hear the scratching of the chickens in my closet, warm and cozy. They're listening to country music, along with my parents downstairs. My father told me that chickens need to keep warm to grow and that music helps them relax and lay more eggs. The problem is, their warmth and relaxation is taking place in the closet of my bedroom during my last two exciting years of high school in Deckerville.

Chickens grow fast, especially when they're dancing to country music, getting more heat than us kids, and have a hot pan of chicken food at their disposal. In fact, I think Bill, the practical man, underestimated just how fast chickens grow under these conditions! Soon we have to move them into every closet in the upstairs: twenty chickens to a closet is what we decide will work. Soon we have one-hundred full-grown chickens dancing and scratching at five a.m.

I know my parents need help with their retirement, but maybe we need to think this through again. The chickens are not cute and fuzzy any more. They've grown so much that they can almost reach my dresses now. Sometimes when I come home from school, there are a few of them outside the closet and I have to catch them and shut them up again before I can start my homework. They're big and smelly, with feathers flying in the air when they fight. I have to clean up chicken droppings from the floor. They're on plastic, but chicken droppings on hot plastic have a pungent smell. They have totally taken over my bedroom, and I won't be surprised if they're wearing my clothes soon. When Hope has friends visiting downstairs, she tells them that the loud and noisy chicken sounds overhead are ghosts we brought from our other house.

Spring comes at last, and we break down the brooder houses and let the chickens live outside. The next year, though, another hundred new babies arrive for the same bedroom closet living arrangements. That year I name them all "little sons-of-bitches." Bill finally makes enough money to build a chicken coop—just in time for me to graduate from Deckerville High School.

My Eighteenth Birthday

"OFF YOUR ASS, AND ON YOUR FEET, ERIN!" Bill yells from the bottom of the stairs. This is a call I hear often from my father.

Sinking deeper into my bed, a huge cradle with many warm blankets, I know that I must move fast. Bill is waiting for a response. "Yes, sir, I'm awake," I yell, loud enough for him to hear. I lie in my bed wondering if I will get the gift my father has given the rest of the kids on their eighteenth birthdays.

I'm the last child left at home. Denise moved out when the chickens moved in, and Charlie joined the army, as he said he would, so that just leaves me. I could move out, too, but feel it would be hard on Bill and Hope being alone. Once when I said I wanted to move out, Bill cried. He told me he had been taking care of kids for thirty-seven years and he hoped I would at least stay until I finished school.

The older kids now have their own families, and Hope and Bill act lonesome. I miss the rest of my family, too. One kid at home doesn't seem like a family. I pull on some too-tight jeans and dance down the stairs with the tune of "I'm Eighteen" by Alice Cooper in my head. Today is going to be a blast! I don't expect anything except for a card with a dollar in it and a kiss on the forehead. I know that my parents don't have any money. Just time with them feels good: the real party will be with my friends.

I open the door at the bottom of the stairs and close it again as fast as I can, not to let the heat escape upstairs, making my parents cold. Standing in front of the chicken wallpaper, I wonder what my life will be like when I'm not surrounded by chickens. The chickens seem to like it when I leave the room and they have it all to themselves.

Bill's back is to me. He is struggling to get two farm-fresh eggs out of the pan without breaking them. Carefully, he gets them out without breaking a yoke. Bill wants me to enjoy my breakfast and share some news about school or my job while I'm eating. Bill is a good father. Hope is putting buttered toast on the corner of the plate. "So, Erin, what are your plans for your birthday?"

"Well, it's a school day, and I have to go to school. But after, I want to spend the night with Nancy and have a pajama party!"

Hope hands me a birthday card. "It's not much, Erin, but it will help out." I open the card and it has one dollar and a card signed, "love, Hope and Bill." I keep the card this time, realizing that it is not just about money any more.

"Erin, there's more."

I wonder what they could afford to get me. Hey, maybe a new dress! I think for a split-second. I see my father washing up the black iron frying pan he has just served me breakfast from and wiping it down. "Here Erin, it's yours now," he says. "You need to take good care of it, but it will last you a lifetime. I want you to have it." I get a lump in my throat. Bill is giving me his black frying pan, the one he uses all of the time.

I say, "No, really, Bill, I could not take the frying pan. You have used this for years!"

Hope stands up, concerned I won't respond appropriately. "Erin, he wants to let you have it. We have had it for eighteen years, and now we can share it with you."

"I'm not sure where I would keep it," I say hesitantly. "I only have a car."

Hope stands next to Bill. "Erin, it isn't much, we realize that. But someday you will be moving out, and it would be a great start on your own life. It's not a family treasure or anything. But it's a practical gift that will feed your family for years to come."

I can see this is important to them, so I get excited and say, "Thanks a million! I mean it!" The pan is heavy, and I do feel special. The last time Bill gave me a gift that I remember was a bike without a seat. That was a blast!

Bill goes over to the counter and opens a drawer. He hands me his invention, still without a label on it. "This is your second surprise," he says, smiling, as I try to figure out just what to do with a tin can with one end open and the other end with nail holes punched in it.

"Hmm, your potato chopper? How did you ever invent this, Bill?"

"Well, I know how much you love my fried potatoes. This is what I use."

"Wow, Bill, this is going to be cool when I move out." Bill is a practical man, not a cheap man. He believes that if he could raise twelve kids on his salary, we can all learn something from him about not wasting.

Bill stands there with his hair parted on the side, all wetted down for the day. "Erin, when the luxuries in life become necessities, we are all in trouble."

He is not trying to give me wisdom for my eighteenth birthday; he is just saying what he thinks.

Not counting on such a moving breakfast, I have to hurry upstairs now to get ready for school. I want to skip school in the afternoon, so I move fast in the super-tight jeans I'm wearing to be seen in later at the bar. I have a nice red turtleneck to go with the jeans.

I get all the snow off my car, and it is a clear beautiful day with the sun out and huge snow piles everywhere on the sides of the roads. Hope and Bill are standing in the kitchen window waving as I pull out to go to school. Music blaring, I'm singing, "I'm eighteen, and I will do what I want!"

I pull into Nancy's driveway. She is ready with a bracelet for me. I pull out of the drive as if I'm Barney Oldfield, a race car driver in the fifties that my father says drove like me, like he really did not care. Bill loves to say, "Let 'er eat, Erin!" as I pull up to the corner of a dirt road and have to give it some gas. My light blue 1963 push-button Chrysler is still in great shape in 1975.

Arriving at school, we move as fast as we can to the girls' bathroom so Nancy can have a cigarette and meet Lorrie to make plans. "Okay, we are going out drinking at twelve noon today! Right?" I kind of stick my chest out in the mirror, teasing my friends. "It is my treat. I have a twenty-dollar bill I made working at the three-in-one Dairy Queen."

"What if we get caught, Erin?" Lorrie flips her red hair back.

"We won't get caught. Jocks skip all of the time."

When we leave school at noon, we take the back roads, the way Hope has taught me, to Ed and Alice's Bar. We walk into Ed and Alice's to the smell of steamed buns and ashtrays. My friends turned eighteen a few months earlier, but they have never been in a bar before. Alice approaches our table as if she is going to have some problems on her hands.

"What will it be, Erin?" Alice asks, short and fast.

"We would all like the same thing—a sloe screw (sloe gin and orange juice) and a cheeseburger with mustard and extra pickles — times three, please."

Alice sticks her pencil behind her ear. "Erin, I'm afraid this won't work!" she says.

"Why? We are all eighteen." We all pull out our licenses to show we are of age.

She looks at us carefully, as if she has never seen me before, and says, "Okay, this is a school day, isn't it, ladies?" As she nods, her head jerks to the side to show me that Hope is at the bar, just two stools down, having a drink with Bobby Arnold. I don't get her signal.

"Yes, it is, but we are on a road trip, and the sun is out."

Alice taps her pencil on the green pad and finally says, "Well, okay!" She leaves to get the drinks. I didn't get the message that Alice was trying to give me because I'm too busy having fun, talking to my friends about Johnny Jack and how I want to marry him. Nancy and Lorrie are good friends. We tell a few dirty jokes and laugh at the fact we have tricked all our teachers and parents.

My back is to the bar, and I'm telling my friends about my touching birthday gift of the frying pan and chopper from Hope and Bill when my friends stare over my head as if they've seen a ghost. Hope, drinking with friends at the bar, heard my voice, and now I feel a strong hand on my shoulder.

"Who do we have here? Doctor Livingston, I presume?" Hope leans towards my face. "Erin, I think you are supposed to be in school, aren't you?"

Knowing that lying means punishment by death, I say, "Well, Hope it's my birthday, and I figured my friends might want to go out for a drink and a cheeseburger." I try to look confident, like an adult.

Hope looks at my friends and asks them, "Do your parents know where you are?"

"No ma'am, they think we are in school," they say, unsure of what is to come next.

"Well, I'm not worried about you missing school," Hope replies. "Most of the teachers are only a chapter ahead of the lesson. You might just as well stay here and have a drink." Hope puts a quarter in my hand to play the jukebox. "Play some Hank Williams, Erin. This is a day of celebration. You're eighteen now!"

As I move across the floor with Hope and my friends, I take Hope's hand and we start to dance. Hope puts her vinyl purse on the table and orders another round for us. "Erin, you looked as if you had seen a ghost when I arrived next to your side. I'm your mother. Why would you be so startled?"

"Well, Hope, it was the response of my friends looking at you when you were behind my back"

"Erin, you've been around ghosts all your life."

"There are no ghosts in our old farm, are there? No, Hope, I think what you're hearing is the chickens dancing in my room."

Back at our table, paying for the round, Hope says, "Erin, most houses have ghosts. In one house we lived in—it was in Lake Orion—they were running up and down our stairs. We lived in that house when you were little. But if you are not open to ghosts, they will not show themselves." Hope slips her change into her purse to set the stage for a good story. She is great at capturing her audience, her eyes all ready for the scene.

"At night we heard giggling coming from within the walls. It was kids giggling and running up and down the stairs. I had told some of my friends. They didn't believe me and said they wanted to drink beer at the top and bottom of the stairs and wait for the ghost to run past them!"

"What happened, Hope?" I ask.

"Well," Hope whispers, "about four of my friends came over, and they waited, two at the top of the stairs and two at the bottom. Arnold was one of the men waiting on the bottom step. They had a case of beer waiting. It got dark, and all of you kids went to bed. The house was silent. Then about eleven o'clock the wind started to blow up the stairs, just like I had told them it did. Your brother Butch was alive then, and he ran into you kids' bedroom, and you were all asleep. As he stood at the doorway, he could hear the giggling from the stairs, too."

"The wind blew past him. Butch and Tony both felt the cold wind and a frigid stiffness in the air as it blew by. My two friends were as white as ghosts, guzzling their beer as if there could not be enough of it.

"Butch said, 'I think the children from Germany are here now!'"

Just as she says those words, Hope looks into my eyes and says, "Erin, the children's spirits ran past all of my friends—ran back and forth, giggling in German!"

"How did you know it was German?"

"At first we didn't know, and then we found many old games in the basement. We would come downstairs, and the games would be out as if they had left them there after playing. The games were in German. We never saw those children, but we heard them almost every night! Sometimes Bill would come home and see a light in the snow, but there was no window it could have been shining through.

"Now, Arnold was at the bottom of those stairs. After he saw the faces of his friends upstairs, he took the case of beer and ran outside, and he would never come to that house again. He still talks about it. I guess it made quite an impression. He likes to have a few beers and talk about it."

"Did it scare you, Hope?"

Hope leans into her hand with her teeth touching her hand, "I don't think I was afraid after I realized the ghosts were harmless kids, giggling and playing. Other ghosts I have seen were older men, and they made me feel uncomfortable. Hell, Erin, one could have been my father, trying to apologize for leaving me when I was twelve years old! I never figured out the old men—just figured it was lost souls—until now."

Hope paused thoughtfully before going on. "When we lived in Carsonville, you walked downstairs and walked right through a spirit that seemed to want something. That one was a man. Remember, Erin? I was crying and said, 'How could you not have seen that man? He needed something!'"

"Yes, I do remember, Hope, and I didn't see anything."

"You have to be at peace to see spirits, and you were just a young kid then. Now I bet you would see him."

"I hope I never do!"

"Ghost are harmless," Hope tells us, "and part of life. They're lost, with their souls in heaven and unfinished business on earth. Sometimes when a person dies, you see, the spirit is trapped on earth, and we need to let it know it's safe so it can pass through. You have to realize, Erin, that we are not the only people who occupy this earth. There are practically layers of souls, some of them waiting for heaven. A lot of people go through life not seeing anything, and that is just fine. But me, I like to know about the other side."

Nancy and Lorrie seemed to be uncomfortable with Hope's story. Lorrie gets up and puts a dime in the jukebox, playing "I'm Eighteen," by Alice Cooper.

This is my nicest birthday party ever. When Hope sits with you, you're in for some honest-to-goodness storytelling, and her stories are always true. I believe her. I have heard the older kids tell ghost stories, too. They were pretty scared when they saw the ghosts.

Hope waves her glass at me, saying, "Drink up Honey. You've got to hit the road."

"I hope you don't tell Bill I skipped school, Hope."

"Don't worry, Erin, I won't tell Bill," she says winking at me. "He wouldn't be happy about this one, and he might blame me."

Interlude: Our Family Reunion

September 1978

TURNING THE KEY TO THE SALON I own in Chicago, it is time to go home. I couldn't be more content with my life. Randy has all of his books packed and we are going home. He rides shotgun, I drive through the city so he can still study his medical books for an upcoming test. If he gets all of his preparations done, it will mean much more celebration at Oleo Acres. Everyone is coming home for this reunion. The trip home is about eight hours to get to Palms, Michigan. With Randy's hand on my knee, we pass the Miracle Mile and beautiful Lake Michigan on the shores of which we have promised ourselves we will someday live. We're back in Michigan. Lots of good conversations about our friends, our dreams and my salon keep the trip moving fast.

Arriving at Palms is a dream come true. Now I am old enough to sit in the kitchen with the whole family, an honor in itself.

We all arrive within a half hour of each other. The music is playing the same old reel to reel music but on a new reel to reel Tony has given Hope and Bill for Christmas the year before. He remade a lot of the old music from Carsonville, those are still the family favorites.

It's hot, but the breeze on the hill makes for an ideal day. Bill looks relaxed, he is smoking his Salem cigarettes still but doesn't have a cough. He has a cold beer in his hand and motions the boys to each grab one from the cooler under the picnic table. It takes four picnic tables borrowed from neighbors to hold us all but it is so good to be back home.

Hope is shucking the corn with her grandkids, while her housedress blows in the wind. Brian and Mike brought their skeet toy that throws out the skeet, and Big Bertha is happy to be used again. The shoulders are being kicked back as we all watch for the next turn. Bored with the boys never hitting the skeet, we decide to recite poetry.

Pat starts with the "Quitter" and then Hope follows. After the proper silence, Hope starts to draw a woman's face on the table as she starts the poem, "The face on the barroom floor." It is one of my favorites. Silence follows Hope's poem.

"I've got one, Hope, how about I do "Sam Magee?" Denise gives a cold stare as she starts to recite. She looks up and at her audience like Hope has taught us. Soon Big Bertha is resting against the bench as Brian captures the audience with "The Dreamer."

Brian is the best story teller so he also starts telling jokes, "to lighten up a bit," he says. I just listen to them all. I don't think they want to hear the prayers I have memorized. Robert Service is Hope's favorite. She used to recite his poems to all of us on hot summer nights to settle us down.

The trees blow hard on the farm, but the barn is still standing and the breeze feels good. The grandkids are taken away with Paul (aka Charlie) to play horseshoes so Hope and Bill can really visit. Hope often gets tears in her eyes to just see us. The Quinlan Clan is stronger then ever, hard times are behind us now, we have good jobs, good educations.

Bill just raises his beer, nodding his head at us all. He doesn't recite poems, but he sure can sing. We are at our own family talent show. Bill captures us with his song, "Jimmy crack corn." The grandkids have heard of this one, and join in. Burl Ives is one of Bill's favorite singers.

Bill tells us stories of the farm they had before I was born. How the cows got out when Brian was in the pathway with a broken leg, and Butch wouldn't drag him out of the way until he was almost trampled. Stories of the big kids before I was alive are pretty funny. You can picture the old farm, and Hope chasing them with a swatter or a wooden spoon. I can see the winter night when Mike has to take the kids on a sledge ride to keep them busy so Hope can give birth to Pat on the farm. Hard times, but the family is so close that you know that was part of the reason why they came through all of their endeavors. Randy just enjoys the big family. He comes from a family of nine kids so he is comfortable in his new family. He is even getting used to the poetry.

Beer flows, stories get confirmed and rearranged for a better telling. Bill stays up late and is still sharing stories into the dark. Hope has shared all of her wine. It is candle lit now, and the family has made a private commitment to each other forever.

Loss of Freedom

HOPE AND I WRITE TO EACH OTHER EVERY WEEK AND TALK on the phone about every other week. She keeps me informed about life at Oleo Acres without us, and I can tell by her letters that she is not doing well. Her thoughts are hard to follow. She seems depressed, disconnected, drinking too much. I know that Hope's health has gotten bad since I left home. I know she struggles with her drinking, that she is lonely, that her health is not good enough for her to travel to visit her kids at their homes. So Randy and I decide that, broke or not, we are going home to see Hope and Bill this Christmas.

Stopping at my sister Pat's house for some laughs the night before we are to arrive in Palms, I know right away that something is not right. Pat is not making jokes. Her house isn't even decorated for Christmas. I have a feeling in my gut that we are heading for new hard times.

Pat tells us that Hope has been scaring Bill with her forgetfulness. She leaves burners on, she is depressed, and she is often drunk before noon. My father can't deal with her any more. "Yes, Erin," Pat says, "we've run out of ideas on how to handle Hope. She's unstable. She's lost her zest for life. She doesn't even want to leave the house. Some days she just cries all day. She has lost her will to live and wants to cash in her chips."

I tuck my purse tight under my arm (for no reason) and look at the clock. I ask, "What in the hell are you even saying? This is not the Hope I know! Doesn't she go to Ed and Alice's anymore? Where are the friends she used to hang out with?"

"Most of Hope's friends are dead, Erin. She had older friends."

"She can't want to cash in her chips! Death is just something she likes to ponder—she always has—but surely she doesn't plan on dying, does she?"

"No, Erin, it isn't even that," Pat explains. "Hope's 'toys are scattered,' as Bill says. She really can't be left alone any more. It's too dangerous."

"I don't believe you, Pat. I know she has struggles, but she is still the strongest woman I have ever known."

"That was true years ago, but not now." A tear has rolled down Pat's face and drops off her chin. Her voice is shaky. "Erin, you are living in the past. Hope is a shadow of her former self. Her closest friends have died, she is lonely, and the drinking is all she enjoys now."

"So what if she wants to drink!" I scream. "Who in the hell cares if she does? She has nothing but booze now—let her keep it! We should not monitor our own mother. She deserves better!"

Pat stares at me, touches my shoulder and says gently, "I don't think you're listening. This is about Bill, her husband, our father, saying he needs the State of Michigan to step in and save her. Bill says he refuses to live like this. He deserves to have a life, too. Bill is over his head, and he has asked for help. I won't turn my back on him, Erin. I understand where Bill is coming from, and he has rights, too. Caro Regency Center is where you send unstable people, and, believe me, Hope is unstable. They'll dry her out, get her off the booze, and teach her how to deal with the pain in her life without alcohol. She needs to go there, even if she doesn't want to. Would you rather have her drink herself to death, Erin?"

"No, of course not. I know she needs help, Pat. It just seems like it's all come on so fast!"

"Erin, you are pretty naïve. This did not come on fast! Hope has been drinking excessively for years. She's living on borrowed time, with the way she's abused her liver." Wiping the tears from her eyes, she continues, "Actually, I'm surprised she's still alive at all. Her heart is not good; she has diabetes. As she herself would put it, Erin, she has 'gone to hell in a hand basket.' I'm not going to let her drink herself to death," Pat says, "so if that is what you want, then you are on your own."

She goes on firmly, "There will be a hearing tomorrow at Caro Regency Center, and I will be there. Do you really think you have the right to fight me on this? Well, you are dead wrong! I'm not the bad guy! Hope has put herself into this mess, and she will be lucky if she can get the help she needs. You can decide what you will do yourself, but I'm tired of being the strong one here. She is my mother, too."

Pat started out calm, but she is all worked up now. "You run off to Chicago and write letters, Erin, and you don't know the pain we are all in over this. For you to come here and tell me to slow down, that we're moving too fast—well,

I'm pissed that you think you are the only one who loves her! Erin, you and Hope are close, but she has lots of other kids, and she loves us all, and we all love her, too. So you either come to the hearing tomorrow and be some help to your brothers and sisters, or stay away and be a cheerleader for Hope. But what she needs is medical help, not ignorance. We have to face it. This is the only way, trust me!"

Tears are flowing down Pat's cheeks. She pulls out a Kleenex. Blowing her nose, she says, "I'm supporting Bill on this one, because he needs us kids now. What Hope needs is help. So suit yourself, Erin. You can beg the judge to change his mind, and then you can take her home with you to Chicago, because Bill can't deal with Hope any more unless she gets dried out. You talk like we are overreacting, and I resent the hell out of that!" She storms over to the opposite side of the kitchen, as far from me as she can get.

Randy looks at Pat, the one who introduced us, and says to her, "Erin doesn't mean to come off like a know-it-all. She's just in shock, and she feels bad that she was not aware things had gotten this bad. You can't really blame her, Pat. Neither one of us knew Hope was so bad. I know you, Pat, and I know you're doing the right thing, and you don't need Erin to come into your house and put some kind of a guilt trip on you. You love Hope—I know you do! When we were at Oakland University together, you always talked of Hope with love. It's really not fair that you are put between two parents. There's no good way to look at the current situation, except for getting Hope the help she needs, and it sounds like she needs it fast."

"You act like we have a choice," Pat says, "but we don't. Erin, the hearing is tomorrow."

Somehow Randy maneuvers the sisters together again. Putting his arm around me, he kisses me on the cheek while he pats my sister on the back and says to her, "Pat, you are a strong woman. I know this is an emotional situation for all of you. I'm sorry that you're put in the middle, but you are doing the right thing. Even Erin knows that."

I retreat to the guest room, thinking I sure don't feel like one. The blankets are too tight, the room too hot, and my heart is pounding to a rhythm that feels like a death march. My throat is closing. I don't want to be held — I just want to kick my blankets to God and make him fix this! I'm sweating, and my eyes are pouring out my private thoughts. I feel that Hope is two hours away, praying on her knees for someone who will save her, and I can't do it.

I can't sleep. How did things get so bad so fast? She always drank! I know she drinks excessively, but I had no idea it had gone this far. Why is the problem worse now? Maybe I should not have left home to start my own life.

Lying in bed, feeling confused, I put my head on Randy's shoulder. Thank God he has big shoulders! I know in my heart that all of us kids love Hope and have her best interest at heart but that Pat, being my older sister, sees the whole picture better than I do. I know it is time to listen to Pat and to God, both of them telling me that the time has come. Hope needs professional help. Randy is supportive; he too is concerned about what the future will hold. Finally I manage to pray myself to sleep.

As Randy and I drive with my sister Pat and brother Mike to Caro Regency Center the next morning, I have a sinking feeling about what the day will hold for me. When we get out of the car, my brother Mike sways and almost loses his balance as he zips up his winter jacket, putting his arm around me at the same time. Gazing up at the ivy growing on the side of the building, I can see and smell desperate people. I hear in my head untold stories of misunderstood people treated there in the past. I think to myself, maybe I belong here! After all, I'm hearing the voices of lonely souls!

Mike (Hope calls him "Mikie") has his hands in his stretch jeans pockets, and his white dress shirt from work shows his name above the pocket. In his world he is important, but he has taken time off work to be here. We all hook arms and run from the cold, but we can't outrun it because the real cold is inside us. It is Christmas Eve of 1979. I wish I were a kid again, waiting for Christmas morning.

Knocking the snow off our sleeves and boots, we enter the building. The heavy metal door has an extra heavy weight to it today, and as the entrance way fills with fresh snow, the wind closes the door for me. We walk up two flights of stairs and dust-filled landings, then down a long hall that echoes as we speak to each other. Randy, holding my hand, says, "Erin, this might be for the best. She will get help." Tears fill his eyes, but I let go of his hand.

Pat is holding my hand as we slowly enter the hearing room. An official-looking woman dressed in a crisp navy blue suit walks me to my seat on the aisle, patting my shoulder with a silent tap. It is almost as if she knows the outcome before it happens. The old oak benches are cold and hard. I look up to see a small chair up front with Hope sitting on it.

Entering the room, the judge nods his head forward, pulling his sleeves out from underneath his robe as he starts to look over his paper work. The court reporter is typing as the judge explains to the family that the State of Michigan is trying to see if Hope is competent. This is a hearing to determine if Audrey Hope Quinlan is a danger to herself or anyone else. The first question the judge asks Hope is, "What is your birth name?"

Hope answers, "Consuela." This is a name she calls herself when she is tired of being Hope, but the judge doesn't know that.

"Hope, how many children do you have?"

Hope looks directly at Mike, Pat and me, saying, "I have nine children now!" Hope says this to make her feelings clear to us, even if it makes her look crazy to the judge.

The judge scoots up his chair to tap the microphone to ask, "Who is the President of the United States?"

Hope smiles at the judge, saying, "Oh, Judge, you should know that!"

The judge, tapping his pen on the paper before him, says, "Hope you are not taking this very seriously. We are trying to see if you are able to take care of yourself, and you are hurting your case. Do you know what your phone number is?"

Folding her arms in front under her breasts, Hope says, "I know some of the numbers but not all of them." Looking into the back of the room she sees Randy and me. She winks, smiles, and then looks away, looking like a different woman. I know she hates authority, but this judge has the ability to have her put away, and she is not being helpful to the judge or to herself.

"Is Bill Quinlan your husband?"

"Yes," Hope replies.

"Do you live on Ridley road?"

"Yes, sir, I do."

The kind-faced, partly bald judge smiled at some of Hope's answers, but he looks at her seriously now, saying, "Hope you are going to stay here at Caro Hospital for a total of no more then sixty days. The paperwork here that your children filled out says you started your husband's bed on fire. Is that true?"

"Yes, sir, I was trying to show Bill the dangers of smoking in bed!"

The judge asks, "Is it true you pulled a gun named 'Big Bertha' on Bill?"

"Yes, sir, but Bill knew I would never shoot him, and the gun wasn't loaded. I don't think it was, anyway."

"Well, do you leave burners on all of the time?"

"Yes, sir. But that is to keep warm!"

"Did you take a canning jar full of tomatoes and knock your husband over the head with the jar?" Here the Judge gives her a stern look.

"Yes, sir. I felt a pain in my head, and I thought he had hit me first!"

"Audrey Hope, you leave me no choice. I will be releasing you to the Caro Regency Center in Caro, Michigan. There you will seek treatment for alcohol abuse. It might only take thirty days, but that is up to you, Hope, on how hard you try to get your life together.

"Court adjourned!" he announces, hitting his mallet on the bench before him. The judge stands and looks at Hope. "Do you know what this means?" he says as he looks right at her.

The room is silent. Hope turns to the judge and says, "Yes, sir, I do understand what this means." With a smirk on her face, she says, "There ain't no niggers votin' in Alabama today!" The courtroom seems to understand her humor, but it is too late.

Even when Hope is against the wall, and the law is locking her up, she is her own person. Her sense of humor lets me know she will rally one more time, as she always has in the past. Still, sitting in silence, I feel an unpleasant heat come over my body. My eyes sting, and tears fall, then jump, to escape my hot face.

The judge shakes his head side to side. "Hope," he says, "I believe this will help you get your life together. Your response is not what I really expected." We all wait in silence. Mike jumps up to his feet, walking out of the hearing room as fast as he can so as not to be seen crying. Pat whispers to me, " She is going to be fine, Erin. Now she can actually get help," but Hope is biting her bottom lip waiting for the orderlies to come and take her to her room. The judge slides back in his chair, waiting for Hope to be taken away.

A female orderly comes over to Hope and takes her by the hand to lead her out. Hope looks back over her shoulder into the hearing room, resisting, and a nurse dressed all in white with white nylons comes to assist the orderly, saying, "If one of you wants to help your mother get situated in her room, come with me." Hope stops in her tracks, her eyes somewhat glassy, looking at the two women but speaking loud enough to be heard by all of us: "One mother can take care of ten children, but ten children can't take care of one mother!" I stand up. Pat and Mike might want to come to be by her side, but I want it to be me. Hope walks hunched over, her black stretch pants and flowered shirt pulled to one side. She acts confused. She is confused.

I'm able to go to her side, to give her a kiss on the forehead and tell her that everything will be okay. We are led to the café, where we wait, talking, as Hope's room is made ready for her. She has a lot of questions about how and why she has been put in Caro Hospital. In one breath, it's fine, even funny, and then in the next breath she turns angry and belligerent. When I leave her side to talk to the nurse, I hear her yelling at me from the other end of the café. "Elmer! Elmer!" (This was always one of her joking nicknames for me.) "You came to save me, right? I knew I could count on you! This woman has gotten my arm and won't let go; she doesn't know you are here to get me. She thinks I'm staying here. I don't belong here! I don't belong here!"

I had thought, at twenty-two years old, that I could save her, and I had come to rescue her, to take her home to my life in Chicago, but now the hearing is over, the judge has made the final decision, and I feel as if I turned my back on Hope. Standing now in disbelief, I realize I didn't do anything to save her. I should have stood up, pleaded for her second chance. Now instead, I'm only keeping her company while they take her away. I have failed the test I was raised to pass.

I run down one side of the café to the other, where Hope is, slipping on the freshly waxed floors. Hope slumps, lost in her thoughts about where she is and how she has gotten here. She still smells of alcohol and pulls away from the nurse trying to take her to her room, the strange nurse who has a hold on her. Rubbing her soft mushy slightly bruised arms, Hope looks at me and starts to cry. "Erin, I mean Elmer, where in the hell am I?"

"I'm here with you, Hope. Don't be afraid. You are in the hospital, Hope. Let's look at the choices in the candy machine." Hope is childlike, and I play to that. "Hope, do you want some candy? How about some orange slices? I know you like 'em, Hope, and diabetes is the least of your worries now!"

Hope starts to cry again. "Erin, there has been a bad mistake! Your father needs me. He can't put wood in the woodstove without me. He will die without my help! Bill needs me to put the chickens back in the chicken coop at night, get the house warm and drag in wood for the next day. His legs don't hold him up very well any more, Elmer. He's too old to live alone. I need to be there with him and remind him to take his medicine. I will bake bread and cook for you kids, too. You are too young to take care of yourselves!"

"Hope, your kids have all left home, and Bill wants you to get some rest here. He is worried about you. He wants the doctors to see why you are leaving burners on, forgetting where you are and who you are. Bill got very concerned when you pulled a gun on him, Hope. He says he's too old to deal with the illness of alcoholism. You are only sixty-one years old, and you have a long life ahead of you. Bill wants what is best for you." She swings at me, as if she wants to strike me, and I hold up my arm to protect myself. "Hope, he only wants his old Hopie back!"

"That bastard, after all I have done! I have raised the bastard's kids! I have given birth to you kids, run a household when there was no money, and now he has turned me in? I never waited for him to come home to punish you kids; I doled out whatever had to be done! I raised you kids alone, practically! I fed one-third of Carsonville. Is that incompetent, Erin? That bastard will never be forgiven!"

"I agree, Hope, you have been treated badly, but you make Bill nervous. He thinks you are going to hurt him; he's afraid for his safety. I think pulling a gun on him was the last straw." I reach out with a bag of orange slices. "Remember how much you love these?"

Hope reaches out to take one, and stops. "Elmer! You can throw that chair through the window and break the glass! I can leave with you and go to Chicago with you! Please Erin, I've been your friend!" She keeps switching back and forth from my childhood nickname to my real adult name.

"I know, Hope, you are a good mother, and you don't deserve this, but this is what needs to happen. You taught me everything I know, Hope, and now I need to return your love to you by keeping you here in the Caro Hospital to get help."

She is running her hands through her hair the way she always does, stopping at the top of her head and pulling for a few minutes. Erin, where are the boys? They would not have put me away! I was there for them during the Vietnam War; we are drinking buddies, for God's sakes. Erin, there is a mistake! Call the boys, Elmer! Call the boys! They must not know what the others have done to me!"

As she pulls Bill's old green sweater up over her shoulder, I realize she doesn't understand what has happened. "Hope," I say, "Caro Hospital is going to dry you out from drinking for at least thirty days. Bill is afraid to death you will hurt him or yourself!"

Hope says, "Well, he should be afraid now! Today, a few minutes ago, there was a hearing, and I'm afraid the wrong kids showed up! I saw you kids who came to get me out of here pulling away from me."

"Hope, the judge asked you how many children you have. Do you remember that?

Rubbing tears from her face with the sleeves of her green sweater, she seems to listen but not understand. "My God, Elmer, I would have never turned my back on you! You came to get me, right, Erin?"

"Yes, Hope, I thought it was all lies until I saw you sitting there. Now I know you do need help. I came to see how bad you are, to see for myself if the others were making a mistake! I believed that if they asked the right questions, you would get to go home with Bill!" Squeezing her soft hand I say, "Hope, you seem lost. Your mind doesn't work like it used to. You do know who the president of the United States is, don't you?"

"Hell, no, Elmer, and I don't need to know!"

"Do you know how many kids you have?"

"Yes, you smart-ass, Erin, I had twelve kids, right?"

"Hope, yes, you gave birth to twelve kids, but you told the judge you only have nine."

"Yes, Erin, I know what I was doing. I just wrote you and Mike and Pat off for turning me in. You kids are turncoats." Hope stands up, staring me straight in the eyes. "You kids should be ashamed of yourselves." Crying again, her head in her hands, she says, "I need to talk to the judge now! This is a big mistake!"

"No, Hope, it's too late now. You didn't know any of the answers to questions the judge asked."

I walk over to the machine and get myself a coke, and Hope moves fast to the next table. "Erin, we could run out that back door! Please, Erin?"

"Hope, they would stop us—this is a mental institution! There are alarms on the doors and windows."

Hope gets up, and I hold her with my arms tucked into hers. Stumbling arm and arm, we try the doors together, and Hope realizes she is locked in. "Erin, I baked bread for you kids! I never complained about the things you kids did wrong! I fed most of Carsonville lunch every day! Surely someone can defend me."

I move my fingers across her face, holding back my own tears. "Hope, you know Bill loves you, and he's been there for you through thick and thin, but he is worried about you! These doctors are going to help you."

Knowing my time is almost up, I put her head against my breast to say good-bye, pressing hard, holding her head. We both start to cry uncontrollably. I wipe my nose, turning my head to take a breath. "Hope, this is hard on me, too. I need to go now. They won't let me stay with you!"

I run down the hall, not wanting to look back. Turning, I see two young men, one on each side of Hope, lifting her with a turn to the long dark hallway. Even though it is a bright sunny day, the shadows follow her as she keeps calling, "Elmer! Elmer!" My cleavage is full of tears. I listen, and the sounds scare me. Why? Because I am in a place that doesn't make sense. They want my mother, and I can't save her. I watch the double doors open, the cold steel doors, and I can see the black rubber on those doors seal Hope's fate as she yells from a distant hallway, "They've hijacked me! You could still save me, but you won't try! Tell that bastard that put me in here that I will never forgive him!"

Hank Williams is in my head singing, "Alone and forsaken by fate and by man."

The next communication I receive from Hope reads:

Dear Erin,

"When you can bear to hear the words you've spoken, twisted by those who make a trap for fools; when you can see the things you gave your life broken, and stoop to mend them up with worn-out tools." — Kipling
All of my ideas of fair play have gone to hell. I trust no one now!

Love,

Hope.

Behind the Double Doors

"LET GO OF ME, YOU LITTLE SON OF A BITCH," Hope screams. "I'll kick you if you don't let me go! You don't know who you're messing with! My boys are on their way! They won't allow me to be treated this way! The charge nurse isn't going to scare me into doing what you fools want!"

Mrs. Ackerman is pulling Hope's (that is, Bill's) green sweater off her shoulder, saying, "Listen here, Mrs. Quinlan, we're not going to allow you to have anything on but a gown we provide. Your sweater will have to be sent home."

Hope yells, "Oh no, you don't! I need the sweater to keep warm outside. It's almost Christmas, and I need to get the presents under the tree. It isn't much, but the kids don't care." Mrs. Ackerman pulls off the green sweater Hope had gotten from Bill while Hope is still screaming. "My kids are coming! There are ten of them! Believe me, you are out of your league," she yells, swinging at Mrs. Ackerman and scratching her face.

"Hope, I'm losing patience with you. We don't tolerate hitting here under any circumstances!" She calls to another staff member, "Quick! Get the restraints! No, Hope, we're not here to make you comfortable, and I see that trying to be nice doesn't work with you."

Hope yells, "I know! I am flat on my ass in front of the holy fountain!"

"You are belligerent and violent." They put leather straps around Hope's wrists and force her down on the gurney. The sun is down, and the moon shines on her face as she is wheeled her into a room, looking for answers about how she came to be here.

Mrs. Ackerman comes back to say, "We will release you from the restraints if you don't swing at anyone." Hope reaches up with her leg and kicks Mrs. Ackerman in her stomach. "That's it," Mrs. Ackerman says. "Jack and Archie, I want her legs tied down, too! Do what you do—just get her out of my sight now!"

Doctor Chung arrives and tells her, "Hope, you are a drunk, and you need to detoxify. Being angry is part of the sickness from alcohol. That's why you're shaking. You are having withdrawal. How long has it been since you have had a drink?"

"None of your goddamn business!" Hope yells.

"Hope, you are making this harder than it has to be!" Doctor Chung states.

"It's not against the law to have a drink is it?" Hope asks, challenging him. "I have never been in such a sober crowd! I could really use a drink, right now!"

Doctor Chung smiles and says, "Mrs. Ackerman, put her in a locked room, but take the restraints off. She is upset with reason. She feels betrayed. She's really more confused then violent! This is hard on her, and we need to allow her some time to adjust."

Rolling her into a private room, Mrs. Ackerman locks the door. The door is kept locked until dinner.

Hope cries as she looks out over the parking lot, seeing no one she knows. Her mouth is dry. Shaking, she is unable to eat dinner when it is brought to her. She gets on her knees and prays.

Later that night, a new nurse, Miss Joanne, arrives. She is pretty with smooth skin, soft pink lips, and a loving manner. Miss Joanne unlocks the door to find Hope in the middle of the floor, screaming. "Someone threw me out of the bed a few minutes ago! Please help me?" Hope is childlike, her big brown eyes distant. Like a very strong child having a tantrum, she tosses her hundred and fifty-four pounds across the dusty floor that has not been cleaned all day.

Miss Joanne sits on the floor next to her. Taking Hope's hand, she tries to make her understand that she will not be allowed with other patients yet. "Hope, we can't take the chance of you kicking the head nurse again! I want to get you back into your bed now."

"No!" Hope swings her legs around and turns her back to Joanne and will not allow herself to be put into bed. She continues to shake and refuses to eat. When Joanne leaves the room, Hope is still holding onto the leg of the bed, looking up at the clock but unable to tell the time.

Finally, Doctor Chung comes to give her a shot. After that she can be put into bed, and she sleeps in peace for a while, with dreams flowing through her head.

Then she begins to fight again in her sleep. The room is cold, but Hope sits up on the edge of her bed and starts whispering methodically for Mike, Butch, Tony, Brian, Marianne, Pat, Shannon, Denise, Erin and Charlie. Archie, a male nurse, comes to calm her down. "Hope, you're in Caro Hospital!"

Hope stirs and wakes. "You get back, you bastard! I don't need your kind of help! You are the man who tried to make plans to kidnap me—I know you're the one!"

"Hope, you're delusional. Your kids aren't here. If you settle down, though, maybe we can allow you some visitors!" Archie says, putting her back in bed. She fractured her hip sometime earlier, but no one has yet realized it. "Hope, you're hallucinating, you're shaking, and we need to get some meds into you so you can sleep."

Archie goes looking for a doctor. He paces the floor for help, but no one seems to care, and he comes back to Hope's room and picks up her hand to calm her. Her brown eyes seem lost, and she falls against his hands to rest. A few minutes later she awakens to say, "They took my clothes, my purse and my glasses! What kind of a place are you running around here? Someone with a gun tried to shoot me! I want to go home. Bill, come and get me now! They're all crazy here!" She kicks her feet almost hard enough to fall out of bed again.

Finally a doctor arrives on the scene. "Hope, calm down," Dr. Miles says soothingly. "We're going to keep you here for sixty days until you get sober and we can see what health problems you have."

"You are not going to touch me, young man! I have boys who will hurt you if anything happens to me! Joe and Brian will hurt you. They know you have hijacked me!"

Doctor Miles says, "Hope, we're trying to make you comfortable."

Hope smiles and says in a wheedling voice, "To make me comfortable you need to put some whiskey in my orange juice! I need a drink. Who is bartending in this place, anyway? Please let me call my kids! This is all one big mistake. The girls probably want me to teach them how to make gravy."

Falling back into dreamland again after another shot, Hope is still restless. The next time she gets up, announcing pain in her hip, her door has been left unlocked, and pain doesn't stop her from going on a booze run, chasing from room to room looking for a drink. Other patients wake up alarmed, yelling back at her to get out of their stuff, but Hope keeps moving from room to room, looking for what life she has left.

The sun wakes everyone up, as the smell of Mr. Clean is wiped from one room to the next. Dressed all in white, different staff members smile at Hope as they enter her room. One man has a pencil in his top pocket and gives it to Hope as a gift. Grateful, she asks for paper to go with it. The man comes back before lunch to give her a small pad of paper with silly expressions on it, drawings of cleaning people. His grandson had given it to him.

Soon Nurse Ackerman enters the room. "Good morning, Hope. How are we today? Better, or do we need to put you back into a seclusion room?" Hope had been a patient for three days now, though her own sense of time was very unclear. "You have been combative, abusive and mean," the nurse went on, "so if today is like last night, you won't last on my shift. I am the head nurse, and I run this place."

Hope has started to write notes to her kids, begging to be rescued. She holds her pencil to her chest and says to the nurse, "I am not your enemy. Just let me write." Sitting still, she looks out the window, trying to gather her thoughts. She sees there is still a chair that could be thrown through the locked window, but Hope is trying to get along. She is able to make a list. She is nervous, afraid she has lost memory of her past except for glimpses. Pushing her hands in her hospital nightgown, she accidentally tears a pocket.

Another nurse straightens Hope's nightie and retightens the strings. "Hope," she says to her, "you have been handed a raw deal. I can't get you out of here, but I went to school with your kids. You're a good woman, and you're going to be fine. Let's get you to lie back now. You don't need to write anyone. Just rest. Please, Hope, your body needs to be at complete rest. You are healing from an addiction. It is hard on a body to go through what you have been through." Fluffing up the pillows, she eases Hope's head back. "Tomorrow will be a better day, I promise." Hope is untied, the restraints slipped off, and she is left in the dark, snoring.

Hope says, "Someone broke my hip in my sleep last night. You can't fool me. It hurts when I walk." Hope wants to walk out to get Christmas presents for her kids; she is begging to go to the store.

"No, Hope, you can't leave to shop for presents for the kids," Archie says. "They are all grown up now, anyway. You're in Caro Hospital, and you're here to get help, so stay nice today, please. Why don't you tell me about your kids?"

"None of your goddamn business. I know men like you, and I don't trust them! They can shoot you!"

"Hope, I'm not going to shoot you or hurt you, but I'm going to put you in a chair to look out the window." Holding onto her back, he moves her over to the window where she can look out.

"I'll wait here for my kids. Surely someone will come."

She has been in the hospital a few weeks now and watches the snow blow across the parking lot.

Later Nurse Joanne enters the room to say, "I want to give you a warm bath and wash you up. It will feel good."

Hope gets up and complains again about a pain in her hip. "Someone broke my hip in my sleep last night! Maybe it was Nurse Ackerman—she is sure mean enough." Starting to test the water with her socks on, she does not feel the heat and sits down in it totally dressed.

"No, no! Wait, Hope! We're not ready yet. You need to take off your clothes."

Hope stands still as if she is a toddler being potty trained, while Nurse Joanne undresses her, then she says confidently, "I'm cold. Is your boiler broken? Because if it is, I could fix it for a drink!"

"No, Hope, it is not, but after your hot bath you will feel warmer for sure."

"How about a candy bar? Can I have that?"

"Yes, Hope, you can." Nurse Joanne orders candy bars for Hope.

Hope wants to let the kids know that "they" have stolen the purse she bought at Gambles store. Looking for booze under the bed and not finding any, she goes to the other rooms and starts going through other patients' personal items looking for booze. One patient gets out of bed, and Hope yells at him, "Joe, you are not even dressed for school! Get dressed now!"

Archie comes to get Hope, with a smile this time. "Hope, I know you think all of these people are your kids, but they are patients here, like you, and you can't keep yelling at them for not having their chores done! Sorry, Hope, but you can't walk the halls if you don't keep out of other people's things. You're upsetting others."

Hope says, "Well, if you would let me go to the store, I would bring back food for everyone here. I am starving! Besides, I know that they took my purse and my glasses and my favorite green sweater that Bill gave me. I'm not stupid, you know. Well?" she asks, with her hands on her hips.

"Hope, as soon as you can be trusted, I promise you I will get your purse and glasses and sweater."

Hope gets close to Archie and whispers, "Archie, if you get me out of here, I will get you large sums of money!" Just as she is leaning over, saying, "Hey, I am going to get a beer, I will be right back!" Mrs. Ackerman comes into the room. Staring at Hope suspiciously, she asks, "What are you up to now, Hope? More escape plans?"

"No," Hope says, "I am planning a party and have invited a lot of people, and you will look foolish when you don't have any wine to serve them!"

"I will take that chance, Hope," Mrs. Ackerman answers and walks out.

Hope looks back to Archie, pleading with him for one more shopping trip. "Please take me to the store! Just drop me off, and I promise I will have the grocery man bring me right back after I am done!"

"No, Hope, I'm afraid I can't do that," Archie answers with a gentle smile.

Giving up for the time being, she naps for a few hours, then wakes with fear in her eyes. She looks around the room, gathers her blankets close to her chest, feeling misplaced. "I'm not stupid," she says to Archie. "This is a boarding house, and I hired you and I can fire you."

Archie says back, "You were doing so well, Hope. What happened — a bad dream?"

"Yes, maybe. I just don't trust you bastards, and I know when I am sleeping you are making plans to get rid of me."

"No," Archie answers, laughing out loud. "We have no such plans! We're trying to get you to conform somewhat, so we can see where your real problems are, and to do that we need you to get free of alcohol. You'll have to humor us, Hope, so we can do our job."

Someone peeks ahead in the door. "Are you all right?" It is Nurse Ackerman again.

"Yes, we're fine. Hope had a bad dream, and I am just reassuring her so she understands this is normal."

"Well, I will tell you one thing. On the night shift she was walking the halls again yelling for the kids and disturbing all of the other residents! I tell you right now, I will not tolerate that here!"

"She is just confused. She told me yesterday that she lost a baby, and she was crying when she told me. Surely you can understand that pain, can't you? She also told me how her house had started on fire and how she almost lost her kids again. She is mourning her children. I am not a doctor, but I do know this woman has been through a lot. When I first arrived in her room, she was on her knees, praying, and tears were running down her face. We need more compassion here," Archie says, looking directly into Nurse Ackerman's eyes. "Hope has been through a lot in her life!"

"Well, I will tell you what she has been through, and that is 'Booze.' In fact, she is still looking for it! And if she causes another disruption I will personally talk to Doctor Miles to have her sedated. Caro Regional Center has a reputation to uphold." Nurse Ackerman tucks a chart attached to a clipboard under her arm. "Hope Quinlan" is the name written on the top of the page.

Hope sleeps better that night, though. She has someone to listen to her, even if it is only Archie. He will not help her escape or get her booze, but he does care.

The next morning Hope gets out of bed, opens her door and yells, "Come on in and drag 'em out! It's the only way. Hi, Mr. Butterfield, how are you doing today?" She says this to a man who is not there! Looking out the window with a dark brown metal frame, she yells, "Bill! Bill, they have hijacked me!"

Hope then goes to the office, looking for her chart to release herself. She yells, "Are you proud of the way you are treating your mother? You make sure you tell your brothers how you have treated your mother, and tell your father too!" She gives a cold, hard stare to a man in his room across the hall.

Next morning Dr. Miles says, "Hope, we have a wheelchair for you. "You do have a fractured hip, and you should not be walking on it. We are sending you to Hurly Hospital tomorrow to get a pin in it. But for now, no more walking."

"I guess the pain was real, Hope," Archie says. "You gave us a lot of confusing messages these first few weeks; I guess we didn't take the pain in your hip seriously. It must have happened the first week here when you were kicking everyone and falling out of bed."

"No," Hope says, "I fell a few days ago in the hallway trying to get the kids to bed. No one here is smart enough to figure that out. I told Dr. Miles, if he was so smart, then why doesn't he know my hip is really hurt? He said he is a physiologist, so it's about time to get this hip fixed. What kind of a joint do you run here, Archie?" Hope slides into the plastic seat of the wheelchair, feeling doomed to recovery. "Fine, fine, I will stay in my chair. But I have kids to take care of!"

A few hours later she is asking to have her hair cut, and Nurse Jones makes the arrangement. Silva comes to wash and cut Hope's hair.

"Thanks so much for the haircut. It makes me feel a lot better."

She is taken to Hurley Hospital and stays there two weeks, returning with a walker, much calmer. The shakes are over. Now she just wants candy. Nurse Ackerman gives permission for her to have a pen and paper to write a few letters, but Hope has already written the kids asking for a quick escape.

When Hope is no longer delusional, great stories start to flow. At break time people come to her room to hear whatever story she is in the mood to tell. One day she tells Archie about a fairy ring we had at our farm before the last few kids were born.

"I would get up in the night to get a drink of water, and the light shone in a circle right in front of my window. I could see them all dancing in their tiny colored dresses, blowing around spreading dust, and sure enough the next day, we would get good news. Then Bill accidentally plowed the ring under, less than one year ago, and it has been nothing but trouble since. I bet that's how I got here."

Hope writes a note thanking Archie for his kindness and for the compassion he showed in her thirty days at Caro Regency Hospital, still commenting about how much nicer it would have been if she could have escaped—even if it had cost her "large sums of money" to get help.

Joe, the counselor, says, "She is an intelligent woman with a strong will and a sense of survival. I would bet she has an IQ of 143 or higher, but the pain in her life led her to drown her sorrows by drinking too much. After witnessing the withdrawals, I feel she has turned the corner, but some rehabilitation would be in order. I think it is time for her to be counseled by Spike Jackson, with a private AA meeting in her room."

Spike Jackson sits down with Hope in private to explain that she needs to stop drinking. Alcohol has almost destroyed her life, burning out many brain cells and keeping her in poor general health. "Hope, how much do you drink?" he asks her.

Hope smiles and says, "Why, Spike, how much do you drink?"

Spike smiles back and says, "Well actually, Hope, I have not had a drink in twenty years!"

Hope, still smiling, says, "That is too bad! I bet you miss it, don't you? Well, I normally drink a fifth of booze a day." She pauses and reconsiders. "Well, at least in my best years I did! Now I am not sure what the drinking will be. But I don't plan to stop entirely."

"Hope, I want you to quit drinking completely! It will kill you if you do not stop drinking. Your liver cannot detoxify your body any more, and that's why it took so long to get rid of the alcohol in your system. You need to think of your health and your family. They love you, and this is too painful to see you go through again. Trust me, Hope! You are in danger of dying the next time around. You've been sober now for thirty days, and that is a new beginning for you. Take this opportunity, Hope! It is a sure bet. If you stop drinking, you will add years to your life."

Hope says, "Listen, Spike, you are a nice enough man, so how about we make a deal? I promise to have only one small glass of wine a day, if you will release me."

Mr. Jackson says, "Hope, they are releasing you today to a local AA office for further follow-up. I will be there waiting for you. Maybe one glass of wine a day is the best you can do, but that does disappoint me."

Hope is calm after the thirty days at Caro. At the end, free of anger and booze, she makes friends even with Nurse Ackerman. When it is time for Hope to leave and she is waiting for her son Tony to come and pick her up, she makes up a sign for the door of her room that reads, "ABANDON ALL HOPE YE WHO ENTER HERE!"

Spike signs Hope's release. (He will also take her to AA after she is out of Caro Regional Center.) Tony picks her up in his Mercedes. She sits in the back seat and smiles all the way home, happy to see the sun and to be on a road trip!

Hope lives for three more years, mostly drinking only a small glass of wine a day. She keeps her promise to Spike Jackson.   Case Number 1116

On the Road Again

Ninety days after her treatment ends, Hope has the right to apply for a new driver's license. She has followed all the rules (except for the daily glass of wine), has been attending her AA meetings regularly, and it's now time for her driver's license test. I'm sitting out on the back fire escape stairs of our Chicago apartment when the call comes and Randy yells, "Erin, it's Hope!"

Hope sounds out of breath with excitement. "This is long distance, Erin, so I'll make it short. I need to borrow your car to take my driving test! Can I borrow it?"

"Hope, what are you talking about?"

"The State of Michigan took my license away, Erin, when Bill put me into Caro Psychiatric Hospital, and I have to take a test to drive again. If I pass, I'll be given back my license. You have a car that will pass the inspection, Erin, and I need your help!"

"Fine, Hope, I'll do it! But get me the time and place so I can drive the car back to Michigan and meet you." Then I ask, " How is Bill feeling, Hope?"

"Well, he is still smoking eighty cigarettes a day and preaching the evils of drinking. Your father is not an easy man to be married to, honey! That's one reason I need to have my own wheels! Please, will you help me?"

"Of course I will, Hope."

Hanging up the phone and walking back into the apartment, I see Randy standing by the stove, frying a special egg sandwich. "Randy, Hope needs me to help her get a new driver's license, and I'm going to do it! She has worked so hard on not drinking. I'm proud as hell of her, honey."

"Erin, you are naïve," Randy says, shaking his head. "Wherever Hope is, she will be drinking! But I don't care—go help her get her license!"

I leave the kitchen and look around our dining room at all of Randy's medical books. Well, I think, you are getting a doctorate degree, and I'm running my own hair salon. Our dreams are coming true. So why not let Hope have her dream of driving again? Hope can't live without hope!

The following weekend I go to Michigan. We have been writing to each other weekly. Knowing of her trials and tribulations and feeling guilty for all she has been through in Caro, even though we all think being there saved her life, I feel this is my chance to redeem myself in Hope's eyes. Hope taps the hood of my car, proclaiming that it is a good car and will pass the test. It is just my little two-door silver Chevette (a "four-banger," as Randy calls it), but it will do the job. Hope says she feels freedom in her soul now!

At sixty-one years old, Hope still looks pretty. Her lips have faded, her eyes dimmed, but she has more warmth than the ordinary human being, and she gathers herself together to make a good impression with the policeman giving the test. He acts very businesslike as Hope makes a few jokes. Then she moves her hair out of her face as if she is on a serious mission, and off they go, while I wait in the parking lot for their return.

Back at last, Hope steps out of my car with a huge smile on her face. The officer (who knew Hope in her prime drinking years) is kind of chuckling to himself and shakes her hand now, saying with a grin, "Hope, good luck now! Here's your permit. You should get the actual license in the mail in ten business days. You don't want to get caught drinking any more, or you'll lose your license for good."

Hope looks up to heaven and says, "Thanks for pulling for me." She is still sober, and her life holds lots of promise. Spike, her mentor, told her that she had been using alcohol to self-medicate. It was the way she dealt with depression. Hope is learning for the first time why she did what she did in her life.

She takes the paperwork for her license, bends it in half, and puts her purse strap over her shoulder. "Erin, let's get something to eat!"

We go to the drive-through at the A&W Root Beer in Lapeer. I have missed Hope and am enjoying our time together. I roll down my window, asking her what she wants, and after thinking for a minute she says, "I'd love a foot-long smothered with onions, chili and pickles, Erin!"

"Wow, Hope, that sounds like a lot!"

"No, make that two foot-longs, Erin. I'm hungrier now that I don't drink any more. And how about onion rings, the big ones, and a root beer in a frosty mug? Erin, it has been so long!"

I'm surprised but put in the order, leaning out my window to speak into the old microphone. "Fine, Hope, you can have whatever you want. I will order the same—no chili on mine!" A scratchy voice confirms the order, repeating everything I've requested. As I order and listen closely while the order is confirmed, I am turned away from Hope and don't notice when she pulls a fast one on me. Leaving the door open, she slips out of the car and runs away while my back is turned!

Collecting the food and paying the bill, I start looking for a place to pull over so I can get out of the car and look for Hope. She is always pulling something! I think as I stomp down the street. But she has outsmarted herself this time because I'm leaving her in Lapeer to teach her a lesson! I get back into my seat and start to drive away, but I can't do it. I can't leave her here. Mad as I am, mad enough to shake her, she is still my mother. So I drive around looking for her as if she is a lost puppy, asking complete strangers, "Have you seen my mother? She's playing a game, and I seem to have lost her." She can't have gone far on foot, I think, so I drive slowly through the connecting downtown parking lots until I spot the sign that says "Michigan Liquor Commission." My heart sinks. I have flashes of the past with Hope, the hiding of alcohol and the drunk driving. Back then she used to start her day with wine in a coffee cup, and I didn't even know she wasn't drinking coffee. But all that is in the past. Now she is using me to get booze, and I'm not going along with it! I walk into the Michigan Liquor Commission Store, hoping I don't find her inside. The bell on the door rings, almost like God is listening.

Hope is at the counter, trying to get the man to give her a loan for a fifth of vodka. He stares at her in disbelief, his arms folded in refusal.

Walking to the counter I say, to save her pride, "Hope, that was a real fun game! You scared the hell out of me! I was worried sick that someone hit you with a car or something!" I'm pretending it was a game, but in my heart I'm so disappointed that I can't let myself look into those faded eyes. I'm afraid that if I look into her eyes, I will buy her some booze!

On our walk back to the car, Hope apologizes for running away and tries to explain herself. "I'm lost without booze, Erin. You have no idea what it's like to need to drink! It's been so long. I just don't enjoy life without it! I have given my life to all of you kids and your father, but for me, I just want to wear rose-colored glasses. Erin, I have a monkey on my back. I would rather live two years with booze then twenty years without it." She turns away from me at the end of this sad speech.

"Come on, let's eat our chili-dogs, Hope," I say to her with a smile. "It will be okay, I promise you." We reach the car where the cold chili-dogs are waiting to be eaten. As I move the food over to get into my seat, I put Hope in on her side and lock the door.

"Hope," I tell her, "I do understand how you feel, but drinking doesn't help you at all. You are going to die if you keep drinking! And don't you care about me? Do you have any idea what it feels like to have your own mother choose booze over you? Don't you ever think of anyone but yourself? Because it feels to me like you could control it but choose not to, and that really hurts me. You will die earlier because of your choices, and it is not fair to me! I love you!"

"Erin, don't be ridiculous! This is not about you at all! I love all of you kids. Why does everything always come down to someone else's feelings? God damn it, this is about me!"

My mind flashes back to being a kid and having Bill mad at Hope and saying to her, "You have a monkey on your back!" Now I know what he meant. Picking up her warm hand, I hold it next to my face, closing my eyes, knowing that someday I will regret this day. "What can I do for you, Hope? I live in Chicago now. I love you, but I can't be watching your back any more. I feel guilty, Hope, but I had to get married and start my own life. Nothing can ever change the love I have for you, not even you, but I'm concerned that you don't take care of yourself. You scare the hell out of me. This will kill you—don't you see it?"

"No, Erin, I will never get as bad again, I promise you. I just want one drink a day to take the edge off. I don't ever plan to get drunk again. I do agree with you about that. Erin, I went through the shakes, and I understand that booze is not my friend, but I can't live without it."

I reach over and pull her head down on my shoulder. "I will get you some, Hope. Here is five dollars. You can buy a pint, but not a fifth! I know this is wrong, but I'm powerless with you on drinking issues."

I want badly to believe that Hope can control her drinking, but in my heart I know she just lost the battle, and I know that everyone in the family will be disappointed in me. The truth is, "I had never walked in her shoes nor saw things through her eyes," to quote a Hank Williams song.

Hope takes the money, wiping away tears as she gets out of my car. The bounce is back in her step as she heads toward the Liquor Commission store with cash in her hand.

We drive home in silence, both of us understanding that she is not cured, and I know that someday the alcohol will take her from me.

Bill is excited that Hope has passed her test, and she brags about how great the chili-dogs were. She has already started back drinking before she even has her license, though I'm the only one who knows it. She does stick to wine in small glasses, though—homemade wine she makes herself. She seems to be able to live with her choices.

Easy Times for Hope and Bill

Living in Sandusky was one of Hope's dreams because it used to be her old stomping ground. Most people there know her and care about her. Now she and Bill have been back in Sandusky for four years, and we kids come as often as we can to share our own lives with them.

Bill and Hope each have their own money, lots of good memories, and a feeling they have lived a good life. Hope is happier than I have ever seen her. She is independent, and her time with Bill is spent reminiscing. One of their favorite pastimes is telling stories. Content to be sharing their lives quietly, they aren't under financial pressure any more and seem happy in their new apartment, the stress and strain of the farm behind them. The building they are in is new and has all new appliances—no more carrying wood, raising chickens, and living in an old hard-to-heat farmhouse. Bill has new fish in his fish tank, and Hope is back to making bean soup (without the oxtail). She has a new friend named Mildred. Mildred cannot take the place of Lena, but she and Hope can visit about their children. Hope and Bill like most of the other people in their building, too. Their only real concern in their new life is their health. Aging is hard on them both.

Grandchildren love to visit Hope and Bill in the new apartment, even though an apartment is not as much fun as an old farm, and they have a lot of company, lots of gifts and thoughtful phone calls. Their life is easier than it has ever been. Usually one of my brothers will drop a hundred-dollar bill on the table to give them a surprise in their day. Once I came home and took Hope shopping at the A&P, and we had a blast, buying anything Hope wanted in the store. She got sardines, crabmeat, frozen dinners, lots of canned goods (with the labels on them), and even fancy coffees that Denise has introduced her to. We filled two carts, and when we got to the register, I said, "Hope, this is on me." She just laughed and said, "Honey, I'll take it! Thanks."

Hope and Bill live now without constant financial struggle. They have money in their checking account—no more bouncing checks. They have money for cigarettes and cheap wine. Both avid readers, they also have time for books and letter writing, and they sneak some low-sugar pies from time to time. Bill is happy to have Hope back home, and Hope is doing the best she can to take care of Bill's high blood pressure. Hope goes to the beauty shop and shares stories with the other women there. Bill is still driving, and he and Hope take a few road trips back to Carsonville to visit old friends. They spend their days warm, safe, and happy.

Much of the time they talk about how proud they are of us kids. They have arrived. They fought the good fight in life and won. Three years pass without a hitch.

Meeting Her Maker

HOPE IS TAKEN TO BAD AXE HOSPITAL in an ambulance, bleeding internally. The bleeding cannot be stopped. Hope's liver is no longer functioning. "She's dying," the doctor says. "Her heart won't hold out long with her diabetes, and her body is worn out." Dr. Chill is just that. When Bill wants more answers, he gets none.

I walk into her hospital room and smell only flowers. She is so loved in this small town! I stand in silence, reading cards from the townspeople. Hope's face is yellow, her lips purple, and she has a swollen look to her body. I start to whisper in my head a Hail Mary over and over, flashing back to memories of holidays around our faith. Hope has God, but she wants to "cash in her chips," she says to me, and I have no response for her. I stand with my hands moving, passing each bead on my rosary in silence. I look up at the sign over her bed that says simply, "Hope." I think that if she dies I will kill myself. I can't live without her, I think. But I can't upset her in her present state by letting her know how closely my heart is connected to hers.

Nurses come and go, and Hope just lies there, looking at the ceiling, wanting to be set free from her life. I lean over her and pour water from the yellow plastic pitcher. "Hope, I'm afraid! I can't live without you, Hope. For God's sake, Hope, you can't leave me! I'm only twenty-five years old!"

"Erin, now is not the time for this conversation. I need you to do me a favor. Talk to Bill. I want to be transferred to Deckerville Hospital, where they have their heads up their asses and couldn't save me if they wanted to. I know the staff there. They're all nice enough, but they're a small hospital without the equipment to save my life. This is not the time for anyone to be heroic! I just want to be someplace where my kids can all be by my side during my last hours. I love your purple hair, Erin! Can you please make this happen for me? I would do it for you. I also want you to promise that you will do my make-up and hair. I don't want Carman to make me look like a clown! I have seen his work over many years, and he doesn't have a knack with high cheekbones. He would make me look like a clown."

Bill makes the arrangements, and Hope gets her wish. The transfer is completed. At Deckerville Hospital, the doctors know Hope and understand her needs and wishes. Keeping her comfortable, they allow her to be in control of her dying, and Hope is at peace.

I drive to Deckerville with Randy and Bill to see her. On the way to the hospital, we talk about different things Hope has said (we have had lots of open conversations about death and Hope's wishes), and I tell Bill about a telephone conversation I had with her a few weeks before I came home to Michigan, not knowing then how sick she was. It was when she asked me what I wanted of hers, and I told her I wanted the picture of Christ in the garden. I told Hope how much it meant to me, that it was what I looked at when I was supposed to be thinking about God on Good Friday. I feel guilty sharing the conversation with my father, but he listens as I explain. Hope had laughed on the phone, saying, "No, honey, that picture should go to your sister, Marianne, because she carried it from house to house whenever we moved, and we moved a lot. Marianne thought that when that picture was hung, we were home. She has to have it. I'm sorry, Erin."

I said then, "Hope, don't worry, no one will ever know we talked about this, but just write my name on the back, and I will deal with Marianne."

"No, Erin, that is not right" was Hope's firm response. "You will not take that picture! But after my death you will find your own picture of Christ in the garden, and it will mean more to you than the one hanging on the wall of our home."

Her refusal to give in made me angry. "Hope, it's fine if you don't give me the picture, but don't play this death game with me! Telling me a picture at a garage sale will mean more than the picture on my wall growing up! That is an insult!"

I get to the end of the story and appeal to Bill to tell me I was right. "Don't you agree, Bill? How can she do that? It makes me pissed at her! I'm twenty-five years old, not a child to be treated like this! Fine, if she has already given the picture to Marianne, but don't humor me! Right, Bill?"

The words are no sooner out of my mouth than I see a picture in the front yard of the house next to the Deckerville hospital. It is there on the side of the road, leaning against a tree. I start to scream at Randy to stop. "That's the picture! Hope is giving it to me!"

Bill turns around and says with his wonderful smile, tired and sad though he is, "Well, honey, that's your mother for you!"

I get out of the car and run to the picture. It's part of a yard sale, and the man running it says, "My wife insisted we put that picture close to the road, and I guess it worked!" Lying next to the picture is a blanket, covered with yellow roses. Hope had told me that yellow roses means "good-bye" so I ask the man the price for the blanket. He says, "Three bucks for the set!" and I reach into my jeans pockets, pulling out all the cash I have on me. It adds up to three dollars.

I get back in the car, knowing Hope has said good-bye to me. God will show me the way to find my own answers, comforting me while I sleep under the blanket. After our hospital visit, I cry all of the way back home.

Shortly after she arrives at Deckerville Hospital, Hope is dying. A loving staff, most of the nurses already knowing and caring about her, make her as comfortable as they can. Her breathing is heavy and labored.

Hope wants to see each one of her kids individually to say good-bye. Realizing that this is the last time she will see her ten living children, Hope seems ready to die but worried about how we will face life without her. Gathered in the waiting room, praying silently, talking among ourselves, not wanting her to die but knowing that she has been through too much in her life, we wait for our names to be called, one by one, from oldest to youngest, to say good-bye to Hope. We were raised with the saying, "Rank has its privilege." Years earlier Hope also said, "If I'm dead and gone and my kids can laugh about me, I have done a good job raising them." We tell Hope stories and laugh and cry and tell each other she has another five lives left, at least, even as we know in our hearts that she might die any moment.

I'm number eleven in the family, so I wait for my turn at the end of the line, with only Charlie—now Paul—to come after me. I think about Hope's crazy stories, her good homemade bread and chicken soup, and the feeling of love that flowed through every day of my life with her. Hope brought more love to this earth than almost anyone else I've ever met. I think about how she never judged her neighbor and how she gave much when she had little. Hope gave me many gifts. I feel proud to be her daughter.

My sister Denise is right ahead of me. Coming out of Hope's room, she touches my arm when she walks by, crying hard, and I walk into the room.

Hope has a mask over her mouth. Her hair is all slicked back with sweat. She has red polish on her nails (most of it chipped off). I want to grab her and carry her out of there. I run to her side, look at her, and start to cry, all at once, knowing this is my only chance to say "Thank you, Hope!" I know I must follow the rules and say good-bye and that if I take too much time, Charlie might not get to see her in time.

She pulls up the mask, and her eyes roll back a little. I look her right in her eyes and say, "Hope, I love you!" She is happy to know we are all there for her. Hope has always cared for her family above all. She has given her life for all of us. She protected us, when the storms of life came, and she taught us, by her example, how to love unconditionally. Hope has given us all a dream of God in our lives. She is our own Hope in life. Now she holds the mask away long enough to say, "Erin, I love you," then puts it back over her mouth.

I say again, "Hope, I love you too!" and run out of the room, afraid that she will be gone before Charlie has his turn.

When he comes out of Hope's room, Charlie stands in the waiting room doorway, white as a ghost. Mike takes charge of us all by standing up and saying, "We are going to say the rosary for Hope." We all drop to our knees, saying the rosary as Mike leads it. Hope is not leading the rosary this time, as she did all through our lives. A nurse shuts the door to give us privacy.

We would all love to go back into Hope's room, but the nurse says, "Your family is big, and Hope needs to rest now." I think to myself, she will rest in heaven! Let me kiss her while she is alive—I'm not ready to lose her yet! I try to be alone with just Randy, but the hospital is small, with no place for all of Hope's children and their mates to be away from each other.

I go to the chapel to be alone, to cry, to pray. I stay on my knees to let God know that I need Him to help Hope make her ascension to Heaven. She is worthy, I tell Him. And she is. After a few hours of crying, I fall into a deep sleep in the chapel.

Like Hope, I rely on my dreams to give me answers in tough times. That night in the chapel, in a deep dream state, I dream I'm in a car with Randy, and there is Hope on the side of the road, hitchhiking. "Stop! Pull over!" I scream. Hope is dressed in a white sheet like a robe. Randy pulls our Chevette over to pick her up, and Hope climbs into the back seat of the car. I look back at her and ask, "Hope, do you want to live or die?" Hope looks at me and says, "Honey, let me rest. I'm tired. Erin, you have to let me go. I will be safe. Let me go. I want to die now."

I wake up and run to her bedside. Hope is resting, it is 3:00 a.m., the room is dark, and no nurses are around. Whispering, leaning over her face, I rub her forehead with my fingertips, softly so as not to scare her, but she acts afraid, disoriented. There is fear in her eyes. "Hope," I whisper. "I got your message. You want to die, don't you? It came to me in a dream."

I feel that Hope was actually talking to me in my dream, trying to have me understand that it is time for me to let her go. I look into her soft, tear-filled eyes of love and forgiveness, and I know she wants to die. She will never see my babies. She will leave me forever except for the memories. Again I have the feeling that I want to take her out of that bed and run as fast as I can, hold her as tightly as she held me when I was a little girl! She belongs to us! But I have no choice. I must allow her to die in dignity with the Lord by her side.

My memory flashes to seeing Hope at the kitchen table, drinking, a smile on her face, happy, talking to me about friends and holding up her hand. "If in your life you have two real friends, Erin, you are luckier then most!" Hope has been my best friend, and I do feel luckier then most. Knowing our friendship would last past her death, Hope would often say, "I have had more than most people. I have you kids and your father, and I lived my life the best way I knew how. You can't ask for more then that, honey."

When I think about the past and the many things Hope has told me over the years, I remember her saying that souls can get trapped on earth in the process of dying and that when that happens, only prayer can release them. Hope used to say that a person might not know how to die and might have to be guided so they're not afraid. It is Hope's time to die now. I struggle with my own pain, yet at only 25 years of age I realize I need to help her die. She needs guidance. I believe she made a deal with God to give me the dream to allow me to come to her side at 3:00 a.m. this morning.

With pain in my throat, tears in my eyes, and heaviness in my heart, I begin to speak to her.

"Hope, look for the light. Look for Mae" (her mother) "and Archie" (her only brother). Hope looks startled and opens her eyes wider. "Can you see God, Hope? Can you follow the white light? Can you?" I stop and take a breath. Tears fall in my mouth, and I lick them off my lips and start to ask Hope to slow down her breathing. "Don't be afraid, Hope. God did not bring you this far to let you go alone. Trust Him, Hope. Let go. God will guide you. He has promised you salvation. Archie is there. Let go, Hope. Let God."

Hope closes her eyes, and her breathing becomes shallow. She can't allow it to happen yet, but she falls into a peaceful sleep. I stand, relieved that she is not yet gone. I hold her hand up to my face, kissing the inside of her palm. Then I make the sign of the cross and leave the room.

In the morning, when my sisters join me, I don't feel as I did the night before. I know now that God is still by Hope's side. My sisters and I stand around, trying to make our time with her important. I think, she almost died last night, but God gave her grace again. One part of me believes that heaven is full of love and the peace of God's tender hands, while the other part, Hope's earthbound child, doesn't believe she will ever leave us.

Hope is sleeping in peace, knowing we are all there. The room becomes silent, the nurse whispering behind the curtain on the other side of the room. The room is full of peace, yet I can't feel Hope's soul leave the room and float up to heaven. I look at my sisters' tears. Tears fall uncontrollably from five pairs of eyes.

We move out of the room together to escape our pain, and when we turn our backs on Hope, walking away, Hope, at last, allows God to take her to heaven. Our special mother, whom God had given so many children, had done the best she could on earth, and now her job was done. We stop but don't turn around, knowing Hope wants to die in privacy. God has granted all her wishes: she had a husband who worshiped her, twelve kids who would have laid down their lives for her, and more friends than she could count on both hands.

We go back to the waiting room to our brothers and husbands. Mike drops to his knees for the last family rosary for Hope. Denise says, "With love for God, our faith will pull us through even the death of our mother." Prayer is always the answer.

The Red Dress

MY HEAD IS NUMB, AND MY EARS ARE RINGING. It's up to me to do Hope's makeup for the viewing at the funeral home, and I can't see through my tears. I separate myself from the task to call Carman, the undertaker from across the street when we were growing up in Carsonville. Carman has shortened his vacation to take care of Hope, who planned her own funeral for years, including the songs, "Whispering Hope" by Willie Nelson and "In the Garden." Over the years Carman had made promises to her about the music and the kind of service she wanted.

Standing next to me at the outside entrance of the funeral home, Carman starts to cry. "I'm gonna miss the old gal, Erin. I'm sorry. You're awful young to have to lose your mother. A little unorthodox, but a great gal. A great gal!" I can't speak. I just try to keep the lump in my throat from coming up into my mouth. My face is swollen, eyes burning.

We walk down a long slope where the hearse backs in. "Erin, stay here for a minute. I need to check on something." I wait, my fear rising. I think about backing out now and explaining it to her in heaven later. Why would she ask such a thing? Was it to have me go crazy later in life, or to keep me busy on the toughest day of my life? She was a spiritual woman; does she think she can comfort me this way? Oh, my God, I feel like I'm going to throw up! Well, it's too late now: Carman is here with the door open. I gather up my bags packed with curling irons, brushes, and makeup.

"Honey, this is going to be tougher than you think," Carman warns me. "She doesn't have any clothes on. She's covered up, but this is pretty emotional work."

200

"I can handle it, Carman."

"I remember you as a little girl, Erin," he says, still unconvinced.

I smile and push the hair out of my face with shaking hands, saying, "Carman, you were her friend. Thanks for coming home early to take care of her. I know this is kind of against the rules to have me down here, but Hope felt strongly about it. I won't be long. She just wants me to do her makeup and hair."

Carman carries my bags. I walk down the hall to where Hope is laid out. He stops one last time and says, "Erin, are you sure? She once told me that if I messed up her makeup she would haunt me for the rest of my life. Then she laughed! But I know it was important to her.

"You know you don't have to do this," he goes on as we take the last few steps together. "It will change you for life, Erin. You're only twenty-five years old, and I'm more than capable." Then, seeing my determination, he counsels me, "Erin, when you're working on her lips, try to be extra careful. Don't let the lips separate."

I gasp for air, with my hands over my mouth, but manage to choke out, "Thanks for the tip, Carman. I'll be careful. She is my life. I'm nervous, Carman, but really, I need to say good-bye. Thanks for allowing me in here. I know it will be hard, but 'a promise made is a debt unpaid, I swore I would not fail.'" The quote from Robert Service seems appropriate.

Carman steps away. "I'll be upstairs if you need me, Erin."

I walk close to her, setting down my bags, saying, "Okay, Hopie, I'm keeping my promise to you, but this is the hardest job you've ever given me!" Tears fall off my cheeks. I'm shaking as I take out my blush and start on the cheekbones. Carman has already applied foundation.

"Hopie, you're looking a little pale," I say, brushing an upward stroke with blush. I start to use my soft brown eyebrow pencil, drawing short lines to look realistic. Soft brown eye shadow is next, to show off her bone structure, and pink shadow under the eyebrow. Remembering about the lips parting, I save her mouth for last. Her own ruby red lipstick glides on, as if she is ready for the dance. Then her hair needs to be curled away from her face in one big wave back, the way she used to wear it.

My stomach aches. She's cold. No, she's not winking, thank God! I remind her of all the times we had hot soup and homemade baked bread with friends at our house. My friends loved her. I remind her of how we laughed at the kitchen table. No, she didn't help us with our homework, but she taught us with life experiences. I'm concerned that I'm taking too long to do her makeup and hair, but the memories keep pouring out. At last, tears falling, I pull away, not to ruin her makeup, and stand back with my hands folded behind me. Once when I was little, Hope came home from a funeral, and I ran to her, asking, "How did the lady look, Hope?" Patting me on the head, she answered, "Like a bride, Erin. She looked like a bride." I want people to say that about Hope.

"Hope," I say, "I know you can't wink, so I'm going to wink at you and walk away. I love you, Hope!" I pick up my bags, looking once again at every detail, at how pretty she looks. "Like a bride," I say out loud, "like a bride."

Carman is coming down the hall, "Are you okay, Erin?"

"Yes, sir, I'm fine. Hope and I were just having a little talk. Does she look like a bride?"

Carman smiles at me. "Yes, honey, she sure does."

I lean over Hope, kiss her lightly on the lips, and pat her hand, walking away backwards, making certain not to turn my back on her. Carman stands with Hope's red velvet dress in hand and smiles apologetically. "I'm sorry, Erin. I don't know if this was a good idea." I throw my bag over my shoulder and break down uncontrollably as I walk down the long concrete hallway to join the rest of my family.

Mike, Brian, Joe and Denise go to pick out the casket. Tony and Randy leave together to help get my father ready. I love my father, but I can't worry about him today. Like him, I am struggling with the loss we both must accept. I'm drowning in grief.

Later, we stand in silence at the funeral home. Bill stands on wobbly legs, keeping close to his children for support. He is vulnerable, tender, much different now that we are all facing the toughest day of our lives. His pale blue eyes have lost their depth. He's crying, shaking, his head down in a silent prayer. He sits in a corner, saying to me, "Honey, when your mother walked across the room, I got a lump in my throat." He takes a long draw from his cigarette and starts to say more but then just puts his head in his hands again, crying. Pat and Marianne lead him by the hand to the front door to accept his friends' condolences. He walks as if he has almost forgotten how.

Willie Nelson is playing and singing "Whispering Hope" and later "In the Garden," just as Hope had always wanted, on Tony's reel-to-reel. Instead of comforting me, the songs are like sharp glass in my heart.

I want to be held tight, but I can't see Randy, and I collapse onto my brother Brian's lap. He runs his hands through my hair as I rest on his chest. Brian understands me. His beautiful dark hair hangs forward in his eyes so no one can see him crying.

The older kids comfort each other, and then we all say the rosary on our knees. Bill prays silently along with us.

Later that night Joe tells me that if any one of us in the family doesn't make it, none of us make it. So we will hold on as a family, the older kids say. They will stay close, the way we were raised. We will keep up the Quinlan traditions.

202

Epilogue
The Abandoned House Game

AFTER SPENDING A WEEKEND with Denise, I leave her house early in the morning to stop off at the cemetery where Hope and Bill are buried. Listening to Hank Williams music on the stereo, the peaceful darkness surrounding me, I accidentally drive past the cemetery and end up at the four corners of Carsonville. Taking a deep breath, I turn left and drive down the street where I grew up.

The address is 44 South Main Street. We had the number "44" on the pillar of the house. I pull up to the place where the county building used to be and look around. The Carsonville Hotel is still there, but the tree we swung on with Dickey Roach is not there: the Tarzan tree and the tire swings are gone, and someone has cut the tree down to a stump about three feet tall. I shine my lights on the tree and feel a sadness come over me. It's not there, that worn spot where we flipped upside-down to hold on with our toes.

It is almost daylight now, and I'm sitting in my car with the lights shining onto the back room of the house. Ladybird gave birth to her puppies there, I'm thinking to myself. It looks smaller and dirtier than my memory of it. I wait for Hope to call my name, but the air is silent. The wind starts to blow.

I close my eyes, waiting to feel something that I have written about, waiting for a friend to appear, a loud voice to ring out, a cheer, perhaps a bit of music from the back door as we kids were arguing about who got the swing first. But everyone left twenty-two years ago or more from this house. It is so quiet that finally I get out of my car to see what more than twenty years have done to this house. Is the old oak door hidden between the walls still pulled out, where Hope used to separate Charlie and me? I remember the time I talked him into looking through the keyhole and then poked him in the eye with a pink pick my sisters used for their curlers. If I could get in, maybe I could hear something. I step onto the bottom concrete step and look up to where I climbed up and sneaked into the house late one night at age fifteen. But no, the music is gone; no Irish broom dances are to be heard.

There is a sign on the front door that reads "CONDEMNED" in big print, and I'm still standing on the bottom step, just looking, when all of a sudden I hear myself say, "It's the abandoned house game!" It is the game we used to play when I was little! With my hands behind my back, like a kid, I say aloud, "Where have all of the people gone?" I flash back to being nine years old, living in this house.

My head and heart are full now of both the worlds I have lived in. My dreams are of home, and now, at age 47, I'm standing in front of my old house, feeling like that child. I say out loud again, "It is the abandoned house game." I had forgotten the game and had never told anyone about it.

"Where did all of the people go?" I ask aloud again, keeping my hands behind my back, like I'm a little kid who doesn't want to touch anything.

I can see the boards of the house almost open up in front of my eyes. I can see the Thanksgiving dinners, the big pretty trees we had for Christmas. I can see the steam on the windows from all of our body heat. (Our house windows were always steamy like that.) I see my sisters' and brothers' faces (they're happy), and I see myself at the age of nine, my favorite year of life, ponytail swinging. I smell the aroma of homemade bread billowing out the kitchen window, and I see the canning jars full of fruit on the counter. Above all the rest, I hear Hope humming in the kitchen. Bill is sitting on his favorite white chair, the one he inherited from his parents, and I have the feeling that life will never end for me in Carsonville at 44 South Main Street.

"What happened to the people?" I hear myself ask, my hands still behind my back. I remember how the game ended. At the end, if you were good, you could keep something from the old abandoned house. Before I can give another thought to all that I see and feel and smell, I reach up with my right hand and snatch the number "44" from the pillar on the porch. I change from woman to kid in my heart as I grab my prize.

Then I run fast, like I'm wearing my red Keds, jump into my silver Cadillac and drive as fast as I can out of Carsonville. The twin numbers on my lap still hold small gray nails in their holes. I drive, crying, and hit Sandusky before I even realize what has happened. Then I start to shake and cry until I realize that I know where all of the people have gone.

I loved Hope and Bill, but some of the situations I was in as a child were not safe. Yet I learned many lessons, and I felt safe, because Hope was with me. Only now do I feel lonely. I'm scared, too, the way I was at the age of nine, riding shotgun when Hope was unable to drive home. I feel it all now, everything I couldn't let myself feel at the time.

I cry until I hit exit number 212 on I –75 North. I cry because of all of the memories, because I have seen once again the life that I lived in Carsonville, because it has all come alive one more time for me. After I stop crying, I realize that Hope and Bill are still with me in a spiritual way. I still have the memories, the love, and the feeling in my heart that life never really ends. I have five living brothers and four living sisters whom God has allowed to stay in my life. I'm grateful for all that Hope and Bill have given me. I cry, "God showed me where all of the people have gone!"

Overwhelmed, I drive back to Suttons Bay to tell my husband, Randy, of my experiences. He can tell instantly that I have been crying for hours and asks, "Are you okay?"

I smile and say, "Honey, shut off the news. I have to tell you something!"

Closing his paper, he looks at me with his beautiful green eyes and says, "Okay, I'm all yours."

I tell him the whole story—my vision, my tears. His eyes are locked on my face. At last I smile and say, "Well, by the time I had driven to Sandusky, I realized that I had taken the numbers."

He says, "Let me see them." I get up and hand the metal numerals to him. Randy looks at our daughter Morgan and says, "Morgan, this is a big deal. We are going to hang the numbers on the wall today! We know where the people are. They're Mom's brothers and sisters, so I'm going to hang these on the wall right now."

(To this day, the number "44" hangs on the oak beam that divides our living room and dining room.)

I talk to my brother Tony later that day, and he thinks that's what Hope was doing all along in the abandoned houses. Hope spent that time teaching us about the "dry run" on death, about ghosts, and not to be afraid when your number is called. Maybe Hope could see souls wrestling with life and death. In a way, she loved to go to abandoned houses to be a part of death. "Where have all of the people gone?" was Hope's way of teaching us yet another lesson in life about death, at a level a child could understand.

I cried for hours after this experience because the truth was in front of me at last. I was looking into my old home where love had flowed freely, and I knew where all of the people were! My brothers and sisters are all professionals, raising their children. We are a very close family, the next generation still asking about Hope and Bill. Stories flow at the Thanksgiving party that grows larger every year. My family's love flowed over me physically, like a tidal wave there at the door of our own abandoned family house. I could see the steam in the windows of fun and laughter, and I could smell the fresh bread baking. That was God showing me that I had lived a life of love and that even if it has been a long time since I lived in that house, the love still exists. The circle of life and love is right here at my fingertips.

I have been given the gift of writing and feeling my life through my thoughts, but it also has become a visual experience now, and God is the center of it all. I'm still reflecting on what this experience means to me. One thing I feel is that if I had gone to the cemetery to see Hope and Bill, as I had planned, my experience would have been about Hope and her death. But I drove past because my subconscious needed to find Erin. I was given the gift of vision. It would have been all about Hope and my loss of her if I had stopped, but instead it became about me, not only my loss but also my love for my life. It became Erin's experience about Erin, about who I am.

I did not realize I had taken the number "44" until I hit Sandusky and called Denise. Then I looked down and saw it in my lap.

I was given a gift of the past. Maybe because I spoke and said, "It is the abandoned house game," God responded and showed me the people inside the house. God gave me my past for a few minutes to show me that my story needed to be written. He showed me "where all of the people have gone."

I was given an incredible experience, the gift of visiting my life through the eyes of a child and also as an adult, all in one day. It feels to me like what Scrooge must have experienced in "Christmas Carol."

I believe that my life has been blessed. Bill and Hope raised twelve children who love, laugh, and live.